LIBRARY OF HEBREW BIBLE/
OLD TESTAMENT STUDIES

435

Formerly Journal for the Study of the Old Testament Supplement Series

PHILOSOPHY AND PRACTICE
IN WRITING A HISTORY
OF ANCIENT ISRAEL

Megan Bishop Moore

t&t clark

NEW YORK • LONDON

T & T Clark International, 80 Maiden Lane, New York, NY 10038

T & T Clark International, The Tower Building, 11 York Road, London SE1 7NX

T & T Clark International is a Continuum imprint.

Library of Congress Cataloging-in-Publication Data
Moore, Megan Bishop, 1972-
Philosophy and practice in writing a history of ancient Israel / Megan Bishop Moore.
  p. cm. -- (Library of Hebrew Bible/Old Testament studies ; 435)
  Includes bibliographical references and index.
  ISBN 0-567-02981-6 (hardcover)
1. Jews--History--To 70 A.D.--Historiography. 2. Bible. O.T.--Historiography.
3. Palestine--History--To 70 A.D.--Historiography. 4. Old Testament scholars--
History--20th century. I. Title. II. Series.
  DS115.5.M66 2006
  933.0072--dc22
                2006007656

Printed and bound in Great Britain by Biddles Ltd., King's Lynn, Norfolk

06 07 08 09 10   10 9 8 7 6 5 4 3 2 1

CONTENTS

ACKNOWLEDGMENTS

Throughout graduate school and the writing of the dissertation that eventually became this book, I have been aided by many people. The professors in Emory's Hebrew Bible department, especially my dissertation director John Hayes, have been exceedingly helpful. Special thanks also to committee members Brent Strawn and Shalom Goldman. In the process of transforming my dissertation into a book, the assistance of Henry Carrigan and Duncan Burns was invaluable.

I have also had the constant support of friends and family, most especially my husband Steve, for which I am most grateful.

ABBREVIATIONS

ABRL	Anchor Bible Reference Library
AHR	*The American Historical Review*
AJSR	*Association for Jewish Studies Review*
ANES	*Ancient Near Eastern Studies*
BA	*Biblical Archaeologist*
BAR	*Biblical Archaeology Review*
BASOR	*Bulletin of the American Schools of Oriental Research*
BE	Biblische Enzyklopädie
Bib	*Biblica*
BJS	Brown Judaic Studies
BWANT	Beiträge zur Wissenschaft vom Alten und Neuen Testament
BZAW	Beihefte zur *ZAW*
ChrCent	*Christian Century*
CurBS	*Currents in Research: Biblical Studies*
ExpTim	*Expository Times*
Hen	*Henoch*
HSS	Harvard Semitic Studies
IEJ	*Israel Exploration Journal*
JBL	*Journal of Biblical Literature*
JNES	*Journal of Near Eastern Studies*
JR	*Journal of Religion*
JSOT	*Journal for the Study of the Old Testament*
JSOTSup	Journal for the Study of the Old Testament: Supplement Series
NEA	*Near Eastern Archaeology*
OBO	Orbis biblicus et orientalis
OBT	Overtures to Biblical Theology
OEANE	*The Oxford Encyclopedia of Archaeology in the Ancient Near East.* Edited by E. M. Meyers. New York, 1997
OTE	*Old Testament Essays*
PEQ	*Palestine Exploration Quarterly*
PJ	*Palästina-Jahrbuch*
QD	Quaestiones disputatae
SBT	Studies in Biblical Theology
SHANE	Studies in the History of the Ancient Near East
SJOT	*Scandinavian Journal of the Old Testament*
TUMSR	Trinity University Monograph Series in Religion
UF	*Ugarit-Forschungen*
VT	*Vetus Testamentum*
VTSup	Vetus Testamentum Supplements
ZAH	*Zeitschrift für Althebraistik*
ZTK	*Zeitschrift für Theologie und Kirche*

INTRODUCTION

Historians of ancient Israel and Judah, like all other historians, come to their work with certain presuppositions and goals in mind. These presuppositions and goals influence every aspect of history writing, from historians' choices of subject and modes of explanation, to their dealings with evidence, to the written form their final product takes. Yet it is rare to find a historian who sets forth his or her philosophy of history writing. "Obviously no historian can be asked to make explicit, let alone embark upon a systematic personal study of, every term, concept, assumption and interrelation he employs. If he were, he could never accomplish anything."[1] On the other hand, the presuppositions on which a work of history is founded cannot be ignored: "Understanding history…requires that we grasp the range of assumptions which historians (and the rest of us) make about historical reality and how it is to be explained."[2]

This study will examine and elucidate assumptions about history writing that current historians of ancient Israel and Judah employ. It is undertaken in the context of the conflict between so-called "minimalists" and "maximalists" within the discipline today. This situation offers an excellent opportunity for analysis and critique since, as philosopher of history William Dray observes, "the presuppositions and conceptual frameworks of historians [are] often…found to emerge most clearly where they cannot agree about what conclusions to draw."[3] For reasons that will be explained more fully in the following chapters, this study will use the terms "minimalist" and "non-minimalist" to categorize historians on different sides of this controversy. In brief, minimalists are scholars who generally distrust the Bible's account of Israel's past because they consider the text late, biased, ideological, polemical, and largely removed from the actual events and circumstances of ancient Palestine, at least until the Persian and Hellenistic periods. Minimalists also argue that archaeology is a better source of information about Israel's past than the Bible, and contend that ancient Israel and Judah should be recognized as only minimally important in comparison to the other cultures of the ancient Near East. "Non-minimalists" are historians of ancient Israel who generally do not adhere to these assumptions. They find value

---

1.   M. I. Finley, *The Use and Abuse of History* (New York: Viking, 1975), 73.
2.   Jonathan Gorman, *Understanding History: An Introduction to Analytical Philosophy of History* (Philosophica 42; Ottawa: University of Ottawa Press, 1992), x.
3.   William Dray, "Philosophy and Historiography," in *Companion to Historiography* (ed. Michael Bentley; London: Routledge, 1997), 763–82 (765).

in the Bible's accounts of Israel's origins and may adopt the Bible's basic timeline and paradigms as frameworks for their own history writing endeavors.

This study will show that although the Bible is the focal point of the opposition of these two approaches, the evaluation and use of the Bible are not the only sources of disagreement or difference between minimalists and non-minimalists. Rather, the issue of the Bible as potential evidence for Israel's past is an issue in which a number of related philosophical and practical concerns are telescoped. In order to identify and understand these related issues, this study will situate the study of ancient Israel and Judah in the intellectual context of academic history in general. It will be organized around categories delineated and discussed by philosophers of history, in an attempt "to clarify and, where it seems appropriate, to offer a critique of the framework of basic concepts and assumptions within which historians conduct their inquiries."[4]

The study begins in Chapters 1 and 2 with general discussions of empiricism, objectivity, representation and language, subject, explanation, truth, and evidence evaluation and use. These chapters do not attempt to provide a comprehensive review of the scholarship on these topics and the development of ideas about them. Rather, they introduce the topics order to establish a framework for the analysis of philosophy and practice in writing a history of ancient Israel. This analysis will then proceed in a semichronological sequence in Chapters 3, 4, and 5. There, evidence for understanding historians of ancient Israel's assumptions about these topics primarily will be garnered from scholars' own theoretical statements about history writing. Sometimes, however, in the absence of explicit indications of assumptions, indications of scholars' presuppositions and assumptions will be drawn from analysis of their historical or methodological works.

---

4.   Ibid. In this work, "philosophy of history" refers to the critical or analytical philosophy of history. Critical philosophy of history is a second-order discipline that is concerned with the assumptions and philosophical premises of historians. Today, critical philosophy of history is the common type of philosophy of history practiced. Another type of philosophy of history is the speculative or substantive philosophy of history, which searches for the overall meaning or trajectory of the past. Its beginnings are commonly attributed to St. Augustine, and it flourished through the nineteenth century, carried on by philosophers such as Hegel. See ibid., 763; see also Patrick Gardiner, "History, History of the Philosophy of," in *The Oxford Companion to Philosophy* (ed. Ted Honderich; Oxford: Oxford University Press, 1995), 360–64, and David Carr, "Philosophy of History," in *The Cambridge Dictionary of Philosophy* (ed. Robert Audi; 2d ed.; Cambridge: Cambridge University Press, 1999), 671–73. Gordon Graham points out that continental theorists such as Heidegger, Foucault, Levinas, and Derrida, as well as Americans Rorty, MacIntyre, and Taylor are in some ways leading a "revival of speculative philosophy of history," since they undertake "the application of philosophical concepts and analysis to history, and especially cultural history, in the belief that an adequate understanding of contemporary thought requires the mutual illumination of the two" (Gordon Graham, "History, Philosophy of," in *The Routledge Encyclopedia of Philosophy* [10 vols.; ed. Edward Craig; London: Routledge, 1998], 4:453–59 [457]). There are at least two meanings of the word history, as well. History can be understood as the study of the past, and usually implies a corresponding literary form. This is the sense in which the word "history" will be used in this study (and the meaning of history that the term "critical philosophy of history" employs). "History" is also used to mean "the past itself" (as meant in the "substantive philosophy of history"), but to avoid confusion this sense will not be used here.

Chapter 3 looks at the schools of William F. Albright and Albrecht Alt, mid-twentieth-century historians of ancient Israel whose work predates, but influences, the current situation. As observed in a recent history of ancient Israel, "much of the ground upon which the newer historians take their stand was prepared for them long ago, in the sense that the governing assumptions and methods of much earlier historiography lead on directly to the place in which we now find ourselves."[5] Albright, an American, found evidence for the Israel and Judah described in the Bible in the archaeological record, and thus formulated historical portraits that fused artifacts from the ancient Near East with Israel's story as told in the Bible. In contrast, Alt and his pupil Martin Noth, both Germans, asserted that a critical reading of the Bible led to a reconstruction of Israel's past that did not necessarily follow the Bible's story line, especially in the case of Israel's origins, and used sociological and other comparative models to formulate different histories of ancient Israel.

These schools of thought persisted alongside each other and dominated the discipline until the 1970s, when Thomas L. Thompson's *Historicity of the Patriarchal Narratives* and John Van Seters' *Abraham in History and Tradition* appeared.[6] Based largely on new ideas about how comparisons between the culture described in the Bible and other ancient Near Eastern cultures should be made, these two books challenged assumptions about the Bible's ability to impart historical information. Thompson's and Van Seters' studies convinced many historians of ancient Israel that turning a more critical eye toward the Bible and the assumed extrabiblical evidence for Israel's past was necessary for history writing.[7] In the 1980s, additional histories taking this more critical approach appeared, including Alberto Soggin's *A History of Israel: From the Beginnings to the Bar Kochba Revolt, AD 135*[8] and *A History of Ancient Israel and Judah* by J. Maxwell Miller and John H. Hayes.[9] Questions about the reliability of the Bible continued to develop, and by the 1990s scholars were

5. Iain W. Provan, V. Philips Long, and Tremper Longman III, *A Biblical History of Israel* (Louisville, Ky.: Westminster John Knox, 2003), 9.

6. Thomas L. Thompson, *The Historicity of the Patriarchal Narratives: The Quest for the Historical Abraham* (BZAW 133; Berlin: de Gruyter, 1974); John Van Seters, *Abraham in History and Tradition* (New Haven: Yale University Press, 1975).

7. Niels Peter Lemche has pointed out that "when Thomas Thompson and John Van Seters in the mid-1970s published their respective books on the world of the patriarchs, these were hailed as a new beginning, although they only played this role as seen from a North American perspective (and not yet shared by Israeli scholars); the German world probably saw it as a confirmation of something with which scholars had been acquainted since the days of de Wette" (Niels Peter Lemche, "The Origin of the Israelite State: A Copenhagen Perspective on the Emergence of Critical Historical Studies of Ancient Israel in Recent Times," *SJOT* 12 [1998]: 44–63 [55]).

8. J. Alberto Soggin, *A History of Israel: From the Beginnings to the Bar Kochba Revolt, AD 135* (London: SCM Press, 1984); trans. of *Storia d'Israele, dalle origini alla rivolta di Bar-Kochba, 135 d.C.* (Brescia: Paideia, 1984). Now in its third edition and retitled *An Introduction to the History of Israel and Judah* (3d ed.; London: SCM Press, 1998); trans. of *Introduzione alla Storia d'Israele e di Giuda* (Brescia: Paideia, 1998).

9. J. Maxwell Miller and John H. Hayes, *A History of Ancient Israel and Judah* (Philadelphia: Westminster, 1986); revised edition forthcoming.

discussing the question of what, if anything, can be known about ancient Israel and Judah given the problems with the biblical evidence. The European Seminar on Methodology in Israel's History was formed in 1996, and brought together minimalists and non-minimalists to address the pressing question that formed the title of their first publication: *Can a 'History of Israel' be Written?*[10] By the end of the twentieth century, historians of ancient Israel were expending much energy on questions related to Israel as a historical subject and the Bible as evidence for the past.

Since the 1970s, historical scholarship about ancient Israel has also seen the increase in social-scientific approaches[11] and in studies of cultural structures such as kingship, law, and death in ancient Israel,[12] as well as the inclusion of women's history in the discipline.[13] At the same time, literary criticism of the Bible has gained popularity, demonstrating that the Bible is "susceptible to a wide variety of readings."[14] As will be seen in the following chapters, these developments reflect trends characteristic of historical studies in general and bring new evidence, expectations, and questions into history writing.

In short, current minimalist and non-minimalist approaches to history writing about ancient Israel can be seen as descendants of the breakdown of Albrightian and Altian norms combined with attempts to incorporate into history other changes in the discipline and in the intellectual climate in general. Chapters 4 and 5 of this study define, describe, and analyze assumptions and practices of minimalist and non-minimalist historians of ancient Israel, respectively. It will be shown that minimalists' claims have been a catalyst for reflection and change, as non-minimalists have altered and sharpened their ideas in reaction to them. Minimalists have responded to their critics, but have shown relative constancy in return.

Chapter 6 then assesses the discipline's self-awareness of and trends in the understanding of the topics presented in Chapters 1 and 2. It includes an exposition of similarities and differences in assumptions about and practices of history among the various types of historians of ancient Israel, critiques flaws in certain approaches, and suggests avenues for further discussion and resolution of some

10.   Lester L. Grabbe, ed., *Can a 'History of Israel' Be Written?* (JSOTSup 245; Sheffield: Sheffield Academic Press, 1997).
11.   The first major contribution in this area was Norman K. Gottwald's *The Tribes of Yahweh: A Sociology of the Religion of Liberated Israel, 1250–1050 B.C.E.* (The Biblical Seminar 66; Sheffield: Sheffield Academic Press, 1999); reprinted with expanded introductory material from *The Tribes of Yahweh: A Sociology of the Religion of Liberated Israel, 1250–1050 B.C.E.* (Maryknoll, N.Y.: Orbis, 1979).
12.   E.g. Keith W. Whitelam, *The Just King: Monarchical Judicial Authority in Ancient Israel* (JSOTSup 12; Sheffield: Department of Biblical Studies, 1979); Baruch Halpern and Deborah W. Hobson, eds., *Law and Ideology in Monarchic Israel* (JSOTSup 124; Sheffield: JSOT Press, 1991); Elizabeth Bloch-Smith, *Judahite Burial Practices and Beliefs About the Dead* (JSOTSup 123; Sheffield: JSOT Press, 1992).
13.   E.g. Carol Meyers, *Discovering Eve: Ancient Israelite Women in Context* (New York: Oxford University Press, 1988).
14.   Gottwald, *The Tribes of Yahweh*, xl.

contentious issues. In particular, it will be shown that ideas about objectivity have a direct bearing on the evidentiary debate, which, in turn, affects what subjects and modes of explanations historians see as available to them. Criteria for attempting objective history writing will be proposed, and potential benefits of a clearly defined objective approach to history writing will be demonstrated. It will also be argued that current historians of ancient Israel are beginning to work with a beneficial and useful notion of historical truth that attempts to take into account the many contingencies for the concept and writing of history that twentieth-century discussions about history have introduced.

Chapter 1

CURRENT PHILOSOPHICAL ISSUES IN HISTORY WRITING

Introduction

Any examination of history and historians' practices must begin with the question: What is history? While historians and non-historians may have a general sense of what constitutes history, no simple definition exists. The following examples illustrate a range of ideas about history and provide a glimpse into how historians and philosophers of history have described it. Johan Huizinga wrote, "History is the intellectual form in which a civilization renders account to itself of its past."[1] Wolfgang von Leyden asserts that history is "not the past but knowledge of the past."[2] Moses Finley is a bit more specific; he says that history is "a systematic account over a long enough period of time not only to establish relationships, connections, causes, and consequences but also to show how change occurs and to suggest why."[3] Hans Kellner offers a definition that might be called "postmodern"; he calls histories "formalized aesthetic objects which make certain claims about the world and our relation to it, and which we take as provisional guides in making sense of experience."[4] All of these definitions suggest that knowledge of the past is intrinsic to history. Further, most historians would agree that history writing endeavors to represent the past in an understandable and meaningful way. Put slightly differently, history "helps us to understand human existence in relation to the dimension of time."[5] Or, as Huizinga says of history, "Its purpose is to understand the world *in* and *through* the past."[6]

---

1. Johan Huizinga, "A Definition of the Concept of History," in *Philosophy and History: Essays Presented to Ernst Cassirer* (ed. Raymond Klibansky and H. J. Paton; Oxford: Clarendon, 1936), 1–10 (9).
2. Wolfgang von Leyden, "Categories of Historical Understanding," *History and Theory* 32 (1984): 53–77 (54).
3. M. I. Finley, *Ancient History: Evidence and Models* (London: Chatto & Windus, 1985), 5–6.
4. Hans Kellner, "Introduction: Describing Redescriptions," in *A New Philosophy of History* (ed. F. R. Ankersmit and Hans Kellner; Chicago: University of Chicago Press, 1995), 1–18 (18).
5. Michael Stanford, *An Introduction to the Philosophy of History* (Oxford: Blackwell, 1998), 261–62.
6. Huizinga, "A Definition of the Concept of History," 5.

General definitions of history are important to understanding the practices of historians because such statements elucidate some of the perceptions historians have about what they are doing and why they are doing it. Yet definitions cannot fully describe the process of establishing "relationships, causes, connections, and consequences," promoting meaning and understanding, or helping a civilization "render an account to itself." History writing is predicated on a number of assumptions and decisions that play a role in achieving these goals. Sometimes, historians will disclose their presuppositions and methods; often, however, presuppositions and methods are left undisclosed or even unexamined. Therefore, in order for practices and products of history writing to be optimally described and understood, philosophical and methodological issues pertaining to history writing must be examined in some detail.

This chapter will introduce and summarize a number of philosophical issues related to history writing that philosophers of history and historians have discussed in recent decades. Modern history's dependence on empiricism, objectivity, and the conviction that the past can be represented will be examined, as will methods of explaining the past and the subjects historians choose for their histories. Also, the concept of truth in history will be introduced. This discussion will show that theoreticians' ideas about each of these topics vary, and that postmodernism has spurred reconsideration of what might be called traditional presuppositions about history. The expositions of these topics are brief and do not give justice to the full range of philosophical and methodological discussions that have taken place around them. Nevertheless, these sections aim to serve as a guide and a framework by which assumptions and practices of historians of ancient Israel can be analyzed in the following chapters.

Empiricism

Empiricism, both in its epistemological and methodological forms, is the basis of history as it is currently practiced. As an epistemology, empiricism requires that knowledge be based on observable phenomena. Empiricism is of course recognizable as the theory of knowledge on which modern science is founded. Beginning in the nineteenth century, historians, striving to be scientific themselves, adopted empirical epistemology as a philosophy, and empirical, or scientific, methodology as their technique. The scientific method requires rigorous examination of empirical evidence, impartiality, and inductive reasoning.[7] In the past several decades, however, many assumptions of empirical history have been challenged, in large part due to the decline of modernism and the rise of postmodernism as the prevailing intellectual climate.

---

7. A discussion of empiricism as both epistemology and methodology can be found in Anna Green and Kathleen Troup, eds., *The Houses of History: A Critical Reader in Twentieth-Century History and Theory, Selected and Introduced by Anna Green & Kathleen Troup* (New York: New York University Press, 1999), 1–11.

Postmodernism

The term "postmodernism" is used in this study to describe an intellectual climate that critiques the assumptions and results of modernist thought. The assumption that history can be in some way empirical or scientific was at home in a modernist worldview where fact and value, history and fiction, and object and subject were distinct from each other. Postmodernism challenges the validity of such separations, and thus brings into question many assumptions of science, and by extension, scientific history. Specifically problematic for history are postmodernism's contentions that an object such as the past or reality cannot be defined or separated from the observer's perception of it, and that the language one uses to represent the past in some ways creates the past's reality as well as knowledge about it. It follows that in light of postmodernism, truth in history can no longer be positivistic, in other words, a record of what happened and when and why it happened. Rather, postmodern truth is contestable, seen as part of a narrative that historians create "to justify the knowledge they produce."[8] How postmodernism and postmodernist theories have prompted historians to make accommodations to their understanding of history and their practice of writing will be discussed in the remainder of this chapter and throughout this study.

Objectivity

The concept of objectivity presupposes that the external world can be known and "exists independently of our perception, conception, or judgment of it."[9] Objectivity also requires a "sharp separation...between fact and value."[10] Objectivity's opposite is subjectivity, which allows the "biases, feelings, and personal judgments"[11] of the thinking subject, in this case the historian, to affect his or her perception of the world. Therefore, in order to be an objective observer, the researcher must strive to abandon all biases and to apprehend and present information in a value-free manner.

For historians, objectivity has been a difficult concept to understand clearly, as well as to achieve. Peter Novick, who undertook a study of the concept of objectivity among American historians in the twentieth century, finds ideas about objectivity to be "essentially confused."[12] Novick also claims that, beginning in the 1960s, a cognitive "crisis of historicism"[13] that had major repercussions for the idea of objectivity occurred. Though he does not name it as such,

---

8.   C. Behan McCullagh, *The Truth of History* (London: Routledge, 1998), 298.
9.   Peter A. Angeles, ed., *The HarperCollins Dictionary of Philosophy* (2d ed.; New York: HarperCollins, 1992), 209.
10.   Peter Novick, *That Noble Dream: The "Objectivity Question" and the American Historical Profession* (Ideas in Context; Cambridge: Cambridge University Press, 1988), 1–2.
11.   Angeles, ed., *HarperCollins Dictionary of Philosophy*, 209.
12.   Novick, *That Noble Dream*, 6.
13.   Ibid., 523.

this crisis could be called nascent postmodernism. Postmodernism has forced historians to reconsider some of the optimism they had placed in the concept of scientific or objective history. First of all, the past cannot be observed directly, and thus objective knowledge of the past, that is, knowledge based on direct observation, is technically impossible.[14] The indirect and inferential nature of knowledge about the past leaves history particularly vulnerable to postmodernism's contention that personal values and other subjective factors affect the apprehension, description, and explanation of the past. Furthermore, if, as postmodernism claims, knowledge requires justification and facts are value-laden, it follows that objectivity in history is either an impossible goal or a moot concept. Philosopher of history C. Behan McCullagh explains:

> The suggestion that historical descriptions, interpretations, and explanations could be biased would strike [postmodernists] as either self-evident or nonsense. It is self-evident to them that historians' accounts of the past reflect their personal interests and vision of past events; and they would think it nonsense to suppose that there is some objective standard of interpretation against which some accounts could be judged biased and others not.[15]

Put differently, "One way to understand the revolutionary inversion of 'normal' historiography by postmodern historiography...is to say that the ontological question (what actually existed and happened) is now secondary to the epistemological issue (what historians claim to know about what might or might not have existed or happened)."[16]

Postmodernism has thus raised formidable challenges to the goal of objectivity in history, and indeed has made objectivity, in its strictest sense, an impossible goal. Historians, however, have not accepted the claim that objectivity is a moot concept and likewise have not given up on objectivity as a practice. Instead, they have proceeded by considering objectivity to be a "regulative ideal."[17] In other words, although historians realize that the "noble dream" of pure objectivity can never be realized, they maintain that considering objectivity a regulative ideal allows it to be maintained in principle and negotiated in practice.

In order to keep history as close as possible to the ideal of objectivity, historians and philosophers have attempted to identify and eliminate bias that can occur in history writing. McCullagh, for instance, asserts that bias is rooted in historians' desire "to further certain interests"[18] or for something to be true.

14. R. F. Atkinson (*Knowledge and Explanation in History: An Introduction to the Philosophy of History* [Ithaca, N.Y.: Cornell University Press, 1978], 52) has pointed out that like our knowledge of the past, much of our knowledge of the present is indirect and inferential, as well. We have not observed much of what we think we know or everything we consider to be real.
15. C. Behan McCullagh, "Bias in Historical Description, Interpretation, and Explanation," *History and Theory* 39 (2000): 39–66 (39). McCullagh defends evaluating historical interpretations further in idem, "What Do Historians Argue About?," *History and Theory* 43 (2004): 18–38.
16. Fred W. Burnett, "Historiography," in *Handbook of Postmodern Biblical Interpretation* (ed. A. K. M. Adam; St. Louis, Miss.: Chalice, 2000), 106–12 (109).
17. Stanford, *Introduction to the Philosophy of History*, 55.
18. McCullagh, "Bias in Historical Description," 40.

These desires may spring from individual concerns, or from class or other social interests. McCullagh notes that a historian's cultural background may also contribute to bias in history, since there may be a "culture-wide interest in information of one kind rather than another."[19] Regardless of the source of bias, McCullagh argues, bias manifests itself in the practice of history primarily in four ways:

1. misinterpreting evidence;
2. omitting significant facts about a subject;
3. implying facts which are known to be false; and
4. not mentioning all important causes of events in an explanation.[20]

In order for historians to avoid bias in their own work, McCullagh suggests that they hold "a commitment to standards of rational inquiry which is stronger than one's commitment to a certain outcome."[21] McCullagh does concede, however, that biased history could still be written even if historians adopted this principle since "Sometimes...when investigators who want a certain outcome to be true are challenged to be accurate, the result is not improved accuracy but more elaborate defenses of their preferred result."[22] Nevertheless, he asserts, there are already checks in place that can help limit the number of intentional or unintentional manifestations of bias: an appeal to "the consciences of historians to produce socially responsible history" and "their interest in obtaining favorable peer reviews."[23] In the case of historians of ancient Israel at least, it is not clear that either of these checks actually motivates them to attempt to keep bias at a minimum. In the following chapters, allegations of bias and suggestions for increased objectivity from historians of ancient Israel will be examined, and a more comprehensive list of checks on bias will be suggested.

Even if historians' desires are kept in check, history writing still requires historians to make decisions and value-judgments that are necessarily subjective to some degree. For instance, selection "represents a central and ineliminable feature of historical procedure."[24] Patrick Gardiner argues, however, that "[t]o

19. Ibid., 41. For example, Dray ("Philosophy and Historiography," 771) has observed that many of the changes history experienced in the twentieth century, such as the "shifts from religious to secular emphases...from political and military to social and economic ones; from the activities of social elites to more everyday concerns" can be attributed to culture-wide changes in the value placed on such perspectives.

20. McCullagh, "Bias in Historical Description," 40. For a discussion of objectivity in research in general, see Wayne C. Booth, Gregory G. Colomb, and Joseph M. Williams, *The Craft of Research* (2d ed.; Chicago: University of Chicago Press, 2003), 145–48. Their criteria for responsible use of evidence is similar to McCullagh's. Personal, class, social, and cultural biases of individual historians are not the only potential sources of bias in historical accounts. How evidence, particularly textual evidence, can be biased and how reliance on biased sources can contribute to biased history will be addressed beginning in Chapter 2.

21. McCullagh, "Bias in Historical Description," 55.

22. Ibid., 56.

23. Ibid. McCullagh notes that cultural bias would be hardest to eradicate, even with these checks.

24. Patrick Gardiner, "History, Problems of the Philosophy of," in Honderich, ed., *The Oxford Companion to Philosophy*, 364–67 (365).

maintain that history can...be considered to have an irreducibly evaluative dimension is not, of course, equivalent to suggesting that it is subjective in the pejorative sense of implying personal idiosyncrasy or prejudice."[25] In addition, scholars have noticed that there are advantages to retaining some subjectivity in history writing. In Michael Stanford's view, a certain amount of subjectivity is required if a historian is to understand the human factors, particularly emotions, that affected the course of past events.[26] Another common sentiment is that histories that are highly detached may be boring.[27] Stanford observes that indeed "almost every social scientist today lives and works somewhere between the two poles of positivistic objectivity and insightful subjectivity."[28] Thus, the general consensus appears to be that historians should write history with an appreciation of the difficulties involved in doing history objectively as well as with self-awareness of the subjective factors they bring to their work.

Representation and Language

Perhaps the most simple statement that can be said about history is that it is concerned with representation of the past. Stanford notes, however, that representation of the past "is not as simple a matter as many historians have assumed."[29] Indeed, historians and philosophers disagree on how fully the past can be apprehended and represented. Huizinga claimed that, "In reality history gives no more than a particular representation of a particular past, an intelligible picture of a portion of the past."[30] He also argued that history "is never the reconstruction or reproduction of a given past. No past is ever given."[31] Most historians or philosophers would agree with Huizinga's implication that access to the past requires discovery and interpretation. Yet there are differing conceptions of how complete a particular representation, or intelligible picture, of the past can be. For instance, Perez Zagorin has argued that most historians are (and should be) realists who believe that "history's object is the knowledge of the past as a vanquished reality which is capable of being reconstructed."[32] History writing is thus the practice that can "literally" reconstruct the past.[33] In contrast

25. Ibid., 366.
26. Stanford, *Introduction to the Philosophy of History*, 56–57.
27. Novick, *That Noble Dream*, 14.
28. Stanford, *Introduction to the Philosophy of History*, 22.
29. Ibid., 231.
30. Huizinga, "A Definition of the Concept of History," 5.
31. Ibid.
32. Perez Zagorin, "History, the Referent, and Narrative: Reflections on Postmodernism Now," *History and Theory* 38 (1999): 1–24 (10). For other defenses of writing history with a traditional outlook in the climate of postmodernism, see idem, "History and Postmodernism: Reconsiderations," *History and Theory* 29 (1990): 263–74, and Richard J. Evans, *In Defense of History* (New York: Norton, 1999).
33. Zagorin is here subscribing to ideas about history writing that are decades old. For example, J. B. Bury ("The Science of History," in *Selected Essays of J. B. Bury* [ed. Harold Temperley; Cambridge: Cambridge University Press, 1930], 3–22 [17]) once described the historian's work as contributing brick and mortar to the structure that is the reconstructed past.

is the antirepresentationalist perspective, one of several related postmodernist perspectives that will be discussed in this study. Antirepresentationalists argue that the conventions of representation, particularly language, interfere with one's ability to know or express anything about an object such as the past. Richard Rorty writes that the antirepresentationalist "denies that it is explanatorily useful to pick and choose among the contents of our minds or our language and say that this or that item 'corresponds to' or 'represents' the environment in the way some other item does not."[34] Further, though language cannot represent the past, it can be understood as mediating knowledge about the past, even creating the past in some way.[35] By taking away the hope of correspondence between language and reality and making language responsible for literally creating the past, antirepresentationalism questions the basic premises of most histories.[36]

Historians and philosophers have sought a middle ground between the extreme positions advocated by Zagorin and Rorty. Holding on to the idea that representation is possible, they use insights from antirepresentationalism to mediate potentially oversimplistic notions of representation. For example, Leyden has argued that there is a distinction between the real past and the historical past, that is, the past created by history writing. He states: "that the real past is logically independent of anybody's subsequent thoughts about it is a categorical principle" of history,[37] and thus "historical knowledge can claim logical priority in any attempt to ascertain and construct the past, without however literally creating it."[38] For Leyden, recognizing that language "mediates"[39] the real past and knowledge about it moderates claims about the completeness of historical reconstructions as well as "denial that historical writing refers to an actual historical past."[40]

34. Richard Rorty, *Objectivity, Relativism, and Truth* (2 vols.; Cambridge: Cambridge University Press, 1991), 1:5.

35. Burnett, "Historiography," 107; see also W. J. T. Mitchell, "Representation," in *Critical Terms for Literary Study* (ed. Frank Lentricchia and Thomas McLaughlin; Chicago: University of Chicago Press, 1995), 11–22 (16).

36. Kellner ("Introduction," 1–2) has observed that the ideas that language is "something to be looked *through*" or, conversely, is "something to be looked *at*" have fluctuated in popularity over the course of Western cultural history. He asserts that the tension between the two philosophies "seems as permanent as we can imagine things to be." Cf. Mitchell, "Representation," 14–15.

37. Leyden, "Categories of Historical Understanding," 54.

38. Ibid., 55.

39. Ibid., 56.

40. Georg Iggers, *Historiography in the Twentieth Century: From Scientific Objectivity to the Postmodern Challenge* (Hanover, N.H.: Wesleyan University Press, 1997). Iggers claims that this denial is central to postmodernism, but other scholars argue that the inaccessibility of the referent in antirepresentationalism does not imply its nonexistence. For instance, Keith Jenkins ("A Postmodern Reply to Perez Zagorin," *History and Theory* 39 [2000]: 181–200 [185]) claims that no postmodernists are antirealists, though they are all antirepresentationalists. Also, the views of some of the most vocal antirepresentationalist philosophers such as Ankersmit seem to be mellowing toward the idea of representation. Ankersmit (*Narrative Logic: A Semantic Analysis of the Historian's Language* [Martinus Nijhoff Philosophy Library 7; The Hague: Martinus Nijhoff, 1983], 86) once claimed that "Not according to any current interpretation of the words 'projection' or 'picture' can the narratio be called a 'projection' or 'picture' of historical reality." He later wrote that "the visual

Difficulties in describing and explaining the real past through language have also been observed on the level of historical narrative. Narrative is the literary device that ancient and modern historians have most commonly used to organize and formulate their final product. Philosopher Louis Mink contends that narrative is "a way of making a subject-matter intelligible which is essential and natural in historiography."[41] Narrative is thus a form of historical explanation, yet it is a concept whose appropriateness as a form for describing and explaining the past has been debated heavily in the past decades. In order to understand theorists' concerns about narrative and representation, more general matters of historical explanation and history's subject first must be introduced.

Explanation and Subject

The word "explain," says R. F. Atkinson, has three common uses: to make something known; to make something intelligible; and to account for something.[42] The definitions and statements of history's goals given at the beginning of this chapter reflect history's desire to accomplish all three of these goals of explanation:[43] Leyden called history "knowledge of the past"; Kellner's definition asserts that history makes experience intelligible; and Huizinga's definition of history includes the idea of a civilization accounting for itself. History's goal of promoting understanding also is furthered by explanation.[44]

Since forming explanations is clearly part of the practice of writing history, what history explains—history's subject—and how history explains will be

and optical metaphors which we encounter so often in historical theory show a correct insight into the nature of the historical text after all" (idem, "Statements, Texts and Pictures," in Ankersmit and Kellner, eds., *A New Philosophy of History*, 212–40 [223]).

41. As described by William Dray, *On History and Philosophers of History* (Philosophy of History and Culture 2; Leiden: Brill, 1989), 131; see Louis Mink, "The Autonomy of Historical Understanding," in *Philosophical Analysis and History* (ed. William Dray; New York: Harper & Row, 1966), 160–92.

42. Atkinson, *Knowledge and Explanation in History*, 98–99. Atkinson presents these meanings of explanation in order to examine philosophically historians' conceptions of explanation and see if they indeed operate in the way that explanations are commonly understood. He determines that "The ordinary meaning of 'explanation' is thus wide enough to accommodate all the types of explanation which have been claimed to be characteristic of history" (p. 99).

43. See Arnaldo Momigliano, "Ancient History and the Antiquarian," *Journal of the Warburg and Courtauld Institutes* 13 (1950): 285–315, where he argues that explanation distinguishes "history" from "chronicle" or "antiquarianism."

44. In fact, all three definitions of explanation could be considered ways of promoting understanding. It should be noted here, however, that for philosophers of history, explaining and understanding have in the past connoted different processes and goals. Explanation was associated with causal explanation in the positivist, neopositivist, and postpositivist traditions. Causes, then, were explained, but reasons were understood (see Carr, "Philosophy of History," 672). In current scholarship, the process of understanding reasons is often called rational explanation, assuming a broader meaning of the term explanation that does not limit it to the discovery of causation. See, e.g., the introductory discussion in Gardiner, "History, Problems of the Philosophy of," 364–65. For a discussion of the possibility of reasons being causes, see Atkinson, *Knowledge and Explanation in History*, 141–87.

considered next. As with many of the topics discussed in this study, notions of subject and explanation changed over the course of the twentieth century. Human actions were the purview of traditional modernist-empirical history.[45] History's explanations for the human actions that prompted events were usually expressed in narrative. In the early twentieth century, however, historians of the *Annales* school introduced a focus on nonhuman factors into the study of the past, thereby initiating a shift in history's subject away from human-driven events and individuals.[46] Their subject-less or structural histories replaced narrative with analytical historical writing that appeared to be more suited to its aims. Structuralist tendencies persisted and evolved into poststructuralist history. Each of these types of history involve different assumptions about subject and explanation.

Human Action, Explanation, and Narrative
Until the mid-twentieth century, without much exception, the actors of import to historians were powerful persons whose actions had political and social ramifications. The past often was presented as a succession of leaders such as kings, emperors, senators, knights, popes, and warriors whose deeds were scrutinized, praised, and criticized. In the late twentieth century, power shifts such as the women's rights and civil rights movements occurred in Western societies, laying claim to power for new groups and raising awareness of the importance of the less powerful, including the subjugated and oppressed, to the understanding of the past. Consequently, the range of history's human subjects broadened. By the 1980s, the term "history from below" was understood to connote history which endeavored to include groups outside of the reigning power structure in the story of the past.[47] Since then, the assertion that powerful people were not the only significant actors of the past has found general acceptance among historians, and histories that attempt to involve formerly ignored actors such as women and peasants are now commonplace. Yet writing "history from below" is a formidable task. To begin with, there is no general agreement on where "below" is, or what terms such as "ordinary people," "day-to-day life" and "popular culture" denote. Additionally, historians of these topics often have very little evidence with which to work. Furthermore, this increase in attention to nontraditional

45.   See, e.g., R. G. Collingwood, *The Principles of History and Other Writings in the Philosophy of History* (ed. William Dray and W. J. van der Dussen; Oxford: Oxford University Press, 1999), 44, and Stanford, *Introduction to the Philosophy of History*, 178–82.

46.   For a discussion of whether structures are ontologically reducible to individual actions, see David-Hillel Ruben, "Explanation in History and Social Science," in Craig, ed., *The Routledge Encyclopedia of Philosophy*, 3:525–31 (526–27).

47.   For a discussion of the development of and difficulties of history from below, see Jim Sharpe, "History from Below," in *New Perspectives on Historical Writing* (ed. Peter Burke; University Park: Penn State University Press, 1992), 24–41. For parallels in theology, see Lonnie D. Kliever and John H. Hayes, *Radical Christianity: The New Theologies in Perspective with Readings from the Radicals* (Anderson, S.C.: Droke House, 1968), 32–39. For a discussion of philosophical perspectives and inclusiveness in biblical scholarship, see Martin J. Buss, *Biblical Form Criticism in its Context* (JSOTSup 274; Sheffield: Sheffield Academic Press, 1999), esp. 15–20 and 407–20.

human subjects does not necessarily reflect a change in paradigm. Humans, though now many more of them, are still the actors who performed the actions about which history tells.

Explanations for human action in history fall into two broad categories: "covering-law" explanations and rational explanations.[48] The concept of covering-law explanations in history is associated with the philosopher Carl Gustav Hempel (1905–1997) and has its philosophical roots in nineteenth-century positivism. Covering-law explanations seek to provide causal explanations of human behavior through derived laws. One type of covering-law explanation is statistical, where the laws of probability are cited to explain an occurrence. More familiar to historians are deductive-nomological laws. These claim that the causes of events can be explained through laws of human behavior "which may be social, psychological, and perhaps ultimately biological and physical."[49] Gardiner gives an example of such a law: "Rulers…who pursue policies detrimental to the countries over which they rule become unpopular."[50] Though deductive-nomological laws, like scientific laws, are derived, in history they are not used inductively to predict future events. Rather, prediction in history takes place retrospectively. In other words, an event such as a ruler becoming unpopular is seen as inevitable or highly probable considering the preconditions of the event.

Covering laws may be broad or narrow in scope. Some examples of broad covering-law explanatory paradigms include materialism and idealism. Materialism sees human actions as responses to their material conditions, whereas idealism attributes human actions to the will to live within a system of beliefs. Dray also identifies what he calls "limited-law explanations," which are confined in their reach:

> Historians often explain what happened or was done as characteristic of the period, society, institution or movement which they have in view. Such explanations bring things under generalizations but under generalizations the envisaged scope of which is limited in space and time.[51]

Historical explanation through covering laws has met with much criticism, particularly due to concerns that universal generalizations about human behavior may not be possible. Limited-law explanations could moderate this problem somewhat, but are nevertheless still generalizations. A similar criticism is that covering-law explanations may fail to take into consideration an individual's freedom to act. Thus, since the early nineteenth century, historians have sought alternatives to positivistic universal laws. Leopold von Ranke's famous statement that historians should describe the past "wie es eigentlich gewesen" ("how

---

48.   For a discussion of whether rational explanations are a subset of law explanations, see Atkinson, *Knowledge and Explanation in History*, 115–21.

49.   Carr, "Philosophy of History," 672.

50.   Patrick Gardiner, *The Nature of Historical Explanation* (Oxford: Oxford University Press, 1952), 96.

51.   Dray, "Philosophy and Historiography," 769.

it actually was") made in 1824, was an early expression of the idea that the past should be understood without reference to such overarching concepts.[52] This theory, which offers rational explanation as a way of explaining or understanding human action instead of laws, came to be known as historicism. Historicism's rational explanation seeks to show the reasons behind a person's actions, so that "One can claim to understand what was done when it can be seen as the appropriate thing to have done, given the agent's beliefs about the situation and the goals he was trying to achieve."[53] Philosopher and historian R. G. Collingwood gave perhaps the most well-known suggestion of how to accomplish this, saying that "the historian must re-enact the past in his own mind" by putting himself in the situation of the past agent in order to gain insight into his motives, beliefs, desires, and intentions.[54]

Criticisms of rational explanation include skepticism that naming reasons for a person's action can explain the action fully.[55] Also, Dray points out that rational explanation has not trumped nomological explanation entirely. "If an explanation is to be considered complete, the argument goes, it must show that what happened *had* to happen. And that, defenders of the nomological theory will insist, can only be accomplished by an appeal to laws."[56] Yet rational explanation's assumption that intuition or human experience provides historians with potential explanations for human actions has persisted.

Whether history employs covering-law explanations or rational explanations, narrative is the form of historical exposition that is tied most closely to history with humans and human-driven events as subjects. Lawrence Stone defines narrative as "the organization of material in a chronologically sequential order and the focusing of the content into a single coherent story, albeit with subplots."[57] As mentioned above, narrative is also a form of explanation. Paul Roth says that "A narrative explanation…presents an account of the linkages among events as a process leading to the outcome one seeks to explain."[58] Philosophers discuss narrative in history because, as Roth notes, narrative's explanatory

52.   Leopold von Ranke, "Vorrede der ersten Ausgabe—Oktober 1824," in *Fürsten und Völker: Geschichten der romanischen und germanischen Völker von 1494–1514. Die Osmanen und die spanische Monarchie im 16. und 17. Jahrhundert* (ed. Willy Andreas; Wiesbaden: Emil Vollmer, 1957), 3–5 (4). That being said, Ranke saw God's plan at work in the past. See Ernst Breisach, *Historiography: Ancient, Medieval, and Modern* (2d ed.; Chicago: University of Chicago Press, 1994), 233. A statement of the idea that history should relate "what really happened" can also be found in Heinrich Georg August Ewald, *The History of Israel* (2 vols.; 2d ed.; London: Longmans, Green & Co., 1869), 1:13.
53.   Dray, "Philosophy and Historiography," 767.
54.   R. G. Collingwood, *The Idea of History* (Oxford: Clarendon, 1946), 282. For a discussion of Collingwood's' intellectual predecessors in this opinion, see Provan, Long, and Longman, *A Biblical History of Israel*, 40–41.
55.   Dray, "Philosophy and Historiography," 767–68.
56.   Ibid., 766.
57.   Lawrence Stone, "The Revival of Narrative: Reflections on a New Old History," *Past and Present* 85 (1979): 3–24 (3).
58.   Paul A. Roth, "Narrative Explanations: The Case of History," *History and Theory* 27 (1988): 1–13 (1).

nature is not at issue, but whether it is appropriate for history is.[59] For instance, David Carr has argued that narrative is an ontological category and therefore that history's adoption of narrative is natural. He writes, "As human experiencers and especially as agents we organize temporal sequences into configurations involving beginnings, middles and ends. This is not just the way we tell about our plans and projects after the fact; it is the way they are lived right from the start."[60] On the other hand, Mink argues that the structure of narrative is not something intrinsic to the happenings of the past but is "a pattern *imposed* upon them by the exigencies of story-telling."[61]

Mink's ontological notion was taken into literary criticism by Hayden White in his book *Metahistory*, which spearheaded a revival of the study of the poetics of historical narratives and the relationship of history's narrative form to the organization, explanation, and interpretation of historical data.[62] According to White, historians writing history employ the four classical tropes of metaphor, metonymy, synecdoche, and irony.[63] These are the "deep structural forms of the historical imagination"[64] that not only determine the form of historians' presentations of the past but also their content and the types of explanation and analysis that historians use. In other words, White claims that historians do not start with disjointed information but with a "poetic act" that is the formulation of a framework in which to understand the past. From there the historian moves to research, analysis, and writing, where claims about the past are "emplotted" in narrative form.[65] Under this theory, a historian cannot contribute to the structure of the past without knowing the plan of what he or she is building; the concept of the final structure is in the historian's mind from the start. Additionally,

---

59.   Ibid.

60.   David Carr, "Getting the Story Straight: Narrative and Historical Knowledge," in *Historiography Between Modernism and Postmodernism: Contributions to the Methodology of Historical Research* (ed. Jerzy Topolski; Amsterdam: Rodopi, 1994), 119–33 (122); cf. Jonathan A. Carter, "Telling Times: History, Emplotment, and Truth," *History and Theory* 42 (2003): 1–27. Albert Cook (*History/Writing* [Cambridge: Cambridge University Press, 1988], 9) holds a similar opinion: "The narrative or quasi narrative offers a pattern both that it imposes (it has manifestly selected and organized the data) and that is really there (the pattern has been discovered in the events themselves, as could have happened no other way but in the narrative)."

61.   As discussed by Dray, *On History and Philosophers of History*, 132; see also Roth, "Narrative Explanations," 4–6, where he discusses Mink and similar opinions held by other philosophers, including Maurice Mandelbaum.

62.   Hayden White, *Metahistory: The Historical Imagination in Nineteenth-Century Europe* (Baltimore: The Johns Hopkins University Press, 1973).

63.   Ibid., 31. White demonstrates his theory with case studies from the nineteenth century. Nevertheless, his method of analyzing historical writing has been applied to both ancient and modern histories, and critiques of White's ideas have arisen in the process. See, for instance, Cook, *History/Writing*, 8–9 and 55–58.

64.   White, *Metahistory*, 31.

65.   In *Metahistory*, White also identifies four "modes of emplotment" from which historians can choose (romantic, tragic, comic, and satirical), as well as four modes of argument (formist, mechanistic, organicist, and contextualist) and four modes of ideological implication (anarchist, radical, conservative, liberal).

White argued, "Events in the same set are capable of functioning differently in order to figure forth different *meanings*—moral, cognitive, or aesthetic—within different fictional matrices."[66] In other words, he claimed, historians' literary choices, particularly how they emplot past events, affect the potential interpretations and meanings readers take from historians' constructions of these events.

The examination of the relationship of history to language that has followed the work of White and Mink has been called history's "linguistic turn," and its effect on understanding history has been dramatic. Under the literary lens, history began to look like a creative product of the historian's mind that potentially had little connection to reality and no special claim to knowledge. Consequently, it appeared that history could not hope to tell "what actually happened," but was in fact hard to distinguish from nonhistorical narrative literature, particularly fiction.[67] Worries about history's distinction from fiction are not new, and over the years historians, literary critics, and philosophers have contributed to the discussion. In 1946 Collingwood addressed the issue by arguing that the historian's work and the novelist's work differ in only three ways: a history must be "localized in space and time," it must be "consistent with itself...everything in it must stand in some relation to everything else," and history's truth, unlike the novel's, is justified by an appeal to evidence.[68] Following White's *Metahistory*, however, drawing the history–fiction distinction took on more importance.[69]

Arguments for the distinctiveness of history from fictional literature tend to begin with Collingwood's third rule of historical method, the appeal to evidence. For example, Roger Chartier writes:

> Even when they write in a "literary" form, historians are not making literature. This is because the historian is dependent on two things: first, the archive and the past of which the archive is a trace… Historians are also dependent on the "scientific" criteria and technical operations that are part of their métier. Recognizing variations among them… does not necessarily warrant concluding that such constraints and criteria do not exist or that the only demands on the writing of history are the same as the ones that govern the writing of fiction.[70]

---

66. Hayden White, *Tropics of Discourse* (Baltimore: The Johns Hopkins University Press, 1978), 127.

67. Burnett, "Historiography," 108: "The blurring of the line between history and fiction—for both the production of history and the product—is perhaps the main upshot of the linguistic turn in historical studies." Iggers (*Historiography in the Twentieth Century*, 9–10) claims that discussion of how the use of narrative in history writing requires preconceived frameworks that affect selection and interpretation of information about the past became as least as important as, or perhaps more important than, examination of how rational, law-abiding, or scientific historical explanations are.

68. Collingwood, *Idea of History*, 246.

69. The change from the distinction being a worry to an impetus for a change of focus in the philosophy of history is a postmodern development, since postmodernism challenges modernist assumptions by driving "an epistemological wedge between what an historical account tells us and what actually happened in the past" (Dray, *On History and Philosophers of History*, 133).

70. Robert Chartier, *On the Edge of the Cliff: History, Language, and Practices* (Parallax Revisions of Culture and Society; Baltimore: The Johns Hopkins University Press, 1997), 25–26. It appears that Chartier here equates literature with fiction when he states that historians do not produce literature.

Dorrit Cohn has taken up the discussion of history's distinctiveness from fiction by employing narratology to explore the unique aspects of nonfiction. Using historical narrative as her test case, Cohn names three signposts of fiction that distinguish it from nonfiction. Like Chartier, the first difference between fiction and nonfiction that Cohn notes is historical narrative's "referential level of analysis."[71] This level exists in historical narrative alongside two other levels that are commonly seen in literary texts: "story" and "discourse." Cohn does not deny a certain referentiality in fiction, but observes that "the idea that history is committed to verifiable documentation and that this commitment is suspended in fiction has survived even the most radical dismantling of the history/fiction distinction."[72] The recognition of this level of reference in nonfiction/historical narrative requires a clarification of terminology. Histories, she says, can be described as emplotted, but a novel can not be called "emplotted" since "its serial moments do not refer to, and can therefore not be selected from, an ontologically independent and temporally prior data base of disordered, meaningless happenings that it restructures into order and meaning."[73] Fiction, then, is properly described as "plotted." Cohn's second signpost of fiction is the independence of the subjects from their author. She writes, "The minds of imaginary figures can be known in ways that those of real persons can not."[74] History then "cannot present past events through the eyes of a historical figure present on the scene but only through the eyes of the (forever backward-looking) historian–narrator."[75] In discussing fiction's third signpost, Cohn contends that the author and the narrator of historical narrative are univocal whereas they are distinct in fiction, and she challenges deconstructive readings that collapse the author–narrator distinction for all texts. Thus Cohn, like Chartier, ultimately concludes that a boundary exists between history and fiction.

Another question that has arisen from history's linguistic turn is: How should historians chose the best way to emplot their data, if emplotments reflect ideological choices and thereby influence interpretation? In the nineteenth century, when the substantive philosophy of history was considered vital to the discipline, overarching frameworks for understanding the past and its trajectory in a broad sweep were seen as normal and necessary. History was didactic, and historians were expected to guide interpretation for the advancement of understanding. Sometimes, however, the outcomes of this practice were conclusions or implications that would now be considered too biased for history, such as the implication that Western civilization was the height of human societal evolution and accomplishment. Thus, grand narratives and the substantive philosophy of history fell out of favor. Yet White argues that historians' literary choices always influence interpretation, whether they intend to write a grand narrative or

71. Dorrit Cohn, *The Distinction of Fiction* (Baltimore: The Johns Hopkins University Press, 1999), 112.
72. Ibid., 112–13.
73. Ibid., 114.
74. Ibid., 118.
75. Ibid., 119. Cohn recognizes that historical novels may adopt the manner of fiction, but claims they are "different in kind, not merely in degree" (p. 121).

not. In response, historians have sought ways to suppress or eliminate features of history that might oppressively guide interpretation and prevent readers from being able to draw their own conclusions based on the evidence.

Postmodern theorist Jean-François Lyotard has suggested that historians can avoid giving the false impression of authority by producing small-scale narratives.[76] Indeed, throughout Europe, microhistory has arisen as a way of checking generalizations, especially those made under the influence of social-scientific theory.[77] To other scholars, however, microhistory appears to be inadequate history, since it seems antiquarian, romantic, and ill-equipped to explain change.[78] Other possibilities for historians who wish to remove the authoritative voice from history include writing from the standpoint of many different people, and announcing up front that their work is but one interpretation of the data.[79] McCullagh, on the other hand, rejects the suggestion of including multiple voices, claiming that "the historian's task is to create an account of the history that will explain why each group had the views of it which it had."[80] In addition, Roth argues that an ideal chronicle, in which all voices relevant to understanding the past are included, would necessarily contradict itself.[81] These scholars imply that a desire to let readers interpret meaning from the past themselves should not cause history to devolve into meaningless record keeping, but that history should remain a genre that promotes understanding. Thus, many historians are returning to narrative, attempting to write histories of human-driven events that discuss and explain changes over a long period of time.[82]

In summary, historians working since history's linguistic turn remain committed to representing and explaining the past. They have expanded the actors of interest from aristocrats to "everyday people" and have retained descriptive narrative as the mode of choice for exposition of history with humans as its subject.[83] Historians largely have left the debate over their own narrative history's resemblance to fiction to literary critics and philosophers, though they have had to consider such issues when looking at ancient texts (see Chapter 2). Current affirmations of humans as valid subjects for history and narrative as a valid mode of historical exposition and explanation, however, can only be understood fully in the context of the changes ideas about history's proper subjects and modes of explanation that have occurred under the influence of structuralism and the *Annales* school of history.

---

76.   Jean-François Lyotard, *The Lyotard Reader* (ed. Andrew Benjamin; Oxford: Blackwell, 1989), 132–33.

77.   Discussed in Iggers, *Historiography in the Twentieth Century*, 110.

78.   Ibid., 113.

79.   Peter Burke, "History of Events and the Revival of Narrative," in Burke, ed., *New Perspectives on Historical Writing*, 233–48 (238–40).

80.   McCullagh, "Bias in Historical Description," 59.

81.   Roth, "Narrative Explanations," 9.

82.   See, e.g., Stone, "The Revival of Narrative," and Burke, "History of Events."

83.   Stone, "The Revival of Narrative," 3. He argues that as long as history's "central focus is man not circumstances," descriptive narrative will remain the primary mode of historical exposition and explanation (ibid.).

Annales, *Structuralism and Structures as History's Subject, Poststructuralism, and Historical Explanations Involving Structures*
In 1929, French historians Lucien Febvre and Marc Bloch founded the journal *Annales d'histoire économique et sociale.* They promoted an idea of history which rejected the focus on prominent men and events and instead considered factors such as geography and social structures to be important agents in the past.[84] This new *Annales*-style history reached a pinnacle in Fernand Braudel's *La Méditerranée et le mode Méditerranéen à l'époque de Philippe II.*[85] Here Braudel presented the history of the Mediterranean using three timelines. The slowest was geographical time, where the rate of change was so slow that individual humans rarely were aware of the impact that geographical change had on their lives. The second timeline contained cycles of human activity, such as population fluctuations and economic patterns, that could only be observed over many decades (in what Braudel called "social time"). The third layer of time, individual time, was where events, or *histoire événementielle*—the concern of traditional human-action-oriented historians—took place.[86] To Braudel, human actions and their consequent events primarily were interesting because of what they revealed about the deeper structures of culture.

Developments in the *Annales* type of history were occurring as structuralism became part of the human sciences. Structuralism originated in linguistics with Ferdinand de Saussure (1857–1913), who looked for an internal structure of language that bound together its signs.[87] Saussure considered linguistic signs to be referential but individually arbitrary. Saussure's ideas found their way into other disciplines when "structuralist thinkers extrapolated from structural linguistics to analyse the deep universal mental structures represented by any system of signification."[88] In history, *Annales* historians and structuralists began to explore cultural structures, including *mentalités. Mentalités* were in essence descriptions of collective psychology—for instance, what the community "thought" about religion or work, or its perceptions of the geographical features around them. According to these historians, a culture's shared conceptions inform the behavior

84. For a summary of the *Annales* school and criticisms of it, see Green and Troup, eds., *Houses of History*, 87–97. For a history of the movement up until the early 1970s, see Traian Stoianovich, *French Historical Method: The* Annales *Paradigm* (Ithaca, N.Y.: Cornell University Press, 1976). For a current critical analysis of the contributions of *Annales* historians to history, see George Huppert, "The *Annales* Experiment," in Bentley, ed., *Companion to Historiography*, 873–88. For an account of German historical scholarship at the time of the rise of the *Annales* school, see Iggers, *Historiography in the Twentieth Century*, 65–77. Working class movements and the social history of labor were of particular concern to German historians at this time.

85. Fernand Braudel, *La Méditerranée et le Monde méditerranéen à l'époque de Philippe II* (2d ed.; Paris: Armand Colin, 1966). Published in English as *The Mediterranean and the Mediterranean World in the Age of Philip II* (New York: Harper & Row, 1972).

86. Braudel, *The Mediterranean*, 21. For a current discussion of history that involves placing human history in the context of universal and galactic history, see David Christian, *Maps of Time: An Introduction to Big History* (Berkeley: University of California Press, 2004).

87. Ferdinand de Saussure, *Cours de linguistique générale* (Lusanne: Payot, 1916). Published in English as *Course in General Linguistics* (Glasgow: Fontana/Collins, 1977).

88. Green and Troup, eds., *Houses of History*, 298.

of individuals and provide a broad, complex context for their actions and other ephemeral historical events.

Perhaps the greatest difficulty for historians who make social structures history's subject has been integrating *mentalités*, geographical information, and social time with the events of human history. How is geographical time, for instance, important to explaining the occurrence of an event? Further, is an event truly ephemeral to understanding the past and the important insights only to be found in the study of the larger structures and *mentalités*? Despite these criticisms, the contributions of *Annales* and historians writing about structures are highly regarded, and awareness of the impact of such factors as geography and social structures on human behavior has been absorbed into mainstream historical practice.

Structuralism was followed by poststructuralism. Structuralism had claimed that signs are primarily self-referential within their set, though they do secondarily refer to the external world or reality. Poststructuralism, an important facet of postmodernism, took this notion a step further, arguing that signs are entirely self-referential and that the external world or reality is absent from any system of signification. From a poststructuralist point of view, then, a historian's reconstruction does not refer to reality; "a poststructuralist might argue that the house is still only visible from one side; for all the observer can tell the far wall may be unfinished."[89] One poststructuralist theory particularly relevant to history is deconstruction. Deconstruction was introduced into philosophy by Jacques Derrida (1930–) and applied to literature by Paul de Man (1919–1983). To deconstruct is to recognize that part of language's meaning lies in oppositions rather than in direct references. Derrida called this opposition *différance*. For literature, deconstruction argues that texts can have meanings that rely on concepts to which they do not refer. For example, a deconstructionist reading could be an examination of what a text's construction of masculinity indicated about femininity. History, too, can be read deconstructively, that is, as if the apparent referent of history were simply one possible construction of many in the text.

There is no doubt that deconstruction has challenged and frustrated historians, and effects of deconstructionist readings of the Bible on the history of ancient Israel and Judah will be discussed in the following chapters. Be that as it may, some elements of poststructuralism have been incorporated into the general practice of history. According to poststructuralism, any system of signification such as class construction, attitudes about death, or attitudes about the body can be considered a self-referential "text." Using this concept, Michel Foucault (1926–1984) advocated a type of history that he called the "archaeology of knowledge," or a history of systems of thought.[90] His work is based on a critique of the viability of the notion of the self-present subject in philosophy and history, or "the subject's ability to declare itself self-evidently independent of

---

89. Ibid.
90. Michel Foucault, *The Archaeology of Knowledge* (New York: Pantheon, 1972); trans. of *L'archéologie du savoir* (Paris: Gallimard, 1969).

the external conditions of its own possibility."[91] Foucault paid special attention to the dynamics of power surrounding systems of thought and power's repressive possibilities. Systems of thought relevant to self-determination that Foucault investigated include constructions of madness and sexuality.[92]

With cultural constructions being read as texts and the self-present subject receding in history, poststructuralism has offered the possibility of a history of "virtually every human activity" and idea.[93] Poststructuralism also affords historians the opportunity to compose long analyses of structures of past societies without writing a traditional historical narrative with subjects, plot, and a timeline. Historians and philosophers, however, have never entirely accepted the idea of subject-less histories, worrying that they could "attribute so much power to social structures that it no longer seems possible to imagine subjects exercising…power."[94] Thus, the critique of the self-present subject requires a return to a question posed to the *Annales* historians: How can the existence of social structures be used to explain an action or event?

One opinion, expressed by David-Hillel Ruben, is that "Social structure cannot have an effect on the agents' behaviour directly; its effect must be mediated through, or combined with, the psychology of the agents."[95] Consequently, says Mark Bevir, "the most we can allow is that structure influences or restricts performance."[96] In other words, one way to understand the relationship between structures and events is that structures, while forming the conditions of an event, do not determine the event; the explanation of a specific event must return to the specific human agent. On the other hand, McCullagh argues that historians can use social structures and general processes in their explanations of social change over time, since "social changes can cause not only changes in properties of a community, but also changes in individual behaviour that may include changes in belief and action."[97] How historians of ancient Israel have negotiated the relationship between structures and human actions will be seen in the following chapters.

91. Laura Hengehold, "Subject, Postmodern Critique of the," in Craig, ed., *The Routledge Encyclopedia of Philosophy*, 9:196–201 (196). A review of Foucault's ideas about historiography can be found in Mark Bevir, "The Subject and Historiography," *Giornale di Metafisica* 22 (2000): 5–28.

92. Michel Foucault, *Madness and Civilization: A History of Insanity in the Age of Reason* (New York: Vintage, 1973); trans. of *Folie et déraison: Histoire de la folie à l'âge classique* (Paris: Plon, 1961); 2nd ed. (Paris: Gallimard, 1972); idem, *The History of Sexuality* (3 vols.; New York: Vintage, 1980); trans. of *Histoire de la Sexualité* (Paris: Gallimard, 1976–84).

93. Peter Burke, "Overture: The New History, Its Past and Its Future," in Burke, ed., *New Perspectives on Historical Writing*, 1–23 (3). This book includes sections entitled "History of Reading," "History of Images," "History of Political Thought," and "History of the Body."

94. Hengehold, "Subject, Postmodern Critique of the," 200. It is worth noting, however, that Foucault never abandoned the idea of the subject entirely, and at the end of his life was reconsidering the possibilities of the subject's self-determination. See Deborah Cook, *The Subject Finds a Voice: Foucault's Turn Toward Subjectivity* (Revisioning Philosophy 11; New York: Peter Lang, 1993).

95. Ruben, "Explanation in History and Social Science," 528.

96. Bevir, "The Subject and Historiography," 18.

97. McCullagh, *The Truth of History*, 296.

Another aspect of the shift to history focused on structures rather than human action returns to literary considerations. The form of histories about structures and poststructuralist nonsubjects usually is analytical rather than narrative, as it does not overtly follow a timeline or necessarily seek to tell a story chronologically. Paul Ricoeur has argued, however, that poststructuralist, non-event-centered histories never fully escape narrative. Chartier sums up the reasons Ricoeur considers all works of history to be narratives:

> The entities that historians manipulate (society, classes, mentalities, etc.) are "quasi characters" implicitly endowed with the properties of the singular heroes and the ordinary individuals who make up the collectivities designated by the abstract categories. Moreover, historical temporalities remain largely subservient to subjective time.[98]

In other words, Ricoeur argues that characters and a chronological framework exist even in histories with nonhuman subjects, allowing for plot and, therefore, for narrative. Furthermore, Stone contends that the study of structures such as *mentalités* has in fact contributed to the revival of narrative: "More and more of the 'new historians' are now trying to discover what was going on inside people's heads in the past, and what it was like to live in the past, questions which inevitably lead back to the use of narrative."[99] Thus, issues of narrative pertain to history writing and explanation regardless of history's subject, though the broadening of history's subject has caused the concept and application of historical narrative to change.

As will be discussed at the conclusion of this section, history has begun to meld subjects and explanatory models from both traditional human-driven paradigms of history and history with structures as subjects. First, due to the prevalence of interest in the social sciences among historians in general, including historians of ancient Israel, the use of the social sciences for theories and models of culture that become sources of explanation for historians must be examined also.

The Social Sciences[100]

Several issues must be addressed by historians who wish to draw upon social-scientific research for their history writing, the first being the potential benefits of such an endeavor. One justification for interaction between history and the social sciences is their similar interests, particularly those of history compared

---

98. Chartier, *On the Edge of the Cliff*, 16–17; Paul Ricoeur, *Time and Narrative* (3 vols.; Chicago: University of Chicago Press, 1984), 1:208; trans. of *Temps et récit* (3 vols.; Paris: Éditions du Seuil, 1984).

99. Stone, "The Revival of Narrative," 13.

100. A large body of literature has debated the use of the social sciences in history writing, as well as the value of history for sociology and anthropology. A number of challenges emerge in either case. Since the historian's practice is the object of this study, the role of the social sciences in history is the sole focus of the discussion here. For an overview of this topic, see the section "Anthropology and History in the 1980s," *Journal of Interdisciplinary History* 12 (1981): 227–78. For a detailed analysis of history's potential contribution to the social sciences, see John Comaroff and Jean Comaroff, *Ethnography and the Historical Imagination* (Boulder, Colo.: Westview, 1992).

to those of sociology and anthropology.[101] For instance, historians are usually interested in what anthropologist Sherry Ortner defines as "traditional anthropological concerns," namely, "the actual organization and culture of the society in question."[102] In addition, like historians, anthropologists ask "how we are to understand people culturally different from ourselves" and how one puts an event "within its full cultural context, so that it can be studied on an analytical rather than merely a descriptive level."[103] More concretely, historian Natalie Davis says anthropology can help the historian by offering:

> close observation of living processes of social interaction; interesting ways of interpreting symbolic behavior; suggestions about how the parts of a social system fit together; and material from cultures very different from those which historians are used to studying.[104]

In addition, for some scholars, interaction with the social sciences offers a way to write history without adopting a European-empiricist model. Put in terms of poststructuralism, these historians use the social sciences to aid them in entering, describing, analyzing, and even adopting for history writing a set of self-referential signs that is foreign to them. For instance, Bernard Cohn advocates an anthropological history in which documents are examined "not to establish chronologies or to sift historical fact from mythical fancy, but to try to grasp the meanings of the forms and contents of these texts in their own cultural terms."[105] Similarly, Jordan Goodman envisions a method "in which classifications and categories are not pre-selected," that is where the subject's self-conception and ways of organizing the world are considered valid modes of presentation and explanation.[106]

The second step for historians hoping to borrow insights from the social sciences is understanding exactly what the social sciences can offer history.

---

101. The traditional demarcation between cultures studied by anthropology and those studied by sociology is industrialization. Economics and political science are also generally concerned with postindustrial societies. Consequently, anthropology is the social science considered to have the most potential to aid historians of the ancient world in their research. Economic and political insights, however, can be found in anthropology, as well. Psychoanalysis has also been used in a manner similar to the social sciences, that is, as a mode of understanding and explaining human action in the past. Psychohistorical analysis differs from evaluation of psychological motives in human subjects (discussed above) because psychohistorical analysis depends on laws derived from the discipline of psychology, not casual or experiential psychological observations by historians. Psychohistory is "one of the most controversial areas of twentieth-century historiography" (Green and Troup, eds., *Houses of History*, 59). For this reason, and because psychohistorical analysis rarely takes place in ancient history, it will not be treated in this study.

102. Sherry B. Ortner, "Theory in Anthropology Since the Sixties," *Comparative Studies in Society and History* 26 (1984): 126–66 (143).

103. Sharpe, "History from Below," 35.

104. Natalie Zemon Davis, "The Possibilities of the Past," *Journal of Interdisciplinary History* 12 (1981): 267–75 (267).

105. Bernard S. Cohn, "Toward a Rapprochement," *Journal of Interdisciplinary History* 12 (1981): 227–52 (247).

106. Jordan Goodman, "History and Anthropology," in Bentley, ed., *Companion to Historiography*, 783–804 (798).

Social scientists collect empirical data, but the data may be very far afield in time and/or space from the object of historical study. Furthermore, social scientists usually compile deductions from their data as models, not laws. Models are best understood as highly generalized theoretical portraits of human societies that explain some aspects of their workings. When forming them, anthropologists too must grapple with questions of how structures and human action relate to each other, as well as the relationship of laws and models to rationality in explaining events and culture.[107] Thus, Goodman asserts that historians must understand the theories behind the models they choose to adopt and the "profound issues of interpretation of culture and its meaning" on which they are based.[108] Also, claims Davis, historians need to remember that theoretical models cannot answer historical questions of who, what, where, or when. What they can do is provide "relevant comparisons,"[109] particularly of social structures and processes.

Comparison is a process that depends on the assumption that the objects being compared have individual integrity and are yet relatable in some way. Therefore, before comparing a past society to a social-scientific model, the historian must consider the types and amount of information available about the past society under study, especially whether information about its structures and social processes is available. Also, the appropriateness of a particular social-scientific concept for comparison must be examined. For instance, as anthropologist John Adams observes, some historians have enthusiastically adopted the anthropological notion that societies have a "focal institution" and tried to identify such institutions in past societies.[110] Adams notes that the "possible universality [of the idea of the focal institution] has never been discussed by historians."[111] Indeed, anthropologists have found such focal institutions in very few societies, which further highlights the caution with which historians should appropriate it or other such concepts. In addition, historians must remember that many social-scientific theories emanate from observation of a postcapitalist, postcolonial world. For instance, since Marxist analysis pertains to postindustrial societies, a historian wishing to perform a Marxist-like analysis of an ancient culture would have to define entities like social classes for preindustrial societies and show that these existed in the society in question.

107. For example, Max Weber advocated a type of explanation that involved comparison along with singular causal analysis aided by counterfactual reasoning. Weber claimed that this type of explanation could be used for both human actions and structures. For discussion, see Fritz Ringer, "Max Weber on Causal Analysis, Interpretation, and Comparison," *History and Theory* 41 (2002): 163–78.

108. Goodman, "History and Anthropology," 787.

109. Davis, "The Possibilities of the Past," 267.

110. John W. Adams, "Consensus, Community, and Exoticism," *Journal of Interdisciplinary History* 12 (1981): 253–65 (257). The premier example of a focal institution is the Balinese cockfight, which was described and analyzed by Clifford Geertz (*The Interpretation of Cultures* [New York: Basic Books, 1973]). In cockfighting Geertz saw a text "built out of social materials" that drew "on almost every level of Balinese experience" (p. 449).

111. Adams, "Consensus, Community, and Exoticism," 257–60.

Scholars recognize other limits to how helpful the social sciences can be in providing explanatory models and theories for history, as well. Finley said about the two: "[D]ialogue is useful in so far, and only in so far, as it is useful. Because anthropology illuminates one period (or one aspect) of the classical world, it does not automatically follow that it also illuminates all other periods (or aspects)."[112] Goodman also addresses historians' occasional overenthusiasm for the social sciences when he notes that historians sometimes look to anthropology, especially popular individual anthropologists, to escape from problems within their own discipline.[113] As Davis says, anthropology is not, then, "some kind of higher vision of social reality to which historians should convert."[114]

Once the entities and boundaries for comparison of a historical culture with social-scientific data and models are established, what does the historian do with the information? Max Weber, whose work on ancient sociology almost single-handedly created and defined historical sociology, recognized early on that comparison must entail more than noticing similarities. He was particularly concerned that unsophisticated recognition of like traits among societies was being used to explain the course of the past by fitting societies into an evolutionary framework that identified superior and inferior cultures.[115] It can be added that emphasis on similarity can tempt historians to forget that models and theories cannot be used as evidence for specific historical questions.[116] Weber said that instead comparison "should be concerned with the *distinctiveness* of each of the two developments that were finally so different, and the purpose of the comparison must be the causal *explanation* of the difference."[117] In other words, when comparing societies, historians should note dissimilarity between two cultures in order to stimulate their explanations and analyses of cultural structures and other traits.[118] In addition, many scholars have argued that simplistic comparison could be avoided if history and the social sciences tested each

112.   Finley, *The Use and Abuse of History*, 116.

113.   Goodman, "History and Anthropology," 788.

114.   Davis, "The Possibilities of the Past," 274.

115.   For a discussion of Weber's ideas on comparison, see Guenther Roth, introduction to *Economy and Society: An Outline of Interpretive Sociology*, by Max Weber (2 vols.; ed. Guenther Roth and Claus Wittich; Berkeley: University of California Press, 1978), 1:xxxiii–cx (xxxviii). For example, Weber discusses the use of comparison to determine causes and argues that "even though the situations appear superficially very similar we must actually understand them or interpret them as very different, perhaps, in terms of meaning, directly opposed" (*Economy and Society*, 10). Referring to ideal types or models used to evaluate economic factors behind an event or action, Weber says, "by throwing the discrepancy between the actual course of events and the ideal type into relief, the analysis of the non-economic motives actually involved is facilitated" (p. 21).

116.   See, for example, Finley, *The Use and Abuse of History*, 116–17 and 61–77. Finley discusses how comparison with data from anthropology resulted in simplistic conclusions about Spartan ritual.

117.   Weber, as quoted in Roth, "Introduction," xxxvii.

118.   Cf. Jurgen Kocka, "Comparison and Beyond," *History and Theory* 42 (2003): 39–44 (41), who notes that comparison helps scholars distance themselves from things they know best. Kocka's article is a philosophical defense of comparison in general.

other's theories and carried on a dialogue about the results.[119] Historians would ask if social-scientific theory holds up against the data of the past culture they study, and social scientists would take into account historical evidence in formulating their models. The result would be increased theoretical discussion and better models for historians and social scientists alike.

In conclusion, a few broad methodological guidelines can be inferred from this discussion of how historians should evaluate and use information from the social sciences. First, historians must decide whether there is enough information to initiate comparison. Recognizing the limits of their historical sources will help determine whether a societal pattern, process, or institution is known well enough to be compared to a similar phenomenon from the social sciences. Second, historians should fully understand the social-scientific scholarship they use for comparison. This includes understanding the theory that underlies particular types of data collection and models, as well as competing theories that the research may address. In addition, historians must examine the potential for universal application of the concepts they borrow from the social sciences. Finally, historians using comparative data and models from the social sciences to explain the past should avoid a simplistic focus on similarities of cultures. They should note differences and use them to think creatively about how and why the past society under study came to its particular social configuration and also potentially to re-evaluate the social-scientific concepts being appropriated.

Summary of Explanation and Subject
In practice, historians do not rely on a single type of explanation. Covering and limited laws, narrative, and social-scientific theories and models may all help provide explanations for events and structures in the past. As Peter Burke writes, "The traditional agreement about what constitutes a good historical explanation has broken down."[120] Put more positively, Gardiner describes how historians now use many types of explanation to help further understanding of the past:

> explanations in history may range from being ones that purport to demonstrate the inevi-tability of a particular event to others that are confined to indicating how an unexpected occurrence was possible in a given set of circumstances, and from being ones that focus on the individual motivation attributable to certain historical figures to others whose chief concern is with the influence exerted by such impersonal factors as environmental conditions or advances in technology.[121]

As Gardiner's assessment of current historiographical practices indicates, the variety of types of explanation historians now use is linked to the variety of subjects now in history's purview.

Noteworthy here also is the fact that all the types of explanation mentioned in this study depend on the assumption of past–present correspondence. Such an

---

119. Opinions on this frequently expressed notion can be found in Davis, "The Possibilities of the Past," 274 and Ortner, "Theory in Anthropology," 126–66.

120. Burke, "Overture," 17.

121. Gardiner, "History, Problems of the Philosophy of," 365; cf. Tor Egil Førland, "The Ideal Explanatory Text in History: A Plea for Ecumenism," *History and Theory* 43 (2004): 321–40.

assumption holds that human behavior, the functions and internal logic of social structures, and the workings of the physical world all operated in the past within the same boundaries and with the same possibilities as they do today. This assumption, implicit in most cases of historical explanations, is not universally held among historians of ancient Israel, as will be seen later in this study. In particular, the role of God in events is a controversial topic for those whose historical endeavors intersect with their religious beliefs.[122] The subjects and modes of explanations used by historians of ancient Israel will be examined beginning in Chapter 3.

Truth

History, writes Chartier, "claims to be a discourse about truth."[123] In this claim lies history's very call to existence, as truth "can be seen as the essence and master concept of all philosophical and, some would hold, all human concerns."[124] There is no such thing as a brief general discussion of truth and history. Philosophers and historians have returned again and again to questions of how a work of history can be true, what kinds of truth a work of history conveys, and whether history is indeed a discourse that can achieve or aspire to truth. Issues of truth in history also include how historians justify their historical descriptions,[125] how one knows "if evidence is sufficient to yield knowledge or rational belief,"[126] how a historical account is meaningful to an audience, and how metaphors and generalizations used by historians can be said to be true.[127] Any complete overview of the topic would have to address these and many more issues. This study, however, will limit its discussion of truth in history to an investigation of how correspondence, coherence, and pragmatic theories of truth appear in histories of ancient Israel in order to help clarify the nature of the truth claims historians of ancient Israel are making.

  Correspondence theories are the oldest theories of truth and the most common ones adhered to by non-philosophers,[128] including historians. Correspondence theories claim that truth is "the correspondence between fact and mind," or perhaps more appropriately for modernity and postmodernity, correspondence between fact and statement.[129] What exactly correspondence means is not

---

122. Of course, the supernatural is also present in explanations for the past given by ancient writers, such as in the Bible.

123. Chartier, *On the Edge of the Cliff*, 45.

124. J. L. Gorman, "Freedom and History" (review of C. Behan McCullagh, *The Truth of History*), *History and Theory* 39 (2000): 251–62 (251).

125. E.g. C. Behan McCullagh, *Justifying Historical Descriptions* (Cambridge: Cambridge University Press, 1984).

126. Richard Feldman, "Evidence," in Audi, ed., *The Cambridge Dictionary of Philosophy*, 293–94 (293).

127. E.g. C. Behan McCullagh, "Metaphor and Truth in History," *Clio* 23 (1993): 24–49.

128. Richard L. Kirkham, "Truth, Correspondence Theory of," in Craig, ed., *The Routledge Encyclopedia of Philosophy*, 9:472–75 (472).

129. Stanford, *Introduction to the Philosophy of History*, 67.

important here;[130] the "common denominator of all correspondence theories of truth" is that "a truth bearer is true if and only if it corresponds to a state of affairs and that state of affairs obtains."[131] Applied to history this means that "the truth of an historical account rests upon its correspondence to the facts."[132] It follows from this theory that appealing to facts is a legitimate way to critique and evaluate a historical account.

There are also ways of understanding truth that do not require a truth bearer to correspond to facts or reality. Coherence theories of truth "make truth a matter of a truth bearer's relations to other truth bearers."[133] For history, coherence theories could have at least two applications. First, coherence requires that in order to be true, a work of history must be internally consistent and coherent. Second, a coherence theory of truth could allow a historical account's truth claim to be boosted by its congruity with other accounts. From the perspective of a correspondence theory of truth, a weakness in coherence theories of truth is their theoretical allowance of two internally coherent sets of beliefs to be called true even if they disagree with one another. An appeal to facts or reality can not, in coherence theory's purest form, be used to combat this potential relativism.

Pragmatic theories of truth constitute a third category of theories of truth relevant to history. Pragmaticism, one pragmatic theory of truth, holds that "a true proposition is one which would be endorsed unanimously by all persons who had sufficient relevant experiences to judge it."[134] It seems impossible that a work of history could be considered true in this way, as it would be very difficult to clarify what "sufficient relevant experience" would mean for scholars and their audiences. Another pragmatic theory of truth, instrumentalism, claims that "a proposition counts as true if and only if behaviour based on a belief in the proposition leads, in the long run and all things considered, to beneficial results for the believers."[135] Beneficial, or useful beliefs, have been defined as those which:

> enable us to manipulate the objects of the world; allow us to communicate successfully with our fellows; provide good explanations for other occurrences; and lead to accurate predictions.[136]

Using pragmatic theories of truth in history writing is problematic. For one, the issue of reality's importance to pragmatic theories of truth is complex. For pragmatic theories, "reality itself is an incidental side effect which distracts from, rather than reveals, the essential nature of truth."[137] Thus, following a

---

130. See Kirkham, "Truth, Correspondence Theory of," for discussion of how this term has been difficult for philosophers to define.

131. Ibid., 473.

132. Green and Troup, eds., *Houses of History*, 3.

133. Richard L. Kirkham, "Truth, Coherence Theory of," in Craig, ed., *The Routledge Encyclopedia of Philosophy*, 9:470–72 (470).

134. Kirkham, "Truth, Pragmatic Theory of," in Craig, ed., *The Routledge Encyclopedia of Philosophy*, 9:478–80 (478).

135. Ibid.

136. Ibid., 480.

137. Ibid.

pragmatic theory of truth, one could argue that useful historical truth does not have to be based in objective consideration of the past. Further, in light of Foucault's claim that historical knowledge is a form of power, historical truth that is considered beneficial to a community can be used as a justification for both building up existing social constructions and suppressing ideas that challenge them.

In response to the recognition of the potential power of history in its community, scholars have suggested theories of truth that take this power into account. James Kloppenberg advocates a theory of truth that employs hermeneutics to address the needs and sensitivities of the modern communities in which historians and their audience are situated while using the scientific method to attend to the facts. This combination, he claims, "make[s] our versions of the past truer because they are more comprehensive, more multidimensional, more frankly tentative in tone, and more sensitive to the diversities of human cultures than our predecessors' accounts have been."[138] Along these same lines, historians recognize that "The duties of the historian are moral as well as epistemological"[139] and therefore that "We should consider not just whether each statement fits the facts… It is proper also to ask whether the whole piece is right, honest, straight, reliable, and even honourable."[140]

Postmodernism's effect on ideas of truth also cannot be ignored. If, as postmodernism asserts, all claims to knowledge are justified and all discourses are discourses of power, "what people believe is what they are invited, forced, or simply choose to believe rather than something external to themselves that they can rationally apprehend" and "truth is simply an ideology that is accepted as true."[141] Such an understanding of truth could be viewed as an expansion of pragmatic truth, as a community may choose to accept truths that are beneficial to it, and is amenable to theories of truth by coherence, since according to postmodernism, truth cannot reference anything external to thoughts or language. Correspondence theories of truth, however, are difficult to maintain in the face of postmodernism, as its challenges to notions of objectivity and representation have undermined certainty in the existence of objective facts to which historians' statements can correspond.

As will be seen in the following chapters, most historians of ancient Israel operate with a notion that history's truth lies in its correspondence to reality and have developed ways to accommodate correspondence, as well as representation and objectivity, to concerns brought on by postmodernism's challenges. Historians of ancient Israel have also addressed pragmatic concerns to some extent. Additional suggestions for a concept of truth appropriate to history will be made in Chapter 6.

---

138. James T. Kloppenberg, "Objectivity and Historicism: A Century of American Historical Writing" (review of Peter Novick, *That Noble Dream: The "Objectivity Question" and the American Historical Profession*), *AHR* 94 (1989): 1011–30 (1028).

139. Stanford, *Introduction to the Philosophy of History*, 70.

140. Ibid. See also Joep Leerssen and Ann Rigney, eds., *Historians and Social Values* (Amsterdam: Amsterdam University Press, 2000).

141. Philip R. Davies, "Biblical Studies in a Postmodern Age," *Jian Dao* 7 (1997): 37–75 (39).

Conclusion

The topics discussed in this chapter—empiricism, objectivity, representation, language, explanation, subject, and truth—provide a general outline of philosophical issues that pertain to history writing. This brief summary of these topics shows that notions about them have changed over the course of the last century. It has also shown that historians can vary widely in opinions about these topics. History is no longer easily defined as a narrative account of human actions, or as a scientific, objective, law-giving study of past human behavior, but has become an amalgam of historicist, structuralist, and poststructuralist concerns that has nevertheless retained a positivistic element in its enthusiasm for social-scientific theory. It is the aim of this study to elucidate what assumptions historians of ancient Israel hold about the aspects of history discussed here. Before that analysis can commence, however, the important and more openly debated topic (among historians of ancient Israel, at least) of how historians should evaluate and use evidence must be considered.

Chapter 2

EVALUATING AND USING EVIDENCE

Introduction

Though assumptions and presuppositions about many of empirical history's tenets changed in the twentieth century, evidence remains the basis for every historical account. The necessary selection and interpretation involved in using evidence for history writing requires many assumptions and decisions on the part of historians. They must select evidence relevant to their goal, but their goal naturally influences their selection, and some argue that historians "do not so much 'discover' as 'create' evidence by using it in the light of the right questions in his mind."[1] When historians find or select evidence, they must evaluate its usefulness or trustworthiness. Standards for verification of evidence, however, are "continually shifting and transforming."[2] Furthermore, in order for evidence to contribute to history's goals of explaining and understanding the past, historians must interpret it, and historians' presuppositions and personal judgments play a large part in this process. Finally, all evidence for the past is inconclusive and "can always be defeated or overridden by subsequently acquired evidence."[3] Thus, historians are constantly searching for new evidence and reevaluating the relationship of new evidence to previous knowledge.

This chapter offers a preliminary examination of the methodology and presuppositions historians bring to evidence, focusing specifically on historians of the ancient world[4] and the two main categories of evidence available to them, texts and artifacts.[5] In the spirit of empiricist methodology, historians rigorously examine both texts and artifacts for information that can help describe and

---

1. Leyden, "Categories of Historical Understanding," 61, describing the position of Collingwood.
2. Ibid.
3. Feldman, "Evidence," 293–94.
4. As in Chapter 1, the description here will exclude historians of ancient Israel in order to present a general picture of the discipline of history to which current practices in the history of ancient Israel can be compared.
5. Historians use other types of evidence, as well. For instance, oral sources, such as storytelling and testimony, may be available to historians of more recent cultures. Historians also seek evidence about natural processes such as climate and geography (see the discussion of the *Annales* school, Chapter 1). Evidence for these processes may be found in texts and in artifacts (such as pollen samples and fossilized tree rings), but also often can be observed in the present day.

explain what happened in the past. These types of evidence, however, offer different types of information about the past, and historians do not agree on their individual value or on the proper relationship of the types to each other.

Texts

For the majority of historians, past and present, evidence and texts have been synonymous. This viewpoint has been summed up as "until there are documents, there can be no proper history."[6] Historians value texts whose shape, storyline, content, and proximity to the events described suggest that the descriptions contained within them are accurate depictions of what actually happened. To be more specific, a valuable text would exhibit "precision in form or genre, precision in chronology," and its claims would be similar to the claims of other texts.[7] In addition, many historians prefer eyewitness or near-eyewitness accounts of the past to other sources. In the spirit of scientific inquiry, these historians look for accounts from observers who were as close to the event as possible.

The textual record also includes accounts of events that occurred some time before the texts' composition. Norman Gottwald has called such texts "depth-dimensional sources."[8] Many histories written by ancient authors are examples of depth-dimensional sources. The ancient historians who wrote them were not necessarily involved in the events they report, but themselves appear to have used more ancient sources as evidence.[9] Thus, an ancient history is depth-dimensional because it is both a relic of the culture that produced it and a potential repository of older accounts. Further complicating the interpretation of depth-dimensional

6. Gwyn Prins, "Oral History," in Burke, ed., *New Perspectives on Historical Writing*, 114–39 (114).

7. Ibid., 119. Prins describes these qualities as the qualities "traditional document-driven historians" look for in their sources, but also discusses how oral sources differ from texts and challenge these notions.

8. Norman K. Gottwald, "Preface to the Reprint," in *The Tribes of Yahweh*, xxxix.

9. Some ancient Chinese writings qualify as histories (see David Morgan, "The Evolution of Two Asian Historiographical Traditions," in Bentley, ed., *Companion to Historiography*, 11–22), but Western scholarship has dubbed Herodotus the "Father of History." For his *Historia*, or inquiries, he interviewed people who had participated in events surrounding the Persian Wars, as well as their descendants. Herodotus also may have traveled around the Mediterranean and observed first-hand many of the people and places he described. His interests were varied, covering topics we would now classify as archaeology, ethnography, geography, religion, and anecdote. See M. C. Howatson, ed., *The Oxford Companion to Classical Literature* (Oxford: Oxford University Press, 1989), 282. Thucydides, the next great Greek historian, had a narrower view of what a history should include; for him there was "no room for anecdote or scandal or hearsay, and certainly no room for romantic" (ibid., 570). Thucydides compared his work to that of a physician, and is considered by many to be the first scientific historian. Nonetheless, Thucydides rarely cited documents, and he added his own perspective and judgments by inventing speeches for historical figures to give on important occasions. The classical world subsequently saw the development of many types of history: local history, such as that written about Athens by the Atthidographers; social history, such as Xenophon's *Anabasis*; moralizing history, exemplified by Isocrates and popular later in Rome; and universal history, to name a few.

sources, particularly ancient histories, is the strong presence of moral, didactic, or propagandistic themes in them, as will be discussed below.

In addition, the textual record from the past includes epigraphic evidence such as inscriptions and ostraca, which may be fragmentary and incidental, as well as longer texts. This type of epigraphic evidence is usually uncovered by archaeologists and requires archaeological interpretation as well as historical interpretation. Before the specific challenges and contributions of the various types of textual evidence are examined, however, it is useful to discuss some general principles for evaluating texts.

General Principles for Evaluating and Using Texts as Evidence
Stanford offers three general steps for evaluation and use of evidence that can be applied to texts (as well as to artifacts). The first step is "to examine the relic and be quite sure that it is what it seems to be," or basically to authenticate the potential relic's status as a relic and not something of the present day.[10] The second step is understanding how the relic came to be what it is and where it is today, which is done by ascertaining "through whose hands it has passed and what they may have done to it."[11] Finally, the historian must consider the origins of the object: "Here the important questions are to ask how and why it was produced, by whom and with what intention, in what context...and in what circumstances."[12] For documents, he says that "it is particularly important in history to try to arrive at the intention of the author."[13] He also mentions that historians should be more skeptical of a document written "for other eyes," such as superiors or posterity, than of personal records, such as diaries or account books. Stanford further argues that the "key concept" pertaining to a relic is meaning, particularly what it meant for its maker (such as an author or gold-smith) or its recipient (such as a community or individual).

Stanford's method touches on many important issues in the evaluation and use of evidence. His steps, however, cannot be followed discretely and he appears to downplay how difficult making determinations about a text's original context, meaning, the intention of its author, and transmission history can be. Historians sometimes have little evidence about such matters and therefore often make assumptions and educated guesses in order to "construct explanations of [a text's] origins that will account for its features as fully as possible."[14] In addition, Stanford's method does not directly address one of the most important questions of historical research, namely: How do historians determine what information found in texts is reliable for describing and explaining what happened in the past? Understanding the circumstances involved in a text's

---

10. Stanford, *Introduction to the Philosophy of History*, 64. Stanford uses the example of verifying that a supposedly ancient object is of stone, not concrete (though the Romans did make cement).
11. Ibid., 65.
12. Ibid.
13. Ibid.
14. McCullagh, "Bias in Historical Description," 60.

production and transmission is certainly essential to knowing whether it contains useful information for historians, but knowing or hypothesizing about when, where, and why a document was written is not the same as determining whether the things the text describes actually existed or occurred in reality. Stanford appears to posit some relationship between intention and reliability when he suggests that historians should be skeptical of documents written for "other eyes," but does not clarify this theory any further. As will be seen below and in the remaining chapters of this study, some historians, including historians of ancient Israel, have addressed the relationship of a text's origin and intention to its reliability, and have attempted to formulate and apply theoretical principles to potential textual evidence for the past.

Postmodernism's Influence on Using Texts as Evidence
Antirepresentationalism and poststructuralism bring additional contingencies to reading texts in order to gain knowledge about the past. If texts are considered incapable of representing reality and absent of clear referents, the historian's ability to claim anything about the past using textual sources is seriously undermined. Put another way, "If the meaning of a text is necessarily uncertain, how much more problematic are the historical facts constructed from that text?"[15] Furthermore, as alluded to above, when ancient texts, especially histories, are examined for their narrative or poetic properties, it becomes apparent that ancient authors often began their writing with certain ends in mind. Thus, their work may not satisfy even generous standards of objectivity. Consequently, poststructuralist readings have made historians ask whether the aim of the text in question overrode accurate reporting of events.[16] Historians appear to have reacted to the challenge postmodernist conceptions of language, narrative, and history bring to establishing the historical reliability of ancient texts in three ways: they continue to prefer eyewitness or near-eyewitness accounts, they

15.   Green and Troup, eds., *Houses of History*, 299.

16.   For an example from Classics and the history of the ancient Greek world, see Detlev Fehling, *Herodotus and His "Sources": Citation, Invention and Narrative Art* (ARCA: Classical and Medieval Texts, Papers, and Monographs 21; Leeds: Francis Cairns, 1989); trans. of *Die Quellenangaben bei Herodot* (Berlin: de Gruyter, 1971). Fehling begins by assuming that "Herodotus' practice is a literary one" that combined poetry (or rhetoric) and truth. This literary practice, he claims, is more comparable to the historical novel than to modern scientific history. Fehling asserts that the new genre that Herodotus invented sprang from a man and a culture more accustomed to fictive or epic understandings of the past than scientific ones (p. 11). Fehling then assumes that invention was an accepted and essential element of Herodotus' genre. With these assumptions in mind, he approaches the text by asking "What was the minimum of genuine historical tradition Herodotus needed to write his book?" (p. 213). This type of analysis reveals a historical "skeleton" (ibid.) surrounded by a rich body of literary invention and technique, leaving very little with which historians of the ancient Mediterranean world who are concerned with actual occurrences can work. For contrasting perspectives, see D. Neel Smith, "Herodotus and the Archaeology of Asia Minor: A Historiographic Study" (Ph.D. diss., University of California, 1987), and W. Kendrick Pritchett, *The Liar School of Herodotos* (Amsterdam: Gieben, 1993). Pritchett claims that Fehling's assessment of Herodotus is faulty and that, in general, "the claims and objective of one who is writing history are quite different from those of one who is writing a work of fiction" (p. 9).

continue to use depth-dimensional sources but are extremely careful when doing so, and they seek information that may be incidentally included in texts and thereby potentially free of bias, at least overt bias.

Strategies for Dealing with Textual Accounts of the Past
Ancient historian M. I. Finley strongly maintains that only eyewitness or near-eyewitness written accounts can be considered primary sources for past events. Furthermore, he argues, such primary sources are the only reliable sources for historians:

> Unless a generation is captured on paper and the framework of its history fixed, either contemporaneously or soon thereafter, the future historian is for ever blocked.[17]

> Unless something is captured in a more or less contemporary historical account, the narrative is lost for all time.[18]

Strict adherence to Finley's criteria would make history of the ancient world very difficult to write. Finley recognizes this problem, but claims that historians cannot work around it. For instance, he says that for Roman history, "it is our incurable weakness that we completely and absolutely lack primary literary sources...down to about 300 BC."[19] Finley does not seem to acknowledge, however, that an eyewitness or near-eyewitness source may not be a reliable source, since the objectivity of ancient authors and the accuracy of their reporting can be called into question. Furthermore, Finley's opinion leaves no room for the use of depth-dimensional sources, such as ancient histories, which have traditionally been considered reliable, especially by historians of the ancient Near East and classical world.

Ancient histories, according to Finley, present a number of problems for the historian. First, they are not primary sources, because in his opinion primary sources must themselves be eyewitness or near-eyewitness accounts of events. Second, he asserts, historians tend to be "seduced" by the idea that "statements in the literary or documentary sources are to be accepted unless they can be disproved (to the satisfaction of the individual historian)."[20] Also, as mentioned above, postmodern theories of historical narrative have made it even more difficult for historians to use depth-dimensional sources, as such theories claim that the aims of the authors naturally caused them to slant their presentation of events. Yet despite these concerns, historians have not stopped using depth-dimensional sources.

Historians use a number of methods and arguments in support of the potential of depth-dimensional sources to supply evidence about the past. They begin by subjecting depth-dimensional sources to the same type of examination that eyewitness accounts receive in order to understand how the needs and goals of the author or audience might have caused creative alteration of historical facts

17. Finley, *The Use and Abuse of History*, 22.
18. Finley, *Ancient History*, 11.
19. Ibid., 10.
20. Ibid., 21.

(or even outright invention). Historians also use criteria such as multiple attestation (i.e. coherence with other sources) to help decide if a source is reliable.[21] Similarly, in many cases, historians seek external evidence to support the text's claims, especially from artifacts (discussed below). Also, historians may find helpful incidental historical information in texts whose accurate portrayal of other aspects of the past is questionable. Incidental, or nonintentional, historical information is, in the words of Marc Bloch, what "the past unwittingly leaves all along its trail"[22] that allows us to know "far more of the past than the past itself had thought good to tell us."[23] Nonintentional evidence potentially can include descriptions of names, places, practices, social patterns, prevailing mores, and general attitudes—anything that was assumed by the writer or inherent in the culture that produced and is reflected in the text. Benefits of nonintentional information for history writing include the potential that it can be found in many types of documents, including texts that appear to have deliberate ideologies or aims, such as histories written by ancient authors. Though nonintentional evidence is not "less subject to errors or falsehoods" than intentional evidence, Bloch claims that "distortion, if it exists, at least, has not been especially designed to deceive posterity."[24]

Incidental information also may be found in texts composed intentionally in the course of day-to-day life. Examples include archaeological discoveries such as graffiti, tablets of scribal exercises, letters, and records of legal and business transactions. These texts had significance in a limited context, and were not intended to record events significant to an entire society for posterity. Nevertheless, details in such records may offer insight into popular piety, commercial activity, and the names of ancient people, among other things. The frequency and types of these texts may also indicate the prevalence of literacy in an ancient society.

Incidental details about life garnered from epigraphic finds, as well as nonintentional evidence found in intentional histories or records, may be especially helpful to historians concerned with people outside of the reigning power structure whom intentional histories did not discuss.[25] For instance, mentions of domestic life may indicate what roles and duties were filled by women, and accounts of religious reform may reveal much about practices that were considered heretical.[26] Some caution must be applied to the optimism Bloch expressed

---

21.   See, e.g., John P. Meier, *A Marginal Jew: Rethinking the Historical Jesus* (2 vols.; New York: Doubleday, 1991), 1:167–95.

22.   Marc Bloch, *The Historian's Craft* (New York: Vintage, 1953), 62.

23.   Ibid., 64.

24.   Ibid., 62.

25.   "To reconstruct the attitudes of heretics and rebels, [official] records need to be supplemented by other kinds of sources" (Burke, "Overture," 5).

26.   Reading for nonintentional evidence preceded poststructuralism's deconstruction, but the two are similar in some ways. Both types of reading ask a text for information it did not intend to convey. However, reading for nonintentional evidence searches for concrete information within the text that is potentially accurate, such as the description of a house plan or a meal. A deconstructionist reading would ignore the questions of intention and historical accuracy and focus on the function of

for the value and objectivity of incidental information, however. In particular, the context of incidental information cannot be dismissed entirely. The overarching aims of an author may cause distortions in details that appear incidental to modern readers. Furthermore, a historically important situation is likely an abnormal occurrence, and thus behavior and conditions around it may be atypical. For example, historian Emmanuel Le Roy Ladurie used nonintentional information found in the records of Inquisition interviews in a French village to tell a story of its everyday life, especially its *mentalités*.[27] He assumed that comments made there were accurate, accurately reported, and could exemplify facets of everyday, normal life, even though an Inquisition trial is an extremely stressful and abnormal situation for the participants.[28]

The three strategies historians have adopted for dealing with problems associated with texts as evidence for the ancient past—privileging eyewitness sources, using depth-dimensional sources with consideration of factors that might mitigate their reliability, and looking for nonintentional evidence of the past in ancient texts—have been adopted by historians of ancient Israel, as well. As will be discussed in the following chapters, minimalists champion the importance of eyewitness sources for reconstructing Israel's past and thus exclude much of the Bible from consideration, while non-minimalists use the Bible and have developed strategies for dealing with this depth-dimensional source. Both look for nonintentional information in texts, though ideas about the texts in which they find it and how they use it derive from their opinions about a number of factors, including, but not limited to, the Bible's reliability.

Summary of Texts as Evidence
In summary, historians make a number of assumptions when dealing with texts as potential pieces of evidence, and they establish corresponding methods and practices. First, they attempt to understand the origin, original intent, context, meaning, transmission history, and veracity of texts they hope to use as evidence. They often consider most useful texts whose form and content appear precise

---

différance in the text and the meanings that can be drawn from the text's constructions of, and silences on, larger philosophical issues. In other words, a deconstructionist reading would be more ideologically oriented and would never aspire to offer historical facts, only an interpretation.

27. Emmanuel Le Roy Ladurie, *Montaillou, village occitan de 1294 à 1324* (Paris: Gallimard, 1975); published in English as *Montaillou: The Promised Land of Error* (abridged and trans. Barbara Bray; New York: Vintage, 1979). Another groundbreaking work that read intentional records from the past for nonintentional information was Ginzburg's *Il formaggio e i vermi*. Here, documents from the Inquisition provided information on the life of Menocchio, a sixteenth-century Italian miller who aroused the church's ire by claiming that "the world had its origin in putrefaction" (Carlo Ginzburg, *Il formaggio e i vermi: Il cosmos di un mugnaio del '500* [Turin: Giulio Einaudi Editore, 1976], xi; published in English as *The Cheese and the Worms: The Cosmos of a Sixteenth-Century Miller* [New York: Penguin, 1982]). The cover of the English edition touts it as "In the tradition of *Montaillou*."

28. For a critique of Le Roy Ladurie's *Montaillou* along these lines, see Renato Rosaldo, "From the Door of His Tent: The Fieldworker and the Inquisitor," in *Writing Culture: The Poetics and Politics of Ethnography* (ed. James Clifford and George E. Marcus; Berkeley: University of California Press, 1986), 77–97.

and similar to other texts and which originated near to the events being described. Depth-dimensional sources, such as histories written by ancient authors, may or may not be considered worthy of use, depending on whether a scholar believes that the aims and context of the document were conducive to the accurate reporting of events. In addition, historians can look to nonintentional information found in all types of texts for evidence about the past. "Systematic methods and categories of analysis through which questions of the validity of referents in historical narrative could be approached are virtually nonexistent,"[29] however, and in all cases, historians must ultimately make judgment calls about whether a text's statements correspond to past reality.

Artifacts

Most of the artifacts available to historians of the ancient world have been recovered through archaeology. Traditionally, archaeology was concerned with the classification of sites and artifacts, but archaeology has undergone major developments in the past century. "New archaeology," which was born in the 1960s, began to change archaeology's method and focus by claiming that archaeology could provide processual understandings of change in society.[30] Proponents of the new archaeology, or processual archaeologists (as they came to be called), also claimed that the types of societal change found in the archaeological record could be generalized into "timeless laws of the cultural process."[31] New archaeology aspired to the status of a science by using a method that moved from observations to hypotheses to testable laws that archaeologists could use to explain past cultures.

The success of new or processual archaeology's theory building and adoption of the scientific method is debated, but the field techniques and data required for its lofty goals drastically changed the practice of archaeologists everywhere. The recovery of monuments, public architecture, art, and other markers of large-scale organization had dominated the discipline of archaeology until the mid-1900s.[32] Processual archaeologists believed that "change in the total cultural system must be viewed in an adaptive context both social and environmental"[33] and consequently sought evidence of these contexts in the archaeological record. Thus, new archaeologists attempted to recover remnants of daily life such as

29. K. Lawson Younger, *Ancient Conquest Accounts: A Study in Ancient Near Eastern and Biblical History Writing* (JSOTSup 98; Sheffield: Sheffield Academic Press, 1990), 37.
30. New archaeology was defined and popularized by Lewis Binford. See his "Archeological Perspectives," in *New Perspectives in Archeology* (ed. Sally R. Binford and Lewis R. Binford; Chicago: Aldine, 1968), 5–32. For examples of studies of artifacts and sites undertaken with the processual approach, see the collected essays in *New Perspectives in Archaeology* and in Lewis R. Binford, *An Archaeological Perspective* (Studies in Archaeology; New York: Seminar Press, 1972).
31. William G. Dever, "The Impact of the 'New Archaeology' on Syro-Palestinian Archaeology," *BASOR* 242 (1981): 15–29 (21).
32. One can see here a parallel to pre-*Annales* historical practice where the grand stories of the past were considered most interesting or important.
33. Binford, *An Archaeological Perspective*, 20.

household implements, animal bones, and microscopic plant remains. Comparison of such deposits over time could indicate changes in peoples' diets and work habits, for instance, and perhaps even in the environment. Similarly, processual archaeologists studied settlement patterns within a site, as well as settlement patterns over a larger area, in order to gain information about relationships of people with each other and with the natural features around them. In addition, processual archaeologists adopted some methods from other social scientists, looking to modern cultures for help in "reconstructing the lifeways" of ancient peoples.[34] Such ethnoarchaeology could provide, for example, information on how an artifact may have been used, and potentially also could help archaeologists understand larger cultural patterns and social structures.[35] These practices of new archaeologists are now accepted and, for the most part, expected in archaeology.

Processual archaeology has been followed by postprocessual archaeology.[36] Postprocessual archaeologists find the new archaeology too functionalist in nature, as it explains almost all cultural processes as "the result of adaptive experience."[37] Postprocessualism "view[s] material culture as part of cultural expression and conceptual meaning."[38] Holding that "understanding material culture is more like interpreting a language" where symbolic meanings are often unconnected to the "physical properties of objects," postprocessualists, like poststructuralists, seek a nonreferential interpretation of symbols.[39] Postprocessualists further believe that symbols can change in meaning over time and that ways of forming symbolic meaning vary from culture to culture. Thus, postprocessualism is built on a fluid view of culture, one that takes "an unabashedly idealist approach"[40] by considering ideology an active agent in culture. In

---

34. Binford, "Archeological Perspectives," 12.

35. For an introductory discussion of method and purpose in ethnoarchaeology see Gloria London, "Ethnoarchaeology and Interpretations of the Past," *NEA* 31, no. 1 (2000): 2–8.

36. Ian Hodder, along with Michael Shanks and Christopher Tilley, are the scholars associated with the definition and promulgation of the ideas of postprocessual archaeology. Statements of postprocessualism and its purpose can be found in Ian Hodder, "Theoretical Archaeology: A Reactionary View," in *Symbolic and Structural Archaeology* (ed. Ian Hodder; Cambridge: Cambridge University Press, 1982), 1–16; idem, *Symbols in Action: Ethnoarchaeological Studies of Material Culture* (New Studies in Archaeology; Cambridge: Cambridge University Press, 1982), especially Chapter 1; idem, *Reading the Past: Current Approaches to Interpretation in Archaeology* (Cambridge: Cambridge University Press, 1986); idem, *Theory and Practice in Archaeology* (Material Cultures: Interdisciplinary Studies in the Material Construction of Social Worlds; London: Routledge, 1992); Michael Shanks and Christopher Tilley, *Social Theory and Archaeology* (Albuquerque: University of New Mexico Press, 1988).

37. Hodder, "Theoretical Archaeology," 6.

38. Hodder, *Theory and Practice in Archaeology*, 11.

39. Hodder (ibid., 1) also notes that postprocessual archaeology, "in the wider world would be termed neo-Marxist, hermeneutic, critical, and post-structuralist"; cf. Guy Halsall "Archaeology and Historiography," in Bentley, ed., *Companion to Historiography*, 805–27 (814): "[p]ost-processualists quickly became post-structuralists."

40. William G. Dever, "Biblical Archaeology: Death and Rebirth," in *Biblical Archaeology Today: Proceedings of the Second International Congress on Biblical Archaeology Jerusalem*

addition, postprocessual archaeologists take seriously the researcher's role in determining what can be considered evidence, noting that "in archaeology, the way in which the data is [*sic*] observed, excavated, recorded and (above all) published is heavily dependent upon the theoretical stance of the excavator."[41] Postprocessualists envision history as a discipline that combines chronology, culture, and environment and have actively sought ways to incorporate their findings into history in order to provide interpretations of events that augment the understanding of culture in ways that derived scientific laws cannot.[42]

Combination of Texts and Artifacts for History Writing

Artifacts and the results of archaeology, if used in writing history, usually must be integrated with textual evidence. There are many ways that historians can go about combining texts and archaeology. Interpreting artifacts using information from texts as the most important information about the artifact and its context is one way, but this method makes "the importance of archaeology...inversely proportional to the number of written documents."[43] In addition, the prioritization of texts has allowed historians to dabble in archaeology without recognizing the scope of information archaeology can provide. Guy Halsall argues that historians who prioritize texts have tended to interpret artifacts in three ways: as illustrative, where artifacts are used to illustrate aspects of daily life they describe; justificatory, where archaeology is said to prove claims made by texts; and to fill in the gaps, where archaeology enlightens things in the past about which texts can tell us very little.[44] These approaches to artifacts are limiting, says Halsall, because when questions that historians pose to archaeological evidence arise from their interaction with texts, there is no room for information that artifacts may provide independently. Since one of postprocessualist

June–July 1990 (ed. Avraham Biran and Joseph Aviram; Jerusalem: Israel Exploration Society, 1993), 706–22 (708).

41. Halsall, "Archaeology and Historiography," 816.

42. Hodder, *Reading the Past*, 77–102; Dever, "Biblical Archaeology," 708. For an example of an archaeological project undertaken with the aims of postprocessual archaeology, see Ian Hodder, ed., *On the Surface: Çatalhöyük 1993–95* (London: British Institute of Archaeology at Ankara, 1996). Hodder's introduction to the volume, "Re-opening Çatalhöyük" (pp. 1–18), describes how the fieldwork at the site relates to the aims of postprocessualist archaeology.

43. Halsall, "Archaeology and Historiography," 819. Other problems with this method include its implicit denial that archaeologists of nonliterate cultures, or archaeologists of literate cultures who do not use textual sources, can say anything meaningful about the sociocultural system of the peoples they study. A common way of expressing this opinion is by saying that artifacts are "mute" without texts to explain them. New archaeology has attempted to refute this charge. See, e.g., Binford, "Archeological Perspectives," 22.

44. Halsall, "Archaeology and Historiography," 819. Halsall also observes a corresponding three-stage progression of historians' attitudes toward archaeological data. First, he says, they tend to be optimistic about archaeology's ability to answer a question posed by their textual research. Second, they become disillusioned when no neat correspondence between the pictures of the past painted by archaeology and texts appears. Finally, "the idea that the two types of evidence can be used together at all is rejected" (ibid.).

archaeology's goals is integration of archaeological and historical knowledge, Halsall looks to it, and to poststructuralist theories in general, for a better method of doing so.

For Halsall, the historical process begins with a poststructuralist evaluation of evidence in which potential data about the past, "whether written document, decorated artefact, settlement or house plan or grave," are considered as "textual, conveying symbolic, coded 'messages' to an audience."[45] Designating artifacts "textual," whether they involve writing or not, expresses postprocessualists' desire to look beyond an artifact's typology or origin to messages that an artifact may "tell," such as its symbolic value. Halsall then names six procedures that can help historians decode evidence, noting that they often cannot be followed in order:

1. frame questions;
2. collect data;
3. assess the reliability of the data (quality of excavation, quality of textual interpretation);
4. examine the context of the data;
5. establish patterning within the data; and, finally,
6. produce conclusions but leave open the possibility of alternative explanations.[46]

Halsall's method has a number of traits in common with methods of evidence evaluation and use already discussed here, and also makes postmodern perspectives on evidence beneficial, and even necessary, contributions to historical research. By stating that the first step of historical reconstruction is to frame explicit questions, Halsall acknowledges that historians' conceptions of evidence depend on their goals and, at the same time, recognizes postmodernism's concern that historians are the ultimate arbiters of data and interpretation. The next steps, assessing the reliability of the data and examining context, patterns, and meaning, have been seen to be important for historians using texts as evidence and are also basic tenets of archaeological interpretation. Specifically, Halsall discusses determining the chronological and social origin of texts and the genre of an archaeological find ("votive pit, midden grave, and so on") as well as its place in the culture.[47]

Next, Halsall advocates looking at the data without its context, or dehistoricizing it, as deconstructionist readers do. This process allows historians to free their evidence from its place in a timeline of the past temporarily in order to be attentive to the internal logic of the text's or artifact's signs.[48] He calls this process "reconstructing the message of the data, as opposed to the context in which the message was made."[49] For documents, Halsall is talking about a basic

45.   Ibid., 822.
46.   Ibid.
47.   Ibid.
48.   This is comparable to some of the goals of anthropological history discussed in Chapter 1.
49.   Halsall, "Archaeology and Historiography."

literary analysis that involves "reconstructing internal semantic patterns, ranges of meaning, [and] narrative strategies"[50] For artifacts, this means "looking at spatial distributions, patterns of correlation and so on."[51] Finally, Halsall's suggestion that historians leave open the possibility of alternative explanations both returns to the historian as the ultimate arbiter of interpretation and recognizes that for poststructuralism and postprocessualism, meaning is never ultimately fixed.

By attending to contextual–historical as well as synchronic–symbolic meanings of texts and artifacts, Halsall increases the amount of information available to historians and allows "each body of data to question, as well as to confirm or complement, the others."[52] One of the drawbacks of such a method, which Halsall recognizes, is its assumption of competence in several disciplines. For instance, establishing the pattern of the data, whether by literary or archaeological methods, requires knowledge that may or may not be part of historians' training. Fundamental but difficult historical questions, such as how one determines a datum's context or origin, also are not addressed. Further, specific discussion of diachronic analysis and historical questions about "through whose hands [the evidence] has passed and what they may have done to it" is absent from Halsall's method, though he may intend for such analysis to take place when assessing a datum's reliability or context.[53] Finally, Halsall leaves open the question of how in practice historians would present alternative explanations. Yet Halsall's method takes into account poststructuralist perspectives and promotes utilization of the independent contributions archaeology can make to the study of the past. As will be seen, both of these issues are important to historians of ancient Israel, and thus Halsall's suggestions offer a framework against which their evaluation and combination of different types of evidence can be considered.

Conclusion

Historians have at their disposal many resources that could provide evidence about the past, and some generally agreed-upon tenets about how historians should evaluate and use evidence have emerged. Texts of many types can provide information about large-scale political events as well as about more mundane aspects of past existence. Artifacts ranging from palace ruins to seed deposits give a fuller picture of the day-to-day existence of many kinds of people. Yet data, whether textual or artifactual, only become evidence for history writing when they are asked to provide information relevant to questions

50.   Ibid.
51.   Ibid.
52.   Ibid., 823.
53.   Lewis R. Binford ("General Introduction," in *For Theory Building in Archaeology: Essays on Faunal Remains, Aquatic Resources, Spatial Analysis, and Systemic Modeling* [ed. Lewis R. Binford; New York: Academic Press, 1977], 1–10 [8]) calls theories of how an artifact arrived in its present condition "middle-range theories."

historians ask. In order to evaluate and use this evidence, historians must know as much about their evidence as possible. Information important to historians includes the origin and context of the evidence as well as the stages it passed through before the historian encountered it. For a text such information includes knowledge, or educated guesses, about authorship, purpose, audience, and transmission history. For an artifact, creator, use, and ownership, as well as context within an archaeological site and assemblage are some of the relevant questions. Further, poststructuralism has influenced evidence evaluation, reminding historians to suspend diachronic questions temporarily and consider symbolic and synchronic aspects of evidence. Determining the relevance and reliability of a certain source for historical reconstruction, however, is a process that ultimately depends on the judgment of the individual historian.

The issue of what relative value historians should place on different types of evidence also cannot be easily resolved. As seen above, Halsall argued for a method of evaluating evidence that theoretically prioritizes no type of information. Yet in practice, historians often elevate one type of resource over another, with texts being historians' pre-eminent sources. In some cases, especially when certain types of evidence are lacking, it may be necessary to weigh one type of evidence more heavily than another. In other cases, historians may simply make choices that support their hypotheses or goals best. Often when the veracity or usefulness of one type of source is in question, historians use other types of evidence to evaluate it. For instance, historians sometimes use archaeological finds to evaluate the veracity of texts, a practice commonly found among ancient historians and, as will be seen, a source of contention among historians of ancient Israel.[54] Others, skeptical of their documentary sources, attempt to write history without documents,[55] or do not attempt to write history at all. In the end, the availability of data and the questions posed by the historian in each historical scenario influence approaches to the potential evidence provided by texts and artifacts. The following chapters describe and analyze the philosophical and practical bases for historians of ancient Israel's decisions about evidence evaluation and use.

54. This is widely practiced in ancient history, especially when the veracity of a depth-dimensional source is questioned. See, for example, Peter Kosso, "Historical Evidence and Epistemic Justification: Thucydides as a Case Study," *History and Theory* 32 (1993): 1–13.

55. Finley, in his *Early Greece*, attempts to do so for some poorly attested periods using evidence such as destroyed cities, burial practices, and pottery.

Chapter 3

ASSUMPTIONS AND PRACTICES OF HISTORIANS
OF ANCIENT ISRAEL IN THE MID-TWENTIETH CENTURY

Introduction

The previous two chapters have introduced recent discussions of philosophical and methodological issues pertaining to history and history writing. Just as a range of opinions about what constitutes history and how it should be written can be found among historians and philosophers, so historians of ancient Israel vary in their philosophy and practice. This chapter focuses on the assumptions and practices of members of the schools of biblical scholarship and history associated with the German Albrecht Alt (1883–1956) and the American William Foxwell Albright (1891–1971).[1] In the mid-twentieth century, the history of Israel was rarely conceived outside of the ideas promoted by these men, and, up until the 1970s, the prevailing questions about Israel's past usually were approached from either an "Altian" or an "Albrightian" perspective. These schools, as will be shown, were grounded in empiricist theory, optimistic about objectivity in history writing, and valued texts and archaeology as evidence, but differed in some critical assumptions about these topics. This discussion of the philosophical and methodological presuppositions of the Altian and Albrightian schools thus will elucidate the framework of the discipline that was prevalent when the first widely discussed works skeptical of these positions appeared and the strains of thought that eventually would become minimalism were born. Following this analysis, Ziony Zevit's recent attempt at synthesizing general developments in history writing in the twentieth century will be discussed in order to introduce the wider intellectual contexts in which Albrightians and Altians worked, as well as to introduce potential modes for understanding current minimalist and non-minimalist historians of ancient Israel (the topics of Chapters 4 and 5, respectively).

---

1.   For discussions of history writing about ancient Israel before Alt, Noth, and Albright see John H. Hayes, "The History of the Study of Israelite and Judaean History," in *Israelite and Judaean History* (ed. John H. Hayes and J. Maxwell Miller; Philadelphia: Westminster, 1977), 1–69, and Niels Peter Lemche, "Rachel and Lea, or, On the Survival of Outdated Paradigms in the Study of the Origin of Israel," *SJOT* 2 (1987): 127–53 and *SJOT* 1 (1988): 39–65.

The Albright School[2]

Albright's Ideas About History Writing
Albright's presuppositions about history and its goals stood simultaneously inside the scientific tradition and outside secular, particularist/historicist paradigms of history research and writing. He conceived of researching and writing history as a science, and maintained that historians could and should employ the empirical method objectively. Albright was also a positivist, believing that historians learned about the past through a "record of factual events that can be understood rationally."[3] Furthermore, he argued that historians should elucidate the past by formulating laws that, like those of science, were universal.[4] In other words, both empiricism and the substantive philosophy of history were, in Albright's opinion, integral parts of the discipline.

Albright's most comprehensive statement of his philosophy of history appeared in his *History, Archaeology, and Christian Humanism*, published in 1964.[5] Here, Albright describes himself as a positivist and defines positivism as "the expression of the modern rational-scientific approach to physical and historical reality."[6] Albright calls his philosophy of history "organismic," meaning that he considered the development of human culture to be akin to that of an organism because it "falls into more or less definite forms, patterns, and configurations, each with its own complex body of characteristics."[7] The title to Albright's only comprehensive historical work, *From the Stone Age to Christianity*, reveals his conception of the scope of history and his desire to connect the development of religious ideas to the course of past events. Indeed, Albright's historical pursuits were undertaken as a means to understanding the Bible and

2.   Albright and the Albright school have been the subject of a number of publications, including Leona Glidden Running and David Noel Freedman, *William Foxwell Albright: A Twentieth-Century Genius* (New York: Morgan, 1975); Gus W. Van Beek, ed., *The Scholarship of William Foxwell Albright: An Appraisal* (HSS 33; Atlanta: Scholars Press, 1989); Peter Machinist, "William Foxwell Albright: The Man and His Work," in *The Study of the Ancient Near East in the Twenty-First Century: The William Foxwell Albright Centennial Conference* (ed. Jerrold S. Cooper and Glenn M. Schwartz; Winona Lake, Ind.: Eisenbrauns, 1996), 385–403; Burke O. Long, *Planting and Reaping Albright: Politics, Ideology, and Interpreting the Bible* (University Park, Pa.: Pennsylvania State University Press, 1997); Mark S. Smith, "W. F. Albright and His 'Household': The Cases of C. H. Gordon, M. H. Pope, and F. M. Cross," in *"A Wise and Discerning Mind": Essays in Honor of Burke O. Long* (ed. Saul M. Olyan and Robert C. Culley; BJS 325; Providence: Brown University Press, 2000), 221–44; and the entire issue of *NEA* 65, no. 1 (2002).

3.   William G. Dever, "What Remains of the House That Albright Built?," *BA* 56 (1993): 23–35 (26).

4.   William F. Albright, *From the Stone Age to Christianity: Monotheism and the Historical Process* (Baltimore: The Johns Hopkins University Press, 1940), vii, 49. The second English edition (Garden City, N.Y.: Doubleday, 1957), does not include the first edition's pp. vii–viii (the Preface), but includes a new Introduction.

5.   Chapter 2 of *From the Stone Age to Christianity* was also devoted to this topic.

6.   William F. Albright, *History, Archaeology, and Christian Humanism* (New York: McGraw-Hill, 1964), 140.

7.   Ibid., 141.

especially the eternal truths that he believed were revealed in the experiences of ancient Israel. Consequently, Albright's pupil David Noel Freedman has asserted that Albright was not primarily a historian.[8] As will be demonstrated further, however, for Albright, history could not be separated from other modes of human thought, especially religion. He believed that religion was the arbiter of all meaning, the way in which humanity organized and expressed its most profound thoughts. Albright thus held that historical research should shed light on religious experiences and truths and should further strive to demonstrate the overall significance of these truths for humanity through the ages.[9] A look at Albright's assumptions about additional aspects of history writing, along with the assumptions of some of his pupils, particularly the historian John Bright (1908–1995), will further elucidate the basic assumptions of the Albright school.

Representation and Objectivity
Albright adhered to a positivistic conception of history that was highly optimistic about the historian's ability to represent the past. As Burke Long explains, this system "posits ancient history as discoverable, amenable to rational method, [and] able to be reconstructed in some objective sense if one pays attention to the sure and unfailing evidence which convicts."[10] Further, Albright asserted that "'facts' are true (or false if our knowledge of them is in error) regardless of an historian's judgment about them."[11] In this understanding of history, it also is possible for the historian-scientist to be free from biases that might compromise the apprehension of facts about the past. As Long notes, for the Albrightians "ideologies of historical and philological science...supposedly made theological commitments irrelevant among scholars fervently devoted to scientific objectivity."[12] Yet, although Albright stressed "the supreme importance of accuracy and completeness" in writing history objectively,[13] he did recognize that achieving objectivity in history writing is difficult. "For some 2500 years," he wrote, "most historians have been reading their own world-view or their own partisan standpoint into history until it has come to be doubted whether it is possible to

---

8.   Albright "was interested in history, especially in historical method, concerned to use its resources and techniques in order to achieve results in other areas" (David Noel Freedman, "W. F. Albright as an Historian," in Van Beek, ed. *The Scholarship of William Foxwell Albright*, 33–43 [33]).

9.   See, e.g., Albright, *History, Archaeology, and Christian Humanism*, 291–94, 298–99.

10.   Burke O. Long, "Mythic Trope in the Autobiography of William Foxwell Albright," *BA* 56 (1993): 36–45 (43).

11.   Albright, *History, Archaeology, and Christian Humanism*, 24.

12.   Long, *Planting and Reaping Albright*, 69. Long claims this ideal broke down when Albright and members of his Biblical Colloquium began to plan to publish a theological dictionary (which never was completed), and Jewish and divergent Christian views caused much tension among the editors.

13.   Albright, *From the Stone Age to Christianity*, 49; here he also calls again for the organization of historical facts and explanations into natural laws, so that history would emulate science. See also idem, *History, Archaeology, and Christian Humanism*, 27, where he asserts that certain types of historical judgments can be made objectively.

write it impartially."[14] This comment, however, primarily implicated ancient historians, and Albright was extremely optimistic about modern historians' potential for objectivity. He claimed that while a writer close to the culture in question may be prone to bias—"The more we love [a culture]...the more prejudiced we become and the less able to see it in proper perspective"—a "sympathetic, yet dispassionate, foreign observer of a culture...could understand ancient Egypt better in some ways than a pharaoh or a learned scribe."[15]

Despite such confidence in modern historians, Albright and Bright accused some of their colleagues of unacceptable bias in history writing. Bright called Noth's "mistrust of the early traditions of Israel...little short of nihilism"[16] and Noth's attitude toward archaeological evidence nihilistic, as well.[17] In terms of the biases identified by McCullagh, then, Albright and Bright suggested that Noth omitted significant facts about ancient Israel. Present-day observers of Albright, however, recognize that his own biases are evident. It would be difficult to argue that Albright was a "dispassionate foreign observer" of ancient Israel, since he favored protestant Christian interpretations of the Bible and Israel's past and saw Christianity as the pinnacle of human religious under-standing.[18] Albright also repeatedly expressed the idea that all great civilizations of the world somehow sprang from the cultures of the "Fertile Crescent."[19] In retrospect, Albright too had a strong desire for a certain portrait of ancient Israel to be true.

Subject and Explanation

As seen above, Albright used the organism as a metaphor to describe the subject of history. He defined this organism by saying that:

> [its] basis must be...a modest one, not rising for operational purposes beyond the level of the culture-unit. By this we mean a geographically and chronologically limited horizon, in which there is a real homogeneity about the aspect of any element or factor, which ceases as soon as we cross these boundaries of space and time.[20]

Albright describes his understanding and explanation of the life of this organism as operating somewhere between instrumentalism, which understood culture by

14. *From the Stone Age to Christianity*, 48.

15. Albright, *History, Archaeology, and Christian Humanism*, 121–22. Albright's optimistic view of objectivity also translated into the political sphere, where he believed he could remain neutral in the many political upheavals that took place in Palestine from the British Mandate period onward. See Neil Asher Silberman, "Visions of the Future: Albright in Jerusalem, 1919–1929," *BA* 56 (1993): 8–16.

16. John Bright, *Early Israel in Recent History Writing: A Study in Method* (SBT 19; London: SCM Press, 1956), 53–54. This charge is repeated several times throughout the book (see, e.g., pp. 62, 72, 82).

17. Ibid., 83, 87. See also William F. Albright, "The Israelite Conquest of Canaan in the Light of Archaeology," *BASOR* 74 (1939): 11–23 (12).

18. See, e.g. Albright, *From the Stone Age to Christianity*, 307–11; idem, *History, Archaeology, and Christian Humanism*, 322.

19. Albright, *From the Stone Age to Christianity*, 6; idem, *History, Archaeology, and Christian Humanism*, 322.

20. Albright, *From the Stone Age to Christianity*, 84–85.

examining its elements separately, and functionalism, which saw all cultural structures as integral parts of a functioning whole.[21] Often Albright believed that religion was the element that provided the culture-unit with its distinctive characteristics as well as its ability to survive, and Albright used scientific terminology to express this idea: "Archaeologists and historians cannot help agreeing that religion is the nucleus of all cultures of the past."[22] It follows, then, that for Albrightians "The history of Israel...*is the history of a faith and its people*"[23] and religious figures, such as Moses, and their concomitant institutions, such as the monotheistic Yahwistic faith, were seen as the proper subjects of and sources of explanation for the history of ancient Israel.[24] It is important to stress that Albright considered explanations using religion to be fully scientific. He reacted strongly against metaphysical or idealist philosophies that classified history as *Geisteswissenschaft* (as opposed to *Naturwissenschaft*), that is, as a humanities discipline and not a science, and maintained that his historical thinking was scientific because it made judgments about reality, including religion's role in that reality, not "existential judgments."[25]

In general, Albright argued, historians' explanatory judgments could be classified into "judgments about typical occurrence," "judgments about cause and effect," and "judgments about personal reactions."[26] All are based in the historian's ability to analogize between what he knows from his own experience and study.[27] As for cause and effect, Albright argued that "while it is true that

21.   Albright, *History, Archaeology, and Christian Humanism*, 177–80. The instrumentalism Albright describes is not the same as the instrumentalist pragmatic theory of truth discussed in Chapter 1 of this study. Albright used the term to refer to a mode of explanation, while an instrumentalist theory of truth claims that what is true is that which is beneficial to the community that judges its truth status.

22.   Ibid., 47.

23.   Bright, *Early Israel*, 114 (italics in original). Nevertheless, Bright's history begins with the Stone Age in Palestine. See idem, *A History of Israel* (4th ed.; Louisville, Ky.: Westminster John Knox, 2000), 23–44.

24.   Other historical subjects that found prominence as the twentieth century progressed, such as the environment and its effect on culture or humans other than powerful men, were rarely discussed by Albright or Bright. However, in 1968 Albright hinted that the historian should be interested in the daily life of past peoples. See William F. Albright, "Archaeological Discovery and the Scriptures," *Christianity Today* 12, no. 19 (1968): 3–5 (3). Albright also wrote a paper entitled "Some Functions of Organized Minorities" for the Fifth Symposium of the Conference on Science, Philosophy and Religion in Their Relation to the Democratic Way of Life (published in his *History, Archaeology, and Christian Humanism*, 195–204).

25.   Albright, *History, Archaeology, and Christian Humanism*, 13.

26.   In *From the Stone Age to Christianity*, 75–77, Albright adopted a classification of the types of judgments a historian makes from Maurice Mandelbaum, and he expanded on them in his *History, Archaeology, and Christian Humanism*, 22–28. Albright cites Maurice Mandelbaum, *The Problem of Historical Knowledge: An Answer to Relativism* (1st ed.; New York: Harper & Row, 1938). Two historical judgments Albright names do not pertain to explanation: judgments about particular facts (whether something happened) and judgments of value (opinion about the event and its impact).

27.   William F. Albright, *Archaeology, Historical Analogy, and Early Biblical Tradition* (Rockwell Lectures: Rice University; Baton Rouge: Louisiana State University Press, 1966), 10–11, 65. This is similar to the position of Collingwood, described in Chapter 1. In theological studies, Ernst Troeltsch had already expressed the idea that analogy is vital to understanding the past. See,

emergent historical situations are often too complex to be reduced to simple formulas, simple causes and effects can often be stated with confidence."[28] On the other hand, judgments about why people behaved the way they did had a psychological component and "ought to be omitted entirely in serious historical writing,"[29] presumably for lack of evidence. Historical judgments formed the basis of the natural laws Albright hoped to construct for history. One example of such a derived law, which he called "empirico-adaptive," is his assertion that "historical experience shows clearly that viable cultures are the product of a series of geographical collocations and reciprocal adaptations."[30] Thus, the best explanations in Albright's view, then, were derived from the study of patterns in past events and recognized religion's role in the formation and continued life of the historical organism.

Language and Narrative
Typical of historians writing before history's "linguistic turn," Albright and Bright appear only minimally aware of the narrative or poetic aspects of their own historical writing. A brief analysis of Albright's and Bright's narrative frameworks in their comprehensive histories, however, can reveal some potential overarching themes and patterns that organized their works. As mentioned above, Albright wrote only one comprehensive narrative history, *From the Stone Age to Christianity*. Its chapter titles indicate much about Albright's perception of the growth and development of Israel. After some introductory material, which includes statements of philosophy and theories about evidence, comes "Praeparatio," a chapter about Early and Middle Bronze Age civilization and religion in the Near East. Next comes "When Israel was a Child," covering the Late Bronze Age, the early Hebrews, and the Mosaic period. Childhood is followed by "Charisma and Catharsis," which covers the united and divided monarchies, the Deuteronomistic movement, and the exile. Finally, Israel experiences "The Fullness of Time," which brought Hellenistic culture to Palestine and "Jesus the Christ" to the Jews. Albright's trope in this work appears to be somewhat Hegelian, with law and prophecy (charisma) serving as thesis and antithesis, the exilic period as a break (catharsis), and the later developments of Judaism, and especially Christianity, as synthesis.[31] Furthermore, in this work

e.g., Ernst Troeltsch, "Historiography," in *Encyclopaedia of Religion and Ethics* (ed. James Hastings; New York: Scribner's, 1908–26), 6:716–23 (718–19), and Mark D. Chapman, *Ernst Troeltsch and Liberal Theology: Religion and Cultural Synthesis in Wilhelmine Germany* (Christian Theology in Context; Oxford: Oxford University Press, 2001), 54–55. For Troeltsch's thoughts on the relationship of faith to historical thinking, see Van A. Harvey, *The Historian and the Believer: The Morality of Historical Knowledge and Christian Belief* (Toronto: MacMillan, 1969), 3–9.
    28. Albright, *History, Archaeology, and Christian Humanism*, 25.
    29. Ibid., 26.
    30. Ibid., 49. Albright also claims that this law is exemplified in the spread of Christianity, which he describes as a religion that brought "new life" to "moribund cultures."
    31. Cf. J. David Schloen, "W. F. Albright and the Origins of Israel," *NEA* 65, no. 1 (2002): 57–68 (60), who claims that Albright's "particular philosophy of history was far more Hegelian than he was willing to admit."

Albright's attention to Christianity and ancient Israel as its background was not hidden, but quite overt.

The narrative structure of Bright's *History of Israel* is similar to Albright's, as it moves from "Beginnings and Antecedents" to monarchy, "Tragedy and Beyond (The Exilic and Postexilic Periods)" to "The Formative Period of Judaism." Though Bright concludes with the end of the "Old Testament Period" and an epilogue that introduces Judaism and Christianity as the major religions descended from the Old Testament ("Toward the Fullness of Time"), he concedes that this later boundary is artificial. Since his stated subjects, Israel and its faith, evolved into religions and communities that continue to exist, Bright decides that the transition point from Israelite religion to Judaism was an appro-priate place to end his history.[32] Thus, in Bright's work, a Christian orientation is not as obvious as in Albright's, but the hiatus at Judaism's beginnings is sig-nificant because it allows for Judaism potentially to be seen as inferior to the prophetic Israelite religion of which the Albrightians were quite fond. In fact, the narrative structure as well as the content of *From the Stone Age to Christian-ity* (and Bright's *History of Israel* to a lesser degree) imply that a somewhat pristine ethical monotheism in early Israel was corrupted by monarchy and poli-tics, lost in exile, and later reclaimed, particularly by the nonlegalistic Christian tradition.

Truth

According to Albright's scientific concept of history, universal laws are the desired, even necessary, outcome of historical research. Since historically derived laws of human behavior and culture are interpretations of reality that describe how patterns repeat themselves, historians formulating them aspire for more than the correspondence of individual facts to reality; they seek to derive eternal truths and patterns from the study of the past. In the case of Albright, the eternal truths and patterns he found in history often supported the essential truth of Christianity, especially Protestantism.[33] Thus, since Albright's historical truth could be seen as attempting to justify modern protestant Christianity, it could be considered true according to an instrumentalist theory of truth. Albright and Bright certainly believed, however, that their historical reconstructions corre-sponded to reality, though Bright apparently recognized the difficulty of describ-ing past reality truthfully. He asserted that in final judgment calls, the historian

---

32. Bright, *A History of Israel*, 458–59.

33. "The scientific, that is, historical, philological, and archaeological exploration into the ancient biblical world could scrape off unwanted encrustations and refurbish the essential truths of Christianity—this meant for Albright the Protestant truths of Christianity" (Long, "Mythic Trope," 42). See, on the other hand, Albright's positive assessment of Catholicism in *History, Archaeology, and Christian Humanism*, 320–22. Correspondence from Albright to his family early in his academic career (around 1920) showed his desire to confirm, or at least not contradict, the Bible in his studies (Long, "Mythic Trope," 37; idem, *Planting and Reaping Albright*, 116). Toward the end of his career, in 1968, Albright ("Archaeological Discovery," 3) felt compelled to explain to a non-academic audience that historians of ancient Israel were no longer primarily concerned with con-firmation of scripture, noting however that that goal "remains important."

"must allow himself to be guided by the balance of probability."[34] Approaches such as Bright's, which explicitly allow probability to factor into historians' conclusions about the past, have been criticized as "established by the extremely undependable principles of analogy and harmonization."[35] In other words, modern critics worry that scholars who seek probable reconstructions of ancient Israel may be tempted to accept intuitively probable statements "unless they can be disproved (to the satisfaction of the individual historian)"[36] and thereby run the risk of producing history that is uncritical of, yet coherent with, the Bible. Minimalists, as will be seen in the following chapter, are particularly opposed to probability substituting for what they understand to be historical certainty.

Evidence
It has been established that Albright was an empiricist and that empiricism is grounded on the postulate that facts are external to the researcher and can be apprehended by scientific methods. Albright does not appear to have recognized the historian's role in deciding what is a relevant piece of evidence and what is not. As discussed above, for Albright facts existed whether the historian recognized them or not. For Albrightians, facts could be found both in textual sources and in artifacts.

Texts
Albright wrote: "In studying written documents from the ancient Near East there are four main stages: decipherment of the script, linguistic interpretation, philological analysis, and historical interpretation."[37] Albright uses the term "philological analysis" to encompass genre/form criticism, textual criticism, and historical-criticism, which includes "fix[ing] its date and authorship if possible."[38] Historical interpretation, the final step, is the use of the text for "reconstructing some phase of human history."[39] Thus, Albright adheres to common procedures for understanding and using an ancient text[40] but goes an extra step by implying that every such text can yield valuable historical information. When applied to the Bible, this assumption allowed Albright and his followers to find facts about the past in almost every biblical story.

Albrightians used considerations of form, genre, and hypotheses about the original context and intent of biblical passages as support for their claims that the Bible was historically reliable. The written form of the Bible, they argued, was in many cases based on oral sources. Albright argued that historical information transmitted orally, presumably from eyewitnesses or near-eyewitnesses, usually took poetic form. Poetry, he believed, uses motifs and patterns to make

34. Bright, *Early Israel*, 122.
35. Thomas L. Thompson, *Early History of the Israelite People from the Written and Archaeological Sources* (SHANE 4; Leiden: Brill, 1992), 5.
36. Finley, *Ancient History*, 21.
37. Albright, *From the Stone Age to Christianity*, 19.
38. Ibid.
39. Ibid.
40. Also Bright, *Early Israel*, 124.

the facts of history "serviceable." In the process of oral transmission of historical poetry, some details, including chronological ones, may be altered, but information is never deliberately falsified.[41] Examples of the application of this theory are the studies of Albright and his student Frank M. Cross that combined observations from ancient Near Eastern literature, and especially Ugaritic poetry, with studies of classical epic poetry to argue for a poetic core to the Pentateuchal narrative traditions.[42]

Although Albright considered the biblical text a composite document, he was not fond of the type of source criticism that Julius Wellhausen (1844–1918) had brought to prominence in the discipline.[43] That method, Albright argued, unjustifiably separated pieces of the text that were not markedly different, such as the "J" and "E" sources.[44] Albright brushed aside the apparent contradictions that source critics attributed to the joining of sources by arguing that the biblical writers' *pietas* led them to include different important traditions,[45] and further that multiple views actually helped the historian gain "true perspective."[46] Albright also opposed the evolutionary view of Israel's religion that was grounded in source criticism. To Albright, the Bible's portrayal of Moses as monotheist and Israel as primarily a monotheistic Yahweh-worshipping society from its beginning was true.

Albright called his method of using ancient Near Eastern texts to elucidate Israel's past "an informed critical approach."[47] For Albrightians, ancient Near

41.   William F. Albright, "Albrecht Alt," *JBL* 75 (1956): 168–73 (172).

42.   Frank Moore Cross, *Canaanite Myth and Hebrew Epic* (Cambridge, Mass.: Harvard University Press, 1973). For a critique, see John Van Seters, *The Pentateuch: A Social-Science Commentary* (Trajectories; Sheffield: Sheffield Academic Press, 1999), 50–57. Van Seters seeks to show, among other things, that the Albrightians' use of parallels to classical epic, their dependence on the myth–ritual school, and their early dating of biblical poetic texts, such as the Song of the Sea and some Psalms, are no longer tenable. For a contrasting opinion, see Baruch Halpern, "Eyewitness Testimony: Parts of Exodus Written Within Living Memory of the Event," *BAR* 29, no. 5 (2003): 50–57.

43.   For a discussion of Wellhausen, see Rudolf Smend, *Deutsche Alttestamentler in drei Jahrhunderten: mit 18 Abbildungen* (Göttingen: Vandenhoeck & Ruprecht, 1989), 99–113.

44.   Albright, *From the Stone Age to Christianity*, 46–47. He also asserted that the variants of texts found in the Dead Sea scrolls proved that the Masoretic text as we have it was a late invention and that the text was constantly changing. Since editorial changes and errors occurred not only in the early stages of composition but continued throughout a text's history, "the Masoretic text cannot be used as a basis for the kind of analysis which sometimes divided a single verse among three different sources" (idem, *Archaeology, Historical Analogy, and Early Biblical Tradition*, 46).

45.   Ibid., 47.

46.   Albright, "Archaeological Discovery," 5.

47.   William F. Albright, *Albright, Archaeology and the Religion of Israel: The Ayer Lectures of the Colgate-Rochester Divinity School, 1941* (5th ed.; Baltimore: The Johns Hopkins University Press, 1968), 59. Albright lamented that "misreading or mistranslation" of some ancient Near Eastern texts had led to false conclusions about Israel's past that found acceptance in nonscholarly circles. In particular, Albright mentioned the hypothesis that posited a common origin for Hebrews and Canaanites in the Negev based on readings of Ugaritic mythic poetry (pp. 59–61). Poor comparative scholarship also contributed to mistakes, he claims, in interpreting sacrifice (p. 61), an oversimplified understanding of Egyptian tales such as the Story of Sinuhe and the Report of Wenamûn (pp. 61–63), and the derivation of the name Yahweh (pp. 63–64).

Eastern texts could help describe the wider historical context of ancient Israel and its culture, such as in his portrayal of Canaanite religion.[48] He and his students also used ancient Near Eastern texts to support specific historical conclusions, such as his contention that Abraham was a Middle Bronze Age donkey caravaneer.[49] In short, for the Albrightians, observations from extra-biblical texts helped support the belief that parts of the Bible were verifiably old and reflective of the reality they described.[50] Further justification for this position was found in artifacts.

Artifacts
The work of the archaeologist, said Albright, can be divided into two tasks: stratigraphy and typology.[51] Stratigraphy is the method by which archaeologists classify and relate finds within a site; typology allows them to make comparisons with other artifactual material. Albright claimed that archaeologists "follow the same basic logical method in experimentation that is characteristic of all valid science."[52] In addition, Albright recognized that archaeology potentially could tell more than a story of changes in pot forms and architecture:

> Hitherto little attention has been paid to one of the richest fields to which archaeology can contribute: the history of the workings of the human mind.[53]

> Archaeology has a direct and obvious bearing on questions of social and political organization, though great care must be exercised not to generalize on insufficient basis.[54]

Albright even referred to archaeological finds as "unwritten documents," though this description was meant to justify their suitability for the historical enterprise, for which texts were the pre-eminent source.[55] In practice, Albright always used archaeology in combination with texts to write history. It is in this combination that Albright and his followers made their most unique contributions to the history of ancient Israel.

Combination of Texts and Artifacts for History Writing
It is well known that Albright, Bright, and others of this school enthusiastically combined the results of archaeological research with biblical stories in order to

---

48.   Albright, *Archaeology and the Religion of Israel*, 68–84, and idem, *Yahweh and the Gods of Canaan: A Historical Analysis of Two Contrasting Faiths* (Garden City, N.Y.: Doubleday, 1968), 110–52. The correlation of Ugaritic culture with Canaanite culture is now problematic. See, e.g., Niels Peter Lemche, *The Canaanites in Their Land: The Tradition of the Canaanites* (JSOTSup 110; Sheffield: Sheffield Academic Press, 1991).

49.   William F. Albright, "Abram the Hebrew: A New Archaeological Interpretation," *BASOR* 163 (1961): 36–54.

50.   Albright, *Yahweh and the Gods of Canaan*, 1–52.

51.   Albright, *From the Stone Age to Christianity*, 24; idem, *History, Archaeology, and Christian Humanism*, 20.

52.   Albright, *History, Archaeology, and Christian Humanism*, 21.

53.   Albright, *Archaeology and the Religion of Israel*, 3.

54.   Albright, *From the Stone Age to Christianity*, 31.

55.   Albright, *History, Archaeology, and Christian Humanism*, 20.

write about Israel's past. Peter Machinist has called their method the "diagnostic detail approach."[56] As Thompson explains, "Albright presupposed that the affirmation of significant details of the tradition by extrabiblical sources established the historicity of the tradition as a whole."[57] This approach resulted from the combination of several practices, which Albright's studies of the patriarchs exemplify. First, Albrightians ignored many literary-critical issues when examining the Bible. Albright read the biblical patriarchal stories as synchronic wholes, with "a resolute avoidance of any discussion of the Abraham stories as narrative, and of any effort to deal with the historicity of these stories by analyzing the shape of the narrative through its putative stages of development in a documentary- and/or form-critical way."[58] Such a reading established the task of the historian as proving (or disproving) the narrative in its entirety. Second, archaeological finds, including texts uncovered by archaeology, were studied primarily for what they could contribute to the biblical story. In the case of the patriarchs, Albright examined the Nuzi tablets and found there names that he considered similar to ones in the biblical stories. Since details in the Bible appeared to match details in an extrabiblical, historical document, Albright argued that the historicity of the patriarchs had been confirmed.

When the Albrightians' practice of combining text and artifacts is examined, it becomes clear that they often used archaeology in a justificatory manner, that is, in order to substantiate the Bible's portrayal of Israel's past.[59] Albrightians sometimes discovered, however, that findings from archaeology required them to reinterpret the biblical story if their historical reconstructions were to be accurate. For instance, Bright dated the exodus from Egypt to the thirteenth century BCE, even though this dating contradicted the biblical chronology.[60] The Albrightian approach to the conquest of Palestine also required some adjustments to the Bible's story. Essentially, Albrightians accepted the stories of Joshua's exploits and sought sites named in the narrative in order to find evidence of their destruction in the Late Bronze Age. Yet 'Ai (Et-Tell), which by the Albrightian chronology should have been inhabited and conquered by

56. Machinist, "Albright," 398.
57. Thompson, *Early History*, 17.
58. Machinist, "Albright," 397.
59. Albright's student George Ernest Wright (1909–1974), who was primarily an archaeologist and theologian, also vocally promulgated the idea that archaeology had substantiated most of the Bible's historical claims. See, e.g., George Ernest Wright, *Biblical Archaeology* (Philadelphia: Westminster, 1957), 17–28.
60. William P. Brown, "Introduction" to the 4th ed. of John Bright's *A History of Israel*, 1–22 (9). Bright did so based on Nelson Glueck's assertion that Edom was too sparsely populated before this time for the Hebrews to want to avoid it. Glueck's theory of a Middle Bronze occupation gap in Edom was later disproved. See Nelson Glueck, *The Other Side of the Jordan* (New Haven: American Schools of Oriental Research, 1940), and Gerald L. Mattingly, "The Exodus-Conquest and the Archaeology of Transjordan: New Light on an Old Problem," *Grace Theological Journal* 4 (1983): 245–62. New artifactual finds and new interpretations of existing data caused Bright to revise his history twice before his death. For a summary of the differences in the first, second, and third editions of Bright's history see Brown, "Introduction," 6–20.

Joshua in the thirteenth century BCE, was, according to archaeology, not inhabited at this time. Instead, Albright argued that the Bible actually reported the conquest of Bethel (Tell Beitin), since it was in the same area and had occupation and destruction layers datable to the thirteenth century. This contention allowed the Bible's essential claims about these episodes to be maintained, as well as the belief that Israel entered its land through an exodus and conquest.

Summary of the Albright School

In summary, the scholarship of William Foxwell Albright combined assumptions and goals that now seem dated or even contrary to that to which history writing should aspire. His unquestioned advocacy of the scientific method for history, with its assumptions of objectivity and explanations by derived laws, appears naive in the face of postmodernism. Furthermore, the Albrightian approach to history and archaeology is now associated with a desire to describe Israel's past in such a way that much of the Bible's story is left essentially intact. As has been discussed briefly here and will be seen in the next chapter, many aspects of the Albrightian approach came under serious attack in the 1970s.

The Alt School[61]

Altians on History Writing

As Albright's ideas became the basis for most North American studies in the history of Israel, the methods and assumptions of Albrecht Alt and his pupils, especially Martin Noth (1902–1968), began to dominate the discipline in Germany and Europe.[62] One noticeable characteristic of the Altians is their lack of philosophical reflection about the historian's task. Albright, as seen above, was exceptional in his production of essays about philosophical topics relating to history. Alt and Noth (and also Bright), more typical of historians in general, primarily produced reconstructions of the past in their writings and only rarely stopped to reflect on presuppositions and method. Alt even boasted that he put little effort into the philosophical issues introduced by Albright in *From the Stone Age to Christianity* and E. Meyer in his *Geschichte des Alterthums*.[63] When Alt and Noth did discuss their assumptions, their comments were brief and usually specifically related to how historians should interpret texts and use

61.   For other studies of the Alt school, see the essays in Steven L. McKenzie and M. Patrick Graham, eds., *The History of Israel's Traditions: The Heritage of Martin Noth* (JSOTSup 182; Sheffield: Sheffield Academic Press, 1994). For Alt, see Smend, *Deutsche Alttestamentler in drei Jahrhunderten*, 182–207; for Noth, see ibid., 255–75.

62.   Siegfried Herrmann (1926–1999) and Herbert Donner were also students of Alt whose methods were similar to Alt's but whose influence was not as widely felt.

63.   "Alt legte Wert darauf, bei der Lektüre von Ed. Meyers *Geschicte des Alterthums* [sic] und W.F. Albrights *From the Stone Age to Christianity* die geschichtsphilosophischen Einleitungen 'mehr oder weniger überschlagen' zu haben" (see Rudolf Smend, "Nachruf auf Martin Noth," in *Gesammelte Studien zum Alten Testament II*, by Martin Noth [ed. Hans Walter Wolff; Munich: Kaiser, 1969], 137–65 [147]); see also Eduard Meyer, *Geschichte des Alterthums* (5 vols.; Stuttgart: Cotta, 1884–1902).

archaeology.[64] Thus, many of Alt's and Noth's presuppositions about history will have to be inferred, and, due to lack of evidence, some will have to be left undescribed.

Goals of History

The essays of Alt, along with the more comprehensive works of Noth, demonstrate that explaining and clarifying aspects of the biblical story were important goals for these scholars. What things happened in Israel's past and how and why they happened are the focus of much of their writing, but how they perceived that their work fit into a larger human quest for knowledge is mostly left undescribed. Noth seems to adhere to the idea that history is a science, as he mentions deduction and "scientifically controlled intuition" as important to learning about the past, especially "the unspoken" of a past culture (what might be called its *mentalités*).[65] Also, though Noth called the Christian Bible "one of the very roots of our understanding of the essential significance of history for life on earth,"[66] neither he nor Alt explained how they believed Israelite history and world history were related. Additionally, neither Alt nor Noth contributed greatly to theology.[67] Timo Veijola claims that Noth's avoidance of theology derived from a belief that history "is the main forum for God's revelation,"[68] and Noth agreed with Schleiermacher's claim that history is the "highest object of religion."[69] Thus, it can be inferred that for Alt and Noth, study of the past had

64.   Smend ("Nachruf," 163) uses such a passage from Noth's *Geschichte Israels* (Göttingen: Vandenhoeck & Ruprecht, 1950) to exemplify how "Aussagen dieser Art begegnen bei Noth oft; sie sind für ihn charakteristisch und geradezu Programm."

65.   Martin Noth, "God, King, and Nation in the Old Testament," in idem, *The Laws in the Pentateuch and Other Studies* (Philadelphia: Fortress, 1966), 145–78 (147). This volume is a translation of *Gesammelte Studien zum Alten Testament* (2d ed.; Munich: Kaiser, 1960). This particular essay originally appeared as "Gott, König, Volk im Alten Testament: Eine methodologische Auseinandersetzung mit einer gegenwärtigen Forschungsrichtung," *ZTK* 47 (1950): 157–91.

66.   Martin Noth, "The Understanding of History in Old Testament Apocalyptic," in *The Laws in the Pentateuch and Other Studies*, 194–214 (194); trans. of *Das Geschichtsverständnis der alttestamentlichen Apokalyptik* (Arbeitsgemeinschaft für Forschung des Landes Nordrhein-Westfalen: Geisteswissenschaften 21; Cologne: Westdeutscher Verlag, 1954). In this essay, Noth does ask whether there are laws in history and what the meaning of history is. Here, however, he seeks to understand how Old Testament Apocalyptic literature, particularly Daniel, answers these questions and does not disclose his views on the subject in general. Noth concludes that Old Testament Apocalyptic saw no *telos* in history, i.e., no trend towards ultimate good or bad. Rather, Old Testament Apocalyptic is of the opinion that "History takes its course in a series of changing phenomena, and God lets it happen in just this way" (p. 214).

67.   Noth "war keine Figur des geistigen Leben im allgemeinen und wollte es auch nich sein... Mit theologischen Äußerungen hielt er sich, von einigen nicht unbeactlichen Ausnamen abgesehen, zurück" (Smend, "Nachruf," 144).

68.   Timo Veijola, "Martin Noth's *Überlieferungsgeschichtliche Studien* and Old Testament Theology," in McKenzie and Graham, eds., *The History of Israel's Traditions*, 101–27 (103).

69.   Martin Noth, "Die Historisierung des Mythus im Alten Testament," in *GS II*, 29–61 (29). For Noth, however, establishing the history of religion and religious ideas was not equivalent to and should not be confused with establishing a "Theology of the Old Testament" (idem, "As One Historian to Another" [review of John Bright, *A History of Israel*], *Int* 15 [1961]: 61–66 [65–66]).

access to truth in part because it addresses the same universal and existential questions as does religion.

Representation, Subject, and Explanation

Judging from the many historical reconstructions Alt and Noth proposed, it can be argued that they were confident in the historian's ability to represent the past in some way, though they do not elaborate on the extent to which representation is possible or how the historian should go about representing the past. In their concept of Israel and in their choices of subjects and modes of explanations for Israel's history, Alt and Noth were indebted to Max Weber. In his book *Ancient Judaism*, Weber described Israel as a covenant community that was the result of the need for three different strata of Palestinian society—the city-dwellers/ plebeians, the farmers, and the bedouins—to co-exist.[70] Noth accepted Weber's idea that Israel was a community formed in the land,[71] and Noth's amphictyony, which explained the unity of the Israel as the outgrowth of a religious community that worshiped at a common sanctuary, was an elaboration on Weber's contention that Israel's unity was covenant-based.[72] Religion, however, was not the only factor in Israel's unity that Noth cited; he named geography, language, and politics as contributors, as well.[73] In line with the human-driven nature of explanation current in history before the rise of the *Annales* school, and the individual agency prominent in Weber's explanations,[74] however, geography and

---

70. Max Weber, *Ancient Judaism* (New York: Free Press, 1952), esp. 10–27. *Ancient Judaism* originally appeared as a series of articles in the *Archiv für Socialwissenschaft und Sozialforschung*, 1917–19, and then as idem, *Gessamelte Aufsätze zur Religionssoziologie*. Vol. 3, *Das antike Judentum* (Tübingen: Mohr, 1922–23).

71. Martin Noth, *The History of Israel* (2d ed.; New York: Harper & Row, 1960), 1–7; trans. of *Geschichte Israels*. Here Noth refers to Israel as a "nation" that originated in Palestine and ceased to function ca. 135 CE when the Romans banned the Jews from Jerusalem and Israel became a diaspora community entirely.

72. Martin Noth, *Das System der Zwölf Stämme Israels* (BWANT 4.1; Stuttgart: Kohlhammer, 1930). Cf. Alt: "If we are in any way justified, then, in arguing back from the later history of the Israelite nation to its origins, we can only conclude that the event on which all further development was based took place when the tribes united in the worship of Yahweh" (Albrecht Alt, "The God of the Fathers," in his *Essays on Old Testament History and Religion* [Oxford: Blackwell, 1966], 3–66 [3]; trans. of *Der Gott Der Väter* [BWANT 12; Stuttgart: Kohlhammer, 1929]). The amphictyony theory was ultimately discredited by scholars who argued, among other things, that the Bible did not describe the same type of religious society that had existed in Greece. See A. D. H. Mayes, *Israel in the Period of the Judges* (SBT 29; London: SCM Press, 1974); John H. Hayes, "The Twelve-Tribe Israelite Amphictyony: An Appraisal," *Trinity University Studies in Religion* 10 (1975): 22–36; C. H. J. de Geus, *The Tribes of Israel: An Investigation into Some of the Presuppositions of Martin Noth's Amphictyony Hypothesis* (SSN; Assen: Van Gorcum, 1976); and Eben Scheffler, "Beyond the Judges and the Amphictyony: The Politics of Tribal Israel (1200–1020 BCE)," *OTE* 14 (2001): 494–509 (499–501).

73. Noth, *History of Israel*, 4–6.

74. Mayes (*The Old Testament in Sociological Perspective* [London: Marshall Pickering, 1989], 42) says that in *Ancient Judaism*, Weber's position is that "the understanding of the individuals who constituted that emergent Israel are of foundational importance."

geographical time played a limited role in Alt and Noth's reconstructions of the past.[75]

Thus, though Alt and Noth explained the formation and existence of Israel partly in terms of religious ideas (as did the Albrightians), their explanations were grounded in social-scientific scholarship. Other examples of social-scientific influence in general, and Weber's influence in particular, on subjects and explanations in their work include Alt's "peaceful infiltration" model for Israelite settlement, which posited early Israelites as seminomads or transhumants,[76] his description of Israel's monarchy as charismatic and Judah's as dynastic,[77] and Alt and Noth's work on Israelite law.[78] Among current historians of ancient Israel, Alt and Noth are credited with being early practitioners of sociological research into the biblical world, and their work forms the basis of reconstructions by current scholars as diverse as Norman K. Gottwald and Niels Peter Lemche.[79]

In the case of historical explanation, Alt and Noth did disclose some of their general presuppositions, and in some cases these indicate thoughts on the subject that moved beyond Weber and ideal-type explanations for historical phenomena. Alt argued that "To give a complete picture, what is missing from the tradition must be provided by hypothetical accounts."[80] Noth, in an approach similar to Troeltsch's and Collingwood's, discussed historians' need to use "scholarly intuition" and common human experience to elucidate the mental or spiritual (*Geistlich*) world of a past culture.[81] Expanding on ideas of G. Ernest Wright, he argued that:

> the possibility of transposing oneself into the mental approach and mode of thought of someone else is the precondition for any understanding between men… This possibility rests, therefore, on the existence of a basic community of thought between man and man, lying deeper than the variable mental approaches and modes of thought.[82]

75. For instance, geographical information about ancient Israel is confined to the introduction of Noth's *History of Israel*, and after that the book does not include discussion of how these factors affected the course of Israel's past.

76. See, e.g., Albrecht Alt, "The Settlement of the Israelites in Palestine," in his *Essays*, 133–69; trans. of *Die Landnahme der Israeliten in Palästina* (Reformationsprogramm der Universität Leipzig, 1925).

77. Albrecht Alt, "The Monarchy in the Kingdoms of Israel and Judah," in his *Essays*, 239–59; trans. of "Das Königtum in den Reichen Israel und Juda," *VT* 1 (1951): 2–22.

78. Albrecht Alt, "The Origins of Israelite Law," in his *Essays*, 79–132; trans. of *Die Ursprung des israelitischen Rechts* (Berichte über die Verhandlungen der Sächsichen Akademie der Wissenschaften zu Leipzig, Philologisch-historische Klasse 86.1; Leipzig: Hirzel, 1934). See also Noth, *The Laws in the Pentateuch*. For detailed discussions of Weber's influence on these ideas, see Mayes, *The Old Testament in Sociological Perspective*, 36–77, and idem, "The Covenant People: Max Weber and the Historical Understanding of Ancient Israel," in *Covenant as Context: Essays in Honour of E. W. Nicholson* (ed. A. D. H. Mayes and R. B. Salters; Oxford: Oxford University Press, 2003), 285–310.

79. Though scholars have challenged Alt and Noth's awareness of sociological theory, Lemche has argued that they were "both well informed of the sociology and anthropology of their day" (Niels Peter Lemche, *Early Israel: Anthropological and Historical Studies on the Israelite Society Before the Monarchy* [VTSup 37; Leiden: Brill, 1985], 37).

80. Alt, "The Settlement of the Israelites in Palestine," 135.

81. See n. 27.

82. Noth, "God, King, and Nation," 146.

Noth emphasized the particularity of cultural presuppositions as well. He held that Israel's cultural structures were related to, yet not the same as, those of other cultures of the ancient Near East. He recognized that the literary corpora of Mesopotamia and Egypt offered a wealth of comparative material that could help explain institutions and practices referred to in the Bible, but cautioned that "the place of the Old Testament within [the ancient Near East] needs to be more precisely fixed before the real connections...can be precisely studied."[83] For example, he warned that the ancient Near East had diverse "viewpoints and attitudes" and therefore that a general Near Eastern outlook could not be invoked as a background for biblical study.[84]

Objectivity
Though Alt and Noth left little indication of their opinions on the possibility and importance of objectivity, a few observations can be made. First, it can be assumed that for them objectivity was obtainable and desirable. Noth recognized that in history, especially in explanations, "there is a very real danger of a subjective and unacceptable viewpoint."[85] Further, in a discussion of trends in German theology, Noth worried that he would not be able to discuss the topic objectively considering his Protestant background. It is not clear, however, that he would apply his admission there that "my portrayal throughout will be a personal one"[86] to his works within Old Testament studies, or if this confession is simply a qualifier for work done in a field outside his own.

As seen in the previous section, Albright and some of his students accused Alt and Noth of being biased by having a nihilistic view of the value of the Bible and archaeology as evidence for history writing. Noth reacted strongly to this accusation, though characteristic of his tendency not to dwell on philosophical matters, he discussed it only in a footnote:

> So wenig es gut is, selbst voreingenommen zu sein, so wenig gut ist es auch, bei anderen eine Voreingenommenheit zu unterstellen... Denn erstens ist die Verwendung des Begriffs 'Nihilismus' im vorliegenden Falle sachlich einfach falsch. Sodann aber kann es nicht für wissenschaftlich halten, mit einem weltanschaulichen oder sogar weltanschaulich-politicschen Schlagwort eine wissenschaftliche Methode abzutun, die—ob überzeugend oder nich überzeugend—jedenfalls wissenschaftlich begründet ist.[87]

This statement implies that Noth considered his own biblical research to be scientific, as did Albright, and considered scientific method to be by nature

83. Ibid., 147. In this article, Noth was specifically opposing the claims of the myth and ritual school.

84. Ibid.

85. Ibid., 147.

86. Martin Noth, *Developing Lines of Theological Thought in Germany* (Fourth Annual Bibliographical Lecture, Union Theological Seminary in Virginia; Richmond: Union Theological Seminary, 1963), 1.

87. Martin Noth, "Der Beitrag der Archäologie zur Geschichte Israels," in *Aufsätze zur biblischen Landes- und Altertumskunde* (ed. Hans Walter Wolff; 2 vols.; Neukirchen–Vluyn: Neukirchener Verlag, 1971), 1:34–51 (35 n. 2); repr. from *Congress Volume: Oxford, 1959* (VTSup 7; Leiden: Brill, 1960), 262–82.

objective, as well. Thus, the two were in agreement on the desirability of import-
ing scientific, and thereby objective, methodology into biblical studies. As will
be seen below, however, they disagreed over the proper objective stance toward
the Bible.

Language and Narrative

As with most historians working in the first half of the twentieth century, Alt
and Noth showed little awareness of the relationship of narrative form to the
creation of historical reconstructions and explanations. As discussed above,
Noth's history told the story of Israel's people and political institutions from
their inception to the time when the Romans effectively put an end to Jewish life
in ancient Palestine, and the rise of Christianity is downplayed in Noth's
description of the Roman period. Alt never produced a large scale history. Nevertheless, history's linguistic turn recognizes that even historical reconstructions
that do not take the form of a book-length narrative can exhibit certain characteristics of narrative structure. For instance, Alt and Noth commonly use an
authoritative voice to tell about happenings in the past.[88] As seen in Chapter 1,
the construction of an omniscient narrator is a technique that is now debated
because it implicitly silences dissenting voices and gives an impression of
detached objectivity that postmodern theorists no longer find tenable or acceptable in history writing.

Truth

Though Alt and Noth never named correspondence to past reality as the goal
of their historical reconstructions, it is clear that they held this assumption.
Furthermore, both express concerns about the possibility of fully achieving this
goal. For example, after finding that inscriptions make it "impossible to doubt
that the Israelite tradition of the God of the Fathers presents us with a type of
religion that was a living force" in the ancient Semitic world, Alt goes on to note
that "It does not yet make it certain that this *must* be the case."[89] Another
example of the belief that correspondence to reality may be impossible for the
historian to obtain can be found in Noth's *Das System des Zwölf Stämme Israels*,
where he states that some of the details of his exposition of the amphictyony
must be understood as "mehr oder weniger wahrscheinlichen Vermutungen."[90]
Yet neither Alt's nor Noth's recognition of the imperfection of correspondence
in historical accounts appears to have swayed them from their commitment to
correspondence to reality as the goal of their histories. In addition, as will be
seen in the discussion of evidence below, Alt and Noth had different ideas from
Albright about the possibility of whether and how history can cohere with the

---

88. For example, "To understand properly the very first Israelite national state, the kingdom of
Israel under King Saul, it is particularly necessary to relate it in this way…" (Albrecht Alt, "The
Formation of the Israelite State in Palestine," in his *Essays*, 171–237 [185]; trans. of *Die Staaten-
bildung der Israeliten in Palästina* [Reformationsprogramm der Universität Leipzig, 1930]).

89. Alt, "The God of the Fathers," 145.

90. Noth, *Das System der Zwölf Stämme Israels*, 87.

biblical story. Finally, it is unclear whether Alt and Noth saw history as potentially providing pragmatic truth, that is, truth that is beneficial to the community that receives history. Their lack of active involvement in theology indicates that the preservation of or justification for modern faith communities were not explicit goals of theirs.

Evidence

Alt and Noth, like Albright and most of their contemporaries, believed that rigorous research could uncover facts for the historian. In addition, Alt seems to indicate that historians determine what data are evidence. For instance, he introduces the problem of Israel's entry into Palestine by noting that the Old Testament alone does not provide a complete picture about this time period and then argues that:

> In these circumstances it is doubtful whether any further light can be shed on the Israelites' settlement in Palestine, except by putting the question differently, thereby bringing to bear on it information hitherto unused.[91]

Most of the evidence Altians used came from textual sources. Although they did use artifacts and archaeology at times in their reconstructions, Alt and Noth generally considered these to be less appropriate or less available for answering historical questions about ancient Israel than did the Albrightians. Fortunately, this disagreement about sources of evidence for Israel's past prompted Alt and his pupils to make some methodological statements about the evaluation and use of evidence.

Texts

The most comprehensive description of the Altians' approach to ancient texts can be found in Herbert Donner's *Geschichte des Volkes Israel und seiner Nachbarn in Grundzügen*. Donner was a student of Alt's and his method and conclusions closely parallel those of his teacher. He divides textual sources into two categories: *Unmittelbare Quellen* and *Mittelbare Quellen*.[92] *Unmittelbare Quellen*, "unmediated" or "direct" sources, provide direct evidence about happenings and people in ancient Israel and come from a time close to the events they describe. *Mittelbare Quellen*, "mediated" or "indirect" sources, may be more geographically or chronologically removed from the culture than *unmittelbare* sources. Indirect sources may also give general information about culture and social structures such as religion. For Donner and others of Alt's school, it is impossible to classify the Bible as either a direct or an indirect source about Israel's past since they consider the Bible to be a collection of both types of sources. Therefore, in order to understand the date, geographic origin, context, and purpose of the stories embedded in the Bible, the embedded sources

91. Alt, "The Settlement of the Israelites," 135.
92. Herbert Donner, *Geschichte des Volkes Israel und seiner Nachbarn in Grundzügen* (2 vols.; ATD 4; Göttingen: Vandenhoeck & Ruprecht, 1984), 19.

had to be separated and interpreted using, among other things, form and tradition criticism.[93]

Much of the Altians' textual method was based on the source analysis of Wellhausen and the tradition-historical scholarship of Hermann Gunkel (1862–1932), which Alt called "a development in the scientific method."[94] Gunkel took a formalist approach to texts and argued that there were separate sources within the narrative material of the Bible that could be classified into types, such as *Sage* and *Geschichte*. These types have distinct characteristics, relationships to reality, and contexts, as well as definable chronological relationships to each other. In particular, *Sage* traditions were believed to have been transmitted orally, and their core traditions were considered historical.[95] Alt and Noth believed that when such traditions became part of a written work, the historical facts in them could be placed out of context or otherwise corrupted. More specifically, they promoted a theory of *Ortsgebundenheit*, considering many of the traditions of the Pentateuch and Israel's prehistory to have been tied originally to particular sanctuaries and the tribes that worshipped there. They believed that stories reflective of the experience and beliefs of these smaller groups were told at tribal gatherings, and from these retellings major themes, such as the guidance out of Egypt and the promise to the Patriarchs, became traditions of the larger group. Eventually the nation that arose from these groups incorporated these traditions into their store of common tradition, the Bible.[96]

These assumptions about the nature of the biblical text and the location of historical information within it permitted Alt and Noth to provide very different answers to questions of the dates, origins, contexts and purposes of biblical narratives from the Albrightians. For instance, the Pentateuch attributes the giving of the law to Moses in the desert after the exodus. Alt, however, claimed that the Pentateuch's casuistic law originated in Canaan and was adopted by the Israelites, while its apodictic law "is rooted in the basic institutions of Israel's early history," particularly Yahweh worship.[97] In addition, Alt argued that the conquest stories of Joshua were misplaced remembrances of military conflicts experienced by the early Israelite "states."[98] Also using form and tradition

93. Ibid., 21–22. For a critique of Noth's use of these approaches in history writing, see Thomas L. Thompson, "Martin Noth and the History of Israel," in McKenzie and Graham, eds., *The History of Israel's Traditions*, 81–90.

94. Alt, "The God of the Fathers," 5. For a discussion of Gunkel, see Smend, *Deutsche Alttestamentler in drei Jahrhunderten*, 160–72.

95. Jay A. Wilcoxen, "Narrative," in *Old Testament Form Criticism* (ed. John H. Hayes; TUMSR 2; San Antonio: Trinity University Press, 1974), 57–98 (60–64); Donner, *Geschichte des Volkes Israel*, 25.

96. Martin Noth, *A History of Pentateuchal Traditions* (Englewood Cliffs, N.J.: Prentice–Hall, 1972; repr., Chico, Calif.: Scholars Press, 1981), 46–62; trans. of *Überlieferungsgeschichte des Pentateuch* (Stuttgart: Kohlhammer, 1948). For another summary of this approach to texts see Siegfried Herrmann, *A History of Israel in Old Testament Times* (2d ed.; Philadelphia: Fortress, 1981), 31–34; trans. of *Geschichte Israels in alttestamentlicher Zeit* (2d ed.; Munich: Kaiser, 1980 [1st ed. 1973]).

97. Alt, "The Origins of Israelite Law," 131.

98. Alt, "The Settlement of the Israelites."

criticism, Noth explored the historical books of the Bible and concluded that Joshua, Judges, Samuel and Kings had an outlook related to that of Deuteronomy and that all five books had common linguistic and literary styles.[99] The author of this Deuteronomistic History, Noth claimed, included old traditions but manipulated them to fit into an already established chronology of Israel's history.[100] The Chronicler, whom Noth considered responsible for Chronicles, Ezra, and Nehemiah, also used sources but was more liberal with corrections and changes.[101] Thus, Noth relied on a detailed and sophisticated understanding of the nature and origin of the Pentateuch and the historical books of the Hebrew Bible when composing his *History of Israel*.

In seeking to distill the biblical tradition down to its historical core, Alt and Noth discarded much information that Albrightians considered to be historical. For instance, Bright believed that etiologies were part of the historical core of the Old Testament, but Noth asserted that etiologies were usually secondary and that their connection to reality was difficult to prove. Both sides agreed, however, that the Bible provided some evidence about the premonarchical period and copious reliable information about the early monarchy, a position which, as will be seen, many scholars find difficult to maintain with confidence today.[102] Altians and Albrightians also agreed that texts from the ancient Near East could help in reconstructing Israel's history. As seen above, Alt used a number of sources to reconstruct the territorial history of Palestine. Noth continued Alt's territorial studies, publishing articles about the land east and west of the Jordan River.[103] Donner cites Egyptian texts and the Mesha inscription to argue that Israel's preoccupation with its origins was unique.[104] As will be seen in the remainder of this section, however, their methods of using the comparative material and the conclusions they drew from it were quite different from those of the Albright school.

Artifacts

As in the case of Albright and his followers, it is difficult to examine Alt's and Noth's ideas about archaeology without discussing how they believed artifacts to relate to the biblical story and the possibility of writing history using both as sources. Both Alt and Noth worked and taught at the German Institute of Archaeology in Jerusalem and knew the discipline and the land well. In general, Noth appears to have had a traditional view of archaeology, understanding it to

---

99. Martin Noth, *Überlieferungsgeschichtliche Studien I* (Tübingen: Niemeyer Verlag, 1948); repr. 1957 and 1967. The first part of this book has been translated as *The Deuteronomistic History* (JSOTSup 15; Sheffield: JSOT Press, 1981); the second part as *The Chronicler's History* (JSOTSup 50; Sheffield: JSOT Press, 1987).
100. Noth, *Deuteronomistic History*, 84–88.
101. Noth, *Chronicler's History*, 89–95.
102. E.g. Noth, "As One Historian to Another," 61: "From the time of David on, the history of Israel is well known, biblical and nonbiblical sources being abundantly available; and the writer of Israel's history can be quite confident of his presentation."
103. Collected in Noth's *Aufsätze*, vol. 2.
104. Donner, *Geschichte des Volkes Israel*, 23–24.

be concerned with typology, stratigraphy, and dating. He claimed that "The significance of archaeology for the understanding of history should not be exaggerated,"[105] and saw the appropriate task of archaeology as illustrative:

> Es wird auch immer eine der wichtigen und schönen Aufgaben dieser Arbeit bleiben, den Hintergrund der biblischen Geschichte des Landes aufzuhellen und so die Ereignisse, die sich da abgespielt haben, für unsere Erkenntnis plastisch und anschaulich zu machen.[106]

Noth names buildings and graves as some of archaeology's most useful finds, and mentions surface exploration, saying that it can expand the general knowledge of the number of *tells* with potential habitation in certain time periods.[107] Siegfried Herrmann claims that pottery also is valuable for showing the "age and importance of a site."[108] Pottery, however, "cannot be an independent historical source" but must be "taken in conjunction with written sources."[109] Further, Herrmann claims, "the most valuable find in any archaeological investigation is, of course, written sources."[110]

Noth also explicitly commented on some of archaeology's limitations. In archaeology, Noth claimed, "history is seen only from the standpoint of cultural development."[111] Further, archaeology's reconstruction of the past has "gaps" and "still needs verification in many details."[112] Dating artifacts, he noted, is very important to history writing, but is difficult and sometimes impossible. At first glance, Altians' theoretical statements about the use of archaeology and artifacts as evidence do not seem to be markedly different from Albrightians' ideas. As will be seen here, Altians, however, in general were skeptical of the Albrightians' methods of combining texts and artifacts in history writing and their concomitant claims that archaeology could confirm the veracity of biblical stories.

Combination of Texts and Artifacts for History Writing
The primary methodological contribution that Noth made to the issue of how texts and artifacts relate was the promotion of the idea that artifacts were of limited use to the historian who was interested in events that involved human action:

---

105. Martin Noth, *The Old Testament World* (Philadelphia: Fortress, 1966), 142; trans. of *Die Welt des Alten Testaments: Einführung in die Grenzgebiete der alttestamentlichen Wissenschaft* (Berlin: Töpelmann, 1964).
106. Martin Noth, "Grundsätzliches zur geschichtlichen Deutung archäologischer Befunde auf dem Boden Palästinas," in *Aufsätze*, 1:3–16 (3); repr. from *PJ* 34 (1938): 7–22.
107. Noth, *The Old Testament World*, 107–44; idem, "Hat die Bibel doch Recht?," in *Aufsätze*, 1:17–33 (18–19); repr. from *Festschrift für Günther Dehn, zum 75 Geburtstag am 18 April 1957* (ed. Wilhelm Schneemelcher; Neukirchen: Verlag der Buchhandlung des Erziehungsvereins, 1957), 7–22. Cf. Donner, *Geschichte des Volkes Israel*, 27–29.
108. Herrmann, *A History of Israel*, 27.
109. Ibid.
110. Ibid., 28.
111. Noth, *The Old Testament World*, 107.
112. Ibid., 109.

> Historical events, namely the activity of historical persons and the course of individual
> historical events, items which form the essential content of the literary tradition, by
> their very nature cannot be explained by archaeology, because they have not always
> produced tangible or visible changes in living arrangements. On the other hand even
> where events have produced such changes, they are not immediately recognizable or
> unambiguous.[113]

Thus, Noth argued, artifacts need information from texts to situate them within the totality of past human events: "The definite historical significance of an archaeological find is determined only by matching it to a recorded event."[114] Even then, considering historical evidence side-by-side with archaeological evidence has its limitations. Alt remarked that "There is a limit to what can be proved scientifically by even the most successful comparison, and we must not forget it."[115] Noth doubted that evidence for most of what the Bible reports actually existed; "Es geht aber wissenschaftlich nicht darum, ob wir 'external evidence' brauchen, sondern ob wir 'external evidence' haben."[116] He also questioned the possibility of artifacts confirming biblical reports, asking, "Was ist vom Inhalt der Bibel überhaupt archäologisch beweisbar?"[117] In short, Noth suggested that archaeology and texts, particularly the Bible, offer different types of information about the past. Noth himself did not take up these issues with much sophistication, but his initial skepticism opened the door for others, as will be seen in the following chapter. Ultimately, both Alt and Noth used findings from archaeology in their historical writings, yet held to the notion that "die archäologische Arbeit uns keineswegs entbindet von einer Untersuchung der alttestamentlichen Überlieferung."[118]

Summary of the Schools of Albright and Alt

Albright, Alt, Bright, and Noth worked on the history of ancient Israel at the same time but saw themselves as representatives of two different currents in the discipline. Albrightians, working mainly in America, eschewed source and historical criticism for the narrative parts of the Bible, placed value on its poetic texts (especially in the Pentateuch), and were optimistic about using archaeology

---

113. Ibid., 142.

114. Ibid., 143. For example, a destruction layer could be imagined by the archaeologist to have many causes, but its actual cause would have to be reported in the literary record.

115. Alt, "The God of the Fathers," 45. Alt here is referring to his combination of inscriptional material and biblical material to describe the religion of the patriarchs, but the idea expressed is consistent with his and Noth's cautious attitude toward the combination of the Bible with any external evidence.

116. Noth, "Der Beitrag der Archäologie zur Geschichte Israels," 41 n. 15; cf. idem, "As One Historian to Another."

117. Noth, "Hat die Bibel doch Recht?," 18. Noth was preceded in this opinion by R. A. S. MacAlister; see his *A Century of Excavation in Palestine* (London: Religious Tract Society, 1925), 266–67. MacAlister also claims that archaeology primarily should be used to illustrate the background of the Bible.

118. Noth, "Der Beitrag der Archäologie zur Geschichte Israels," 47.

to place biblical persons and events on the historical record. In Germany, Altians considered the biblical text a composite record of traditions whose origins varied in time and space, drew on social-scientific scholarship, particularly Weber's, and mostly rejected the use of archaeology in specific historical reconstructions. In retrospect, however, some scholars find the assumptions and practices of the Albrightians and the Altians in fact to have been quite similar, especially with respect to their use of the Bible. For instance, Thompson has pointed out that Albright and Alt agreed that "the biblical tradition was generally historical in origin and that the historical events which lay behind any tradition could theoretically be discovered in the earliest forms of that tradition."[119] In other words, both Albrightians and Altians believed that biblical texts reflected the reality they described in some way, and that biblical sources were more reliable the closer they were to the events they described. Thompson also argues that "Albright and Alt shared a common goal of constructing a history of early Israel on the basis of a critical appraisal and synthesis of biblical, archaeological, and ancient Near Eastern studies."[120] These shared assumptions about evidence led to the creation of what he calls "the Albright–Alt consensus," where:

> The long-standing debate between the schools of Albright and Alt, between the alternative interpretations of 'conquest' or 'settlement' as an explanation of Israel's origins, has not been as important as the common gains and the expanding basis of agreement that have been achieved by the two sides of the issues. Alt and Albright, and Noth and Bright, did not after all stand so very far apart.[121]

Alt and Albright also helped to embed a number of other assumptions into the discipline. Both scholars firmly believed that objectivity in history was possible and that historical writing could represent the past, and drew on empiricism and scientific methodology to guide them. Both schools established the religious community of Israel as the subject of the history of ancient Israel, and thereby cemented religion's role in explaining events in Israel's past. Put in theoretical language, both Altians and Albrightians were more idealists than materialists, and both saw religious ideals as a source of rational explanation for past events. Further, historians of both schools believed that most of the data for understanding Israel's religion and unique self-conception could be found in the Bible, and they used systematic, albeit different, methods of reading in order to uncover ancient, reliable information there. In addition, for members of both schools, background for Israel's ways of thinking could be found in ancient extrabiblical texts, such as in the Ugaritic material. Alt and Albright and their pupils also paid attention to material factors that helped shape Israel, using the artifactual record to understand the land and its settlement history, as well as the wider geo-political context of the Bronze and Iron Ages. Finally, all of these historians strove for historical reconstructions that corresponded to past reality.

As the twentieth century progressed, critiques of the schools of Albright and Alt arose out of critical assessment of the evidence, methods, and conclusions of

119.   Thompson, *Early History*, 11.
120.   Ibid.
121.   Ibid., 26.

both schools. The strongest critique that has persisted over three decades is found in the work of the minimalists. Chapter 4 will examine the presuppositions and practices of this group in detail, and will investigate the relationship of their positions to Albrightian, Altian, and other traditional ideas of history, as well as to postmodern ones. Before that, however, Zevit's recent chronological description of history writing since the mid-nineteenth century will be presented in order to help place the scholars considered in this and subsequent chapters, as well as the development of the issues discussed in Chapters 1 and 2, in wider intellectual contexts.

History in the Nineteenth and Twentieth Centuries

Historian of Israelite religion Zevit recently wrote a comprehensive study of ancient Israel's religions and began it with a survey of approaches to the subject in order to situate the approach he takes with respect to others, past and present.[122] Zevit's analysis touches on many of the issues presented in Chapters 1 and 2, but, in contrast to the topical approach taken here, he organizes developments chronologically. Zevit claims that in 1833, Ranke and his historicism set the foundations of a first paradigm of modern history writing, and that three more paradigms have evolved since then (p. 29). A paradigm, Zevit explains, "may be conceived as a loosely defined, three-dimensional web of ideas and attitudes... It delimits the disciplinary culture within which general questions make sense, the objectives of research agendas are readily comprehended, and correct answers are apparent" (pp. 5–6). Zevit attempts to show that "The fortunes of biblical history and the study of Israelite religion have been tied to each of [the] four paradigms" of history writing (p. 29). A brief summary of his conclusions is presented here, with issues noted in the previous two chapters highlighted.

The first paradigm of academic historical study, according to Zevit, had as a goal "an objective, realistic rendering of what happened and an explanation of why" (p. 30). In addition, historians hoped to "produce new insights into the past on the basis of new facts and not simply to retell in narrative what is already known" (ibid.). The aims Zevit describes are tied to a firm belief in the reality of the past and to the assurance that historians can represent it. In the first paradigm, objectivity in research was assumed to be possible and necessary. Explanation was carried out by "the use of analogies to situations drawn from the historian's knowledge or experience," a practice built on Enlightenment "enthusiasm" for the philosophical premise that human logic and reason had great potential for obtaining knowledge (ibid.). Zevit defines the subjects of this type of history as "political, military, religious and constitutional" (p. 31), citing current interest in those topics among the wider European populace as well as the availability of relevant documents in ecclesiastical and state archives. He

---

122. Ziony Zevit, *The Religions of Ancient Israel: A Synthesis of Parallactic Approaches* (London: Continuum, 2000), 1–80. Subsequent citations will be indicated parenthetically.

mentions narrative only in passing, implying that it was the accepted medium of historical reconstruction. He does not discuss then-current ideas about the nature of truth, but does point out that "the historicist element of the paradigm questioned viewing Christianity as the pinnacle of all religious understanding and the major font of insight into the human condition" (ibid.). In other words, whatever truths objective history claimed had the potential to be very different from those claimed by Christianity.

Texts were the only potential sources of evidence for historians of the first paradigm. Ancient texts, like the histories being written, were considered to be reflective of reality. However, ancient sources needed to be examined closely for facts. Zevit describes the process of "distinguishing reliable from unreliable information" as "sieving" (p. 30). Sieved facts, especially from the Bible, were not necessarily "interpreted as reflecting social reality at the time of their literary setting" (p. 31); information left over from earlier time periods could have been incorporated into a later text. Indeed, according to Zevit, advances made in source criticism were the major developments in the history of ancient Israel and Israelite religion that occurred in the context of the first paradigm. Historians Zevit associates with this paradigm include Georg Heinrich August Ewald (1803–1875), Wilhelm Martin Leberecht de Wette (1780–1849), Abraham Kuenen (1828–1891), and Wellhausen.

Challenges to the first paradigm appeared in the late nineteenth and early twentieth centuries. Some of the changes Zevit notes can be described on a philosophical level as pertaining to the possibility of representing the past. The "complex reality" of the past, along with the limits of documentary evidence, contributed to the realization that "what [the] past was is known only through partial reconstruction in the present" (p. 34). In addition, recognition of the historian's role in determining what a fact is (i.e. selecting evidence) and how it relates to other facts (i.e. creating explanations) "emphasized the many junctures at which nonobjective factors entered into the process of doing history" (p. 35). Zevit claims that some historians capitalized on this climate of uncertainty and produced relativistic histories. He considers Gerhard von Rad (1901–1971) and George Ernest Wright (1909–1974) to be historians in this mold because they focused on certain religious beliefs found in the Old Testament, wrote history as if the course of the past could be explained by changes in religious thought, and had transparent Christian motives.[123]

If the critique of the first paradigm had been taken to its logical end, the possibility of all historical knowledge would have been questioned. Instead, by "sensitizing [history] to some of the limitations of its claims" (p. 39), the critique allowed for the development of a second paradigm of history in the mid-twentieth century. Zevit claims that most historians today still work in the second paradigm. A definition of history or its goals according to the second

---

123. Zevit refers to their work as "theology enwrapped in a comfortable historical garb" (p. 36) that "could be labeled 'history' because the relativistic approach validated applying this high-prestige term in ambiguous and ill-defined ways" (p. 37). Cf. James Barr, "Story and History in Biblical Theology," *JR* 56 (1976): 1–17.

paradigm is absent from Zevit's study, but he considers this paradigm a "refined continuation of the first" (ibid.). For second-paradigm historians, the past was still real and could be accessed through documents and other artifacts, as well. Zevit briefly discusses reading documents "obliquely" (ibid.), which is referred to in the previous chapter of this study as reading for nonintentional information. He also alludes to the interaction of biblical studies with the social sciences but does not discuss opinions on principles of cross-disciplinary research held by historians working in the second paradigm. Structuralism was also a feature of the second paradigm:

> Structuralism provided the intellectual framework for seeing certain types of connections as well as for checking historians' explanations of data. Because many of the complex creations of human culture are interlocked, some historical explanations have to make sense or be verifiable in more than one area. (p. 40)

Zevit also asserts that pure objectivity was no longer considered possible in the second paradigm, but instead that historians' conclusions needed to be "objectively reasonable." This meant that conclusions were made "with no special pleading" and that a historian would "abandon an explanation if fault can be found in the reasoning or when evidence falsifies the conclusion" (p. 29).

According to Zevit's description, historians working in the second paradigm do not appear to have any special awareness of issues of language and narrative. Conceptions of truth in the second paradigm, however, were slightly different from those in the first. The second paradigm, Zevit claimed, accepted that there were a "multiplicity of approaches to similar historical issues...different resources that historians may employ in working out an answer, and...different emphases that they may place on what they consider relevant facts" (p. 41). It was seen as "inevitable that different answers...may be presented for similar questions" (ibid.) The objectively reasonable conclusions drawn by historians thus function as possibilities, creating "a field of right answers while eliminating the wrong ones" (p. 42). Thus it appears that, in Zevit's opinion, the main differences between the first and second paradigms lie in the degree of confidence that historians had in their ability to produce an objective, complete picture of the past and the new sources they turned to as evidence.

Zevit paints the second paradigm with very broad strokes, and the historians said to be working within it are quite diverse. Historians of ancient Israel included in this paradigm are Albright and Noth along with Gottwald, and Miller and Hayes (working jointly in 1985),[124] all of whom have distinct assumptions, methods, and results. In light of the previous discussion in this chapter, it is difficult to assess whether Zevit's classification of Alt and Albright into this second paradigm of history writing is valid. Certainly historians of their schools learned to use new types of evidence and took an interest in the structures of Israelite society, particularly religious and political ones. Yet Albright's fusion of a scientific mindset with a belief that the substantive philosophy of history

---

124. On the side of Israelite religion, Helmer Ringgren, Georg Fohrer, and Yehezkel Kaufmann are among the scholars Zevit sees working within the second paradigm.

was important appears contradictory to the pure historicism implied in Zevit's first and second paradigms. Furthermore, in the opinion of many scholars, Albright had "transparent Christian motives," which would make his work vulnerable to the charge of relativism Zevit places on the period between the first and second paradigms. Also, it does not seem likely that Albrightians and Altians would have accepted that history could only provide "a field of right answers while eliminating the wrong ones."

Just as Zevit saw the second paradigm developing from a critique of the first, he attributes the advent of the third paradigm to reactions to certain aspects of the second. He identifies two scholars, Foucault and Derrida, and two new intellectual movements, poststructuralism and deconstruction, as being central to the critique of the second paradigm. In the second paradigm, historians influenced by structuralism had begun to take notice of social institutions and their intertwined roles in the operation of society. As discussed in Chapter 1 of this study, Foucault took a more suspicious look, seeing "society as comprised of decentralized, disengaged controlling institutions, each of which wielded power" (p. 50). Zevit considers one especially challenging result of Foucault's work to be the hypothesis that knowledge and truth are also governed by "institutional self-interest" (ibid.). Under Foucault's theories, then, objective knowledge, including objective historical knowledge, could not exist, and the "thrust of [Foucault's] thought reduced historical analyses to subjective political statements" (p. 51). In other words, under Foucault's influence, history could be considered an enterprise that legitimated the very existence of the institutions from which it sprang.

Derrida and deconstruction constituted another challenge to history writing. Deconstruction by its very nature resists definition, as it has to do with "undoing, decomposing, [and] desedimentizing" structures and meaning (p. 52). Zevit understands deconstruction as allowing the reader to see both the "overt, primal" meaning of the text "as well as [the text] in its disassembled state, all motifs, ideas, claims bared and comprehended in the fullness of their covert meanings" (p. 53). Zevit sees particular repercussions of deconstruction for history: since deconstruction allows for a "theoretical multiplicity of embedded contexts" (p. 54) in a text, the original meaning of a document from the past is considered unattainable. Likewise, when a historian writes history "a formidable number of potentially disinforming elements stand between the written communication of the historian and the intended addressee" (ibid.). Truth, in turn, is not to be found but becomes a "totally subjectified...private matter" (p. 55).

Zevit considers Foucault, Derrida, poststructuralism, and deconstruction as all part of postmodernism, the intellectual basis of the third paradigm of history. He does not attempt to define postmodernism fully, and unlike his descriptions of the first two paradigms, where he named features common to all types of history writing, in his discussion of the third paradigm he notes postmodernism's effects mainly in biblical studies. On a general level, Zevit appears to claim that in the third paradigm of history writing, ideas about historians' access to past reality and the ability to reconstruct it are dramatically different from those of the first and second paradigms. Third paradigm historians, he writes, exhibit a "general skepticism towards dominant views or metanarratives" (p. 57) and tend to select "ideological topics for study, e.g., feminism, sexuality, class structure and power being the most prominent" (p. 58). In the third paradigm, texts used as evidence are open to a variety of interpretations and meaning is *"produced* primarily by contemporary readers" (ibid.), not found in the text itself. History can thus be considered a "hegemonic instrument of subjugation and domination" (ibid.).

Among historians of ancient Israel and Israelite religion, Zevit finds few scholars adopting all of the "manifestations" of the third paradigm, but sees several adopting at least some of them. He claims that Philip R. Davies' *In Search of "Ancient Israel"* reflects all of the tenets of the third paradigm.[125] Feminist scholars, such as Athalya Brenner and Carol Meyers, show enthusiasm for the broadening of the subject of history but do not subscribe to the idea that meaning is entirely determined by the reader. Zevit attributes the partial acceptance of the third paradigm to its newness, and implies that some of its precepts are so inimical to assumptions made by traditional (first- and second-paradigm) historians that one cannot formulate history at all in the face of them.

The fourth paradigm Zevit proposes is one he feels he is observing at its nascent stages. It has arisen from a critique of the third paradigm, mainly deconstruction's denial of the possibility of communication.[126] Historical reality is still the object of historical study in the fourth paradigm. Potential subjects of fourth paradigm histories include "individuals, ideas, and movements of the past" (p. 71). Historians use "informed reason, logical argument, and inference in making their determinations" (ibid.) or explanations. They recognize that historical narratives are constructed, and can thus "only act as if their conclusions are objective" (ibid.). In order to minimize bias, historians of the fourth paradigm may study "isolatable, minimal topics" and present only the "bare, essential, relevant facts...without statement or ethical consideration" (ibid.) Zevit claims that fourth-paradigm historians strive for "truthful approximations of the past" (ibid.), but does not elaborate on what that means. Potential evidence for fourth paradigm histories ranges from documents to artifacts to socio-cultural ideas, since all can be "read" as "texts" that require interpretation. Zevit's fourth paradigm of history writing seems very similar to the second, with more mature notions of cultural structures and the evidence that can be used to reconstruct them. Of the biblical scholars Zevit sees working in the fourth paradigm, none are historians of ancient Israel or Israelite religion.[127] Scholars such as Cheryl Exum and David J. A. Clines, David M. Carr, and Mark Z. Brettler, who work with rhetoric and historiography and who turn a critical eye towards their own narrative practices and those of the biblical writers, exemplify

125. Philip R. Davies, *In Search of "Ancient Israel"* (JSOTSup 148; Sheffield: Sheffield Academic Press, 1992).

126. Zevit includes his own extended critique of deconstructionism and Derrida (pp. 64–68).

127. Zevit considers himself to be a historian working in a reformed version of the second paradigm (pp. 75–80).

the fourth paradigm for Zevit. Thus, whereas Zevit attempts to define a new paradigm of history writing, it is not clear from his examples that works about Israel's past actually are being written in a way that markedly differs from the previous paradigms.

Conclusion

The paradigms Zevit sets out at the beginning of his history of Israelite religions provide a general framework for mapping the changes history and biblical studies have undergone in the twentieth century. This analysis will not suffice, however, if the many factors bearing on history writing about ancient Israel are to be understood in greater depth. While organizing by paradigms allows Zevit to trace the chronological development of many issues, their combination sometimes obscures important variations in assumptions and methods. In addition, Zevit's observation that many historians have adopted only part of the tenets of the third paradigm and the fact that he finds no historians of ancient Israel working in the fourth paradigm suggests that these generalizations may not be suitable for understanding current issues in the history of ancient Israel. On the other hand, the topics discussed in Chapters 1 and 2, along with the descriptions of the Albrightian and Altian schools of history presented in this chapter, set the stage for a debate in the discipline that has evolved into the so-called minimalist–maximalist controversy. By examining minimalist and non-minimalist assumptions and practices in comparison to each other's assumptions and practices as well as to those of Altians and Albrightians, the remaining chapters of this study will seek a more nuanced analysis and appropriate synthesis of the current state of the discipline.

Chapter 4

ASSUMPTIONS AND PRACTICES
OF MINIMALIST HISTORIANS OF ANCIENT ISRAEL

Introduction: What is a Minimalist?

By the 1970s, some of the historical reconstructions of the Albrightians and
Altians were not holding up under increased critical attention. For instance,
despite Albright's contention that archaeology bore out a Late Bronze Age
Israelite conquest, archaeological finds raised serious questions about the conquest theory, and, as mentioned in the previous chapter, Noth's amphictyony
was being dismantled.[1] At this time also, Thomas Thompson and John Van
Seters published studies that discredited the Albrightian synthesis between
archaeology and the Bible that had confidently placed the patriarchs in the
Bronze Age.[2] Thompson and Van Seters used incidental information, such as
names of places and people, and the recognition of standardized literary patterns
in the patriarchal stories to argue that they were most likely composed in the
Iron Age or later. Thus, they concluded that the patriarchal narratives could not
be used to reconstruct Bronze Age history.

At the time, neither Thompson nor Van Seters represented full-fledged
historical "minimalism," but their challenges to long-held ideas about the
historical reliability of the biblical stories about the patriarchs planted the seeds
of a new view of the Bible. By the 1980s, questions about whether the biblical
stories set prior to and during the united monarchy were reliable sources for
reconstructing early Israel were widespread in the discipline. Opinions about the
usefulness of the stories set after Solomon's death and the division of the
kingdoms started to change, as well. As challenges to the Bible's historical
reliability became more refined, scholars reacted slowly and in different ways,
with the majority holding to the notion that the Bible reports at least some
reliable historical information. On the other hand, a group of scholars whose

---

1. See, e.g., Hayes and Miller, eds., *Israelite and Judaean History*, which was an effort to take
these new developments into consideration. On the conquest specifically, see, in the same volume,
J. Maxwell Miller, "The Israelite Occupation of Canaan," 213–84. Indigenous models for early
Israel were appearing on the scene, though they were not yet fully developed. See also George E.
Mendenhall, "The Hebrew Conquest of Palestine," *BA* 25 (1962): 66–87; Gottwald's *Tribes of
Yahweh* did not appear until 1979.

2. Thompson, *The Historicity of the Patriarchal Narratives*; Van Seters, *Abraham in History
and Tradition*.

ideas constituted a radical departure from the mainstream of biblical scholarship became identifiable. These scholars, often called minimalists or revisionists, believe that there is very little factual information about the period before the fifth or even second centuries BCE that can be separated from invention in the Bible.[3] In addition, the minimalist approach "'downgrades' Israel to the status of one people among many peoples in Palestine and 'de-centers' Israel from the position of dominant subject...to the parity position of being one subject among many interacting subjects."[4]

Scholars with common minimalist ideas about the value of the Bible as evidence and the place of ancient Israel in history have resisted being classified as a unit. Thompson asserts that "What seems to define these scholars as a school... is that none of us shares either the neofundamentalistic-'literary' nor the biblical archaeological-harmonistic presuppositions common to much American [Old Testament] reading."[5] He also points to the "general European orientation to their scholarship."[6] Thompson concedes, however, that he and other scholars called minimalists in this study value evidence external to the Bible, especially from elsewhere in the ancient Near East, and that they promote independent evaluation of it.[7] With deliberate irony, then, Thompson proposes that a school adhering to these principles ought to be called "neo-Albrightian."[8]

Davies, has also reacted negatively to the label of minimalist:

> Such ridiculous terminology only betrays the extent to which the writing of histories of ancient Israel is still driven by an agenda concerned with the reliability of the biblical sources—an issue in which a historian has to be impartial. The related label "sceptic" reveals even more clearly a religious dimension to this debate... The label "sceptic" honours a historian—unless a biblical one, where faith in biblical narratives is expected.[9]

Davies does find common ground with other scholars in "a certain skepticism regarding the value of the Bible in reconstructing the history of the period that the Biblical author is describing (as opposed to the value of the Biblical texts

3.   Niels Peter Lemche, *Prelude to Israel's Past: Background and Beginnings of Israelite History and Identity* (Peabody, Mass.: Hendrickson, 1998), xv; Philip R. Davies, "What Separates a Minimalist from a Maximalist? Not Much," *BAR* 26, no. 2 (2000): 24–27, 72–73.

4.   Norman K. Gottwald, "Triumphalist Versus Anti-Triumphalist Versions of Early Israel: A Response to Articles by Lemche and Dever in Volume 4 (1996)," *CurBS* 5 (1997): 15–42 (30). For a discussion of minimalism among scholars of ancient Babylon, see Alan Millard, "History and Legend in Early Babylonia," in *Windows Into Old Testament History: Evidence, Argument, and the Crisis of "Biblical Israel"* (ed. V. Philips Long, David W. Baker, and Gordon J. Wenham; Grand Rapids: Eerdmans, 2002), 103–10.

5.   Thomas L. Thompson, "A Neo-Albrightean School in History and Biblical Scholarship?," *JBL* 114 (1995): 683–98 (695–96).

6.   Ibid., 695.

7.   E.g. Lemche, *Early Israel*, 415: "I propose that we decline to be led by the Biblical account and instead regard it, like other legendary materials, as essentially ahistorical, that is, as a source which only exceptionally can be verified by other information."

8.   Thompson, "A Neo-Albrightean School?," 696–97.

9.   Philip R. Davies, "Whose History? Whose Israel? Whose Bible? Biblical Histories, Ancient and Modern," in Grabbe, ed., *Can a "History of Israel" Be Written?*, 104–22 (109).

for reconstructing the period when the text was composed, hundreds of years later)."[10] Davies' parenthetical comment raises an important point—minimalists do find evidence for Israel's past in the Bible, but, like Wellhausen, they claim that this evidence elucidates the period in which they believe the account was written. (This position will be discussed in detail in the section on texts, below.) Lemche has put an ironic twist on this notion, arguing that this position requires a broad appreciation of the Bible, and therefore that minimalists should actually be called "maximalists."[11] The term "revisionist" has also been suggested, both positively[12] and pejoratively,[13] to identify these scholars. The designation "Copenhagen School" also appears in the literature, since Thompson and Lemche are on the faculty of the University of Copenhagen.[14]

Despite some scholars' dissatisfaction with the label, "minimalist" is an adequate description of an approach to the history of ancient Israel. As noted above, minimalist scholars minimize the importance of the Bible as a historical source and of Israel as a historical subject, positions that separate them from the mainstream of historians of ancient Israel. Of course, highlighting commonalities among minimalists risks oversimplifying the issues. As Davies points out, "Behind the entertaining joust of 'sceptic' and 'credulist,' 'minimalizer' and maximalizer,' lie fundamental issues which…comprise a number of interlocking components."[15] It is the aim of this study to examine the assumptions of minimalist scholars closely, and in this analysis similarities as well as differences in their opinions will come to light.

As in other chapters of this study, the analysis of assumptions and practices of historians, minimalists in this case, will focus primarily on theoretical statements about history given by the scholars themselves. Also, just as Albright and Alt were considered seminal figures in certain approaches to Israelite history, so the number of minimalist scholars examined will be limited to those who are most easily associated with the moniker and who have written most openly about their presuppositions and assumptions. These include Thompson, Davies, Lemche, and Keith Whitelam. Minimalist scholars' positions on the issues introduced in Chapters 1 and 2 will be summarized and analyzed. It will be asked if minimalists have common assumptions about certain topics such as

10. Davies, "What Separates a Minimalist from a Maximalist?," 24.
11. Hershel Shanks, "Face to Face: Biblical Minimalists Meet Their Challengers," *BAR* 23, no. 4 (1997): 26–42, 66 (28).
12. Niels Peter Lemche and Thomas L. Thompson, "Did Biran Kill David? The Bible in the Light of Archaeology," *JSOT* 64 (1994): 3–22 (17).
13. William G. Dever, "Revisionist Israel Revisited: A Rejoinder to Niels Peter Lemche," *CurBS* 4 (1996): 35–50 (35–37), and idem, "Histories and Non-Histories of Ancient Israel: The Question of the United Monarchy," in *In Search of Pre-Exilic Israel* (ed. John Day; JSOTSup 406; London: T. & T. Clark, 2004), 65–94 (65–71).
14. See, e.g., Lemche, "The Origin of the Israelite State," 44–63; Jens Bruun Kofoed, "Epistemology, Historiographical Method, and the 'Copenhagen School,'" in Long, Baker, and Wenham, eds., *Windows Into Old Testament History*, 23–43 (23–24); and Marc Zvi Brettler, "The Copenhagen School: The Historiographical Issues," *AJSR* 27 (2003): 1–22.
15. Philip R. Davies, "Introduction," in *The Origins of the Ancient Israelite States* (ed. Volkmar Fritz and Philip R. Davies; JSOTSup 228; Sheffield: Sheffield Academic Press, 1996), 11–21 (12).

objectivity, or common methodologies such as for evaluating and using texts as evidence. Also, minimalist positions will be compared to the positions taken by their predecessors, the schools of Alt and Albright, in order to ascertain whether they have radically altered the shape of history writing about ancient Israel. Along these lines, the relationship of minimalism to postmodernism will also be considered. Since at present, comprehensive historical reconstructions built upon the tenets of minimalism are rare and the minimalist approach exists mainly as a response to more traditional approaches to the history of ancient Israel, the minimalists' role in contributing to the body of historical knowledge, or as playing devil's advocate, will be discussed, as well. The information gathered in this chapter will then allow assumptions of minimalists to be assessed by the same criteria as other scholars' assumptions, most importantly, their current non-minimalist colleagues (discussed in Chapter 5).

History/Historiography

Definitions and descriptions of history given by minimalists attempt a sophisticated understanding of history that, as Davies said, involves several interlocking components. One of the noticeable features of the minimalists' conception of history is their preference for the term "historiography" to refer to the written product of historical research. Their use of the term "historiography" highlights the writing done by the historian (or historiographer), subtly points to his or her influence on the product that results, and thereby indicates awareness of post-modern discussions of representation, language, narrative, and meaning. Davies provides the most complete discussion of this choice of terminology, calling historiography a "metagenre" that involves "a particular kind of writing about the past" and including it in many types of narrative "such as myth, legend, historical fiction and autobiography."[16] Thus historiography is, to Davies, a transcultural and transepochal concept; ancient writers of many types as well as modern ones qualify as historiographers.

For minimalists, historiography as it is currently practiced has its own unique characteristics. Davies calls this type of writing "critical historiography," which is a narrative with "plot, sequence, character, point of view,"[17] a beginning, and an ending. It is based on critically examined data, relies on primary sources, excludes bias, employs citation by footnotes, and includes a bibliography and a "discussion of alternative interpretation."[18] The postmodern concept that knowledge must be justified also plays a role in minimalist definitions of present-day historiography: "Historiography—in its modern and useful sense—is the discipline through which we justify the appropriateness of our assertions about the past."[19] Nevertheless, the goals of minimalist historiography are consistent with

16. Davies, "Whose History?," 117.
17. Ibid.
18. Ibid., 119.
19. Thomas L. Thompson, "Lester Grabbe and Historiography: An Apologia," *SJOT* 14 (2000): 140–61 (142).

the statements of history's goals given in Chapter 1: "we attempt to explain and describe these fragments of the past, and in doing so interpret them as evidence for understanding what is still part of our world, namely its past."[20]

With "historiography" being the name of the work the historian does, "history" for minimalists usually refers to the actuality of the past. Davies writes that he finds "the past" the best meaning of "history" since "this sense is…the most basic (logically) … Any definition of 'history' invokes 'the past' in some way."[21] Thus, in *In Search of "Ancient Israel"*, Davies refers to the actual Israel of the past as "historical Israel," while the modern scholarly construction of Israel's past is called "ancient Israel."[22] Such terminology contrasts the historical past to a fictional past that was never part of experienced reality. Put another way, the common minimalist definition of "history" is very close to Ranke's "what actually happened."[23]

The distinction minimalists make between history and historiography begins to exemplify common aspects of a minimalist philosophy of history. As will be seen in the following sections, the implications that minimalists take from this understanding of the relationship between the past and how historians write about it, influence their understanding of many other aspects of their philosophy, beginning with their views on objectivity.

Objectivity

Historians of ancient Israel working in the mid-twentieth century were optimistic that objectivity was possible. As seen in Chapter 1, however, historians now consider objectivity a regulative ideal that mandates rigor in historical research and constant attempts to minimize bias. Objectivity takes center stage in any endeavor to understand the minimalists, as these scholars have claimed that most other historians of ancient Israel hold biases that favor of the Bible as a reliable historical document. Indications of minimalists' ideas about objectivity can be found in their statements about objectivity in general, the objectivity (or lack thereof; that is, the bias) of other scholars, and their own objectivity.

Minimalists accept that scholars cannot be isolated from personal and cultural assumptions that may affect their perception of the world and their scholarship.

20. Thomas L. Thompson, "Defining History and Ethnicity in the South Levant," in Grabbe, ed., *Can a "History of Israel" Be Written?*, 166–87 (181).

21. Davies, "Whose History?," 116. Davies recognizes a third common use of the term "history," namely "the academic discipline that studies historiography and its relationship to history" (115). In this study, this discipline has been called the critical philosophy of history.

22. Another example can be seen in Niels Peter Lemche, "Ideology and the History of Ancient Israel," *SJOT* 14 (2000): 165–93 (174), where Lemche, discussing the Bible's account of the events of 701 BCE, states that "the historical information is embedded in a network of non-historical tales and myths."

23. Of course, not all minimalists adhere to this distinction at all times. For instance, Thompson ("Defining History and Ethnicity," 181) asserts that "History is interpretation of data within the contemporary world of historical scholarship"—an instance where the term "historiography" might be expected.

As Lemche puts it, "No scholar is an island isolated from the world... Scholar-ship is situational."[24] Also, he says, "every person is entangled in a network consisting of his private biases, prejudices, and perceptions of the world."[25] Lemche identifies several self-interested positions that he claims affect history writing, including a modern European fascination with nation states (that causes Israel to be portrayed as a nation state),[26] the identification modern Jews and Christians are taught from childhood to make with biblical Israel,[27] and the national identity of modern Israelis.[28] Lemche goes so far as to claim that anyone who identifies himself or herself with biblical Israel is potentially a "champion of [its] national history," and "it would be a miracle if a scholar from this society should turn out to write detached, positivistic history of his own society."[29] Thus, whereas Huizinga claimed that history was a civilization rendering an account of its past to itself, Lemche argues that history written by interested parties is necessarily compromised.

Subjectivity in the history of Israel, whether religiously or politically moti-vated, has also been discussed by Davies, who, like McCullagh, sees challenges to objectivity in "individual, group, and class interests."[30] Davies says that bias is too prevalent in the discipline and has contributed to the vitriol that is often traded at conferences and in papers. Writing about the debate over the existence of the united monarchy in ancient Israel, Davies observes:

> It does seem to me that the only *necessary* explanation for the violence of the current debate...is that religious value judgments are playing a role. Not only among lay-people...but also among the many practitioners of biblical archaeology whose personal religion determines a prejudice in favour of as high an assessment of the historical reliability of the Bible as their conscience and academic training will permit. I am personally less worried about this prejudice (as we are *all* guilty of prejudices) than about the way it both denies its own existence yet betrays itself so blatantly.[31]

In other words, Davies claims that a religious outlook in and of itself is not necessarily harmful, but that an unwillingness on the part of historians to be self-critical makes this type of bias insidious.[32]

---

24. Niels Peter Lemche, "New Perspectives on the History of Israel," in *Perspectives in the Study of the Old Testament and Early Judaism: A Symposium in Honor of Adam S. van der Woude on the Occasion of His 70th Birthday* (ed. Florentiono García Martínez and Ed Noort; Leiden: Brill, 1998), 42–60 (52).

25. Lemche, "Ideology and the History of Ancient Israel," 191.

26. Lemche, *The Israelites in History and Tradition* (Library of Ancient Israel; Louisville, Ky.: Westminster John Knox, 1998), 3.

27. Lemche, "New Perspectives," 47–49; idem, "The Origin of the Israelite State," 50.

28. Lemche, "The Origin of the Israelite State," 49.

29. Ibid., 50. In a similar vein, Giovanni Garbini (*History and Ideology in Ancient Israel* [New York: Crossroad, 1988], ix–x) has argued that Italy's position "on the periphery of biblical studies" has allowed for Semitic scholars to be "psychologically freer towards the Old Testament."

30. Davies, *In Search of "Ancient Israel"*, 14; cf. idem, "Whose History?," 111.

31. Davies, "Introduction," 13.

32. See also Philip R. Davies, "This is What Happens..." in *"Like a Bird in a Cage": The Invasion of Sennacherib in 701 BCE* (ed. Lester L. Grabbe; JSOTSup 363; Sheffield: Sheffield Academic Press, 2003), 106–18 (108), where he asserts that the religious public's interest in

The most comprehensive castigation of religious and political motives in biblical scholarship and history appears in Whitelam's *The Invention of Ancient Israel: The Silencing of Palestinian History*. Here, Whitelam seeks to expose cultural biases among historians of ancient Israel who worked in the mid- and late twentieth century. Whitelam argues that their biased outlooks, however unaware of them the scholars may have been, resulted in biased history. Alt, he claims, saw immigration as the key to Israel's origins just as the Zionist movement was gaining speed.[33] Around the time of Israel's "wars of independence," Albright championed the conquest model of Israel's origins.[34] George Mendenhall's ethically superior peasants who revolted, Whitelam argues, mirror Israelis in conflict with native Palestinians.[35] In the same vein, he claims, Gottwald portrays all non-Israelites as oppressors.[36] In general, Whitelam contends that biased history of ancient Israel is characterized by disproportionate attention given to the lands of the Bible (particularly the modern day West Bank) and the time span of pre-exilic biblical Israel (1000–586 BCE) over other "Palestinian" areas and nonbiblical time periods. To use McCullagh's terms, Whitelam claims that historians have desired to further religious and political interests and have thereby omitted significant facts about the past. Yet Whitelam deliberately chooses the term "Palestinian" to represent the non-Israelite/Jewish inhabitants of the southern Levant throughout the ages, and allies his quest for Palestinian history with modern-day Palestinians' struggle, making his approach subjective, as well.

In short, the root of minimalists' concerns about objectivity appears to be that cultural, religious, and national allegiances cause some scholars to be biased in favor of the Bible's account of Israel's past. Though minimalists admit that some subjectivity is inevitable in history, bias in favor of the Bible, they claim, is serious enough that it ultimately compromises the integrity of history and the truths it seeks to convey. The minimalists' critiques of other scholars' biases have been so persistent, dogmatic, and all-encompassing that some scholars have questioned the minimalists' own motivations. Zevit, for instance, writes that Davies added a political element to history, and

> challenged his readers to decide if they were truly historians or believers masquerading as historians. In other words, everybody who might disagree with him was either a literary fundamentalist at worst or an unsophisticated reader at best... Davies' statements comprise an attack on the intellectual integrity of those who might disagree with him.[37]

theology has prevented critical history from being taught in institutions of higher learning, but instead requires that history and biblical scholarship in general "deliver a history with an assured minimum salvation quotient."

33. Keith W. Whitelam, *The Invention of Ancient Israel: The Silencing of Palestinian History* (London: Routledge, 1996), 79.

34. Ibid., 82.

35. Ibid., 104–5.

36. Ibid., 113–14.

37. Ziony Zevit, "Three Debates about Bible and Archaeology," *Bib* 83 (2002): 1–27 (15).

The charge of "ideological" has also been leveled at the minimalists.[38] The ideology to which minimalists are said to subscribe is one that is biased against the biblical material as a historical source, especially for Israel prior to the Persian period. Minimalists, however, downplay or justify their own biases (which, as seen above, they admit everyone has) while continuing to call for scholars to abandon their biases. For instance, Davies has turned the charge of ideology back at his opponents. He writes, "My own position...is that in the case of 'ancient Israel' a certain set of ideological notions is interfering with the application of a method [i.e. the historical method] which most scholars fundamentally accept."[39] Also, Lemche asserts that while indeed his opinion about the historicity of the biblical materials may be called subjective "in the postmodern sense," it is based on his evaluation of the source material.[40] Similarly, Thompson has said that the methods of minimalists "are not chosen for ideological purposes but rather are determined by the kind of data and the nature of the evidence that we have for the history of these periods in this part of the world."[41] Further, he writes, "we...do strive to be objective scholars and are not ideologues."[42] In short, minimalists, though they understand that pure objectivity is impossible to achieve, urge historians to strive for objectivity in history and believe that they themselves do so while charging that others' efforts at objectivity are nonexistent or inadequate.

Minimalists have given few indications about how to solve the quandary of writing history objectively when objectivity is elusive. Most common is the claim that historical method followed closely will provide the best chance at objectivity in history. As Davies writes, "It is precisely because I am no more free from subjectivity than any human being that I insist on working to a methodology that will enable me and my fellow historians to agree on what counts as historical knowledge and how we aim to secure it."[43] He has also argued:

> If we want in some sense to be objective and neutral, we can do so by *refusing to tell a story*. We can instead identify the relevant "sources" and expound them as ancient cultural explanations of what really happened. ... Thus, the modern historian in us can maybe fulfil the demand of objectivity to some extent by refusing to interpose, by

---

38. See Iain W. Provan, "Ideologies, Literary and Critical: Reflections on Recent Writing on the History of Israel," *JBL* 114 (1995): 585–606; Dever, "Revisionist Israel Revisited," 36; idem, "Histories and Non-Histories," 71; James Barr, *History and Ideology in the Old Testament: Biblical Studies at the End of a Millennium* (The Hensley Henson Lectures for 1997; Oxford: Oxford University Press, 2000). A compilation of examples also can be found in Lemche, "Ideology and the History of Ancient Israel," 166–74.

39. Philip R. Davies, "Method and Madness: Some Remarks on Doing History with the Bible," *JBL* 115 (1995): 699–705 (702).

40. Lemche, "Ideology and the History of Ancient Israel," 192. Provan, Lemche says, "is attacking a straw man" (p. 193), and Barr "is simply against revisionism" (p. 193).

41. Thompson, "A Neo-Albrightean School?," 687.

42. Ibid., 693. Thompson claims that his *The Mythic Past: Biblical Archaeology and the Myth of Israel* (New York: Basic Books, 1999) is a critique of the rhetoric of objectivity in historicism. See also his "Lester Grabbe and Historiography," 141–42.

43. Davies, "Method and Madness," 704.

refusing, in fact, to be "objective" regarding the "facts" but being objective about the ancient accounts, not taking sides, expressing, like Picasso, several dimensions at once.[44]

This suggestion, that historians collect information but impose minimal personal interpretation on it, has ramifications for explanation in history, the literary form history takes, and historians' concept of the truth they present. Thus, Davies' statement will be reconsidered at the end of this chapter, when minimalists' assumptions about these topics have been discussed more fully. Besides Davies' comments, however, neither minimalists' assertion of their own objectivity nor their critiques of others' biases include comprehensive theoretical or methodological statements that would promote objectivity in some fashion, perhaps by offering criteria to identify and rectify bias. Some suggestions along these lines will be made in Chapter 6. At present, more assumptions of the minimalists must be examined in order that their methods and results may be understood better.

Representation, Language, Subject, and Explanation

Representation and Language

Minimalists are not antirealists. Lemche asserts, "The Copenhagen perspective is not that there was no historical Israel... There certainly was."[45] Minimalists are not antirepresentationalists, either. To be either would make it quite difficult to remain historians. Yet minimalists are aware of the difficulty of historical representation. The past, Davies says, "is the most elusive of all signifiers... As 'past' it seems invulnerable to the manipulations of human consciousness: we experience the present, we create the future: the past we cannot change."[46] He recognizes that all attempts at representation are incomplete; even "the camera cannot present more than an eye can see."[47] Thompson argues that events past "can be directly described on the basis of evidence,"[48] but elsewhere says that "data offers us in the limits and ambiguity of its mirror a fragmented, fractured past: one that is hardly identifiable or reconstructable as a past that was."[49] Poststructuralist ideas about the nonreferentiality of language are also evident in the minimalists' writings. Davies asserts that "Texts cannot reproduce reality except as a textual artifact, crafted by rhetoric and limited by the boundaries of language."[50] Thompson has written, "History is not a past we reconstruct; it is

44. Davies, "This is What Happens...," 114–15 (italics in original).
45. Lemche, "The Origin of the Israelite State," 63.
46. Davies, "Whose History?," 116.
47. Ibid., 117.
48. Thompson, "A Neo-Albrightean School?," 690.
49. Thomas L. Thompson, "Historiography of Ancient Palestine and Early Jewish Historiography: W. G. Dever and the Not So New Biblical Archaeology," in Fritz and Davies, eds., *The Origins of the Ancient Israelite States*, 26–43 (39); cf. idem, "Defining History and Ethnicity," 181.
50. Davies, *In Search of "Ancient Israel"*, 15.

something we make up. It is our understanding, rooted in our world."[51] Lemche agrees: "History will accordingly always be something which we can never reach physically, only construct as part of a tale which we think is interesting and therefore relevant to us."[52] In short, minimalist ideas about representation and language appear to be in the middle of the continuum introduced in Chapter 1, where faith that history writing can reconstruct the past and antirepresentationalism form the two poles. This stance puts them in line with the majority of current historians.

Subject
Already in this study minimalists have been defined in part by their choice of historical subjects. Whereas Albright, Bright, Alt, and Noth considered the proper subject of the history of Israel to be the religious community that the Bible describes, minimalists are unsure about its existence. In response to this uncertainty, Davies has introduced terminology that separates the text's "biblical Israel" from real Israel, which, as seen above, he calls "historical Israel."[53] Historical Israel, Davies says, was a state centered at Samaria in the Iron II period that was called Israel, Samaria, or the House of Omri. Only shades of information about historical Israel can be found in the Bible's description of Israel. According to Davies, scholars have created "ancient Israel," an entity that has little in common with historical Israel but has marked similarities to "biblical Israel." He argues that historians need to abandon the search for "ancient Israel" and either concentrate on "historical Israel" or "biblical Israel." This contention implies that there are two potential types of subjects for the history of ancient Israel: subjects which existed in the real world, such as historical Israel, and ideological concepts, such as biblical Israel, and that these can be differentiated clearly.

If historical Israel is to be the subject of history, minimalists claim, historians must recognize that this community did not encompass everyone who lived in Palestine from the Late Bronze Age to the Hellenistic period.[54] Or, to return to the general description of minimalists given at the beginning of this chapter, minimalists contend that Israel as a subject of history should be minimized. Justifications for this claim include the known reality of ancient Palestine, where historical Israel and the Philistines shared the land with a number of other less well-known groups (some of which appear in the Bible).[55] Further, minimalists

51.   Thompson, "Lester Grabbe and Historiography," 142.
52.   Lemche, "Ideology and the History of Ancient Israel," 50.
53.   Davies, *In Search of "Ancient Israel"*, 13; cf. Thomas L. Thompson, "Text, Content and Referent in Israelite Historiography," in *The Fabric of History: Text, Artifact and Israel's Past* (ed. D. V. Edelman; JSOTSup 127; Sheffield: JSOT Press, 1991), 65–92 (72).
54.   E.g. Davies, "Whose History?," 112.
55.   The existence of evidence that would indicate a unique Israelite ethnicity, long assumed by the Albrightians, also has been discounted by minimalists. See Thompson, "Defining History and Ethnicity," 166–87; idem, "Hidden Histories and the Problem of Ethnicity in Palestine," in *Western Scholarship and the History of Palestine* (ed. Michael Prior; London: Melisinde, 1998), 23–39;

believe that accounts of what actually occurred in Palestine's past must focus on subjects such as social structures and processes, since in their opinion the Bible's information about specific human subjects is unreliable. Along these lines, Whitelam says that written records for Israel's past are lacking, and therefore that a history of ancient Israel "will not be a history that we are accustomed to or even comfortable with, given the common preoccupation with great individuals and so-called unique events."[56] Instead, in order to make real, or "historical," Israel the object of historical research, Whitelam advocates "a broad regional history dealing with questions of trade, settlement, social relations, and so on."[57]

There is also consensus among the minimalists that the biblical text and its construction of the past are worthy subjects for historians. Davies describes this project as a "sociology of the literature" whose purpose is "to address these texts as cultural artifacts, to discern from them the economic, political, social, and intellectual structures that both enabled them to be produced, and then participated in producing them in the forms they have."[58] Or, as Whitelam writes, "The multi-layered nature of the texts, their adaptability and vitality means that the historian needs to ask how they shape and were shaped by their different contexts, what audiences do they address, and what other possible constructions of the past do they deny and thereby silence."[59] Lemche explains that when "The subject of the historian is…such mental structures, to clarify how they worked in the composition of the historical narrative and to use them as analytic tools," the historian can attempt to "find the *Sitz im Leben* of…systematical thinking"[60] such as history writing. Of course, knowledge about the text depends on knowledge about the real past. Historians investigating the literature rather than its referent, however, would ask about the social situation that inspired the writing of the book of Judges, for example, not whether there was a period when judges ruled Israel or how the office of judge related to the development of the monarchy.[61]

The claim that the sociology of the literature and metahuman structures such as trade patterns are proper subjects of history has a number of ramifications for history writing about ancient Israel. First, it establishes the history of the Bible as a discipline of importance and scholars currently working on the composition

Keith W. Whitelam, "The Identity of Early Israel: The Realignment and Transformation of Late Bronze–Iron Age Palestine," *JSOT* 63 (1994): 57–87.

56. Keith W. Whitelam, "Between History and Literature: The Social Production of Israel's Traditions of Origin," *SJOT* 2 (1991): 60–74 (69).

57. Ibid., 70. Whitelam credits the *Annales* school and Braudel for these ideas.

58. Philip R. Davies, "The Society of Biblical Israel," in *Second Temple Studies*. Vol. 2, *Temple and Community in the Persian Period* (ed. Tamara C. Eskenazi and Kent Harold Richards; JSOTSup 175; Sheffield: JSOT Press, 1992), 22–33 (26).

59. Keith W. Whitelam, "The Search for Early Israel: Historical Perspective," in *The Origin of Early Israel—Current Debate* (ed. Shmuel Ahituv and Eliezer D. Oren; Beer-Sheva: Ben-Gurion University of the Negev Press, 1998), 41–64 (58).

60. Lemche, "Rachel and Lea" (1988), 63–64.

61. Davies, "The Society of Biblical Israel," 32.

history of the biblical text, especially those who take a socio-cultural approach, as historians. Consequently, minimalist historians would consider scholars such as Van Seters, Baruch Halpern, David Jamieson-Drake, Marc Brettler, Yairah Amit, Israel Finkelstein, and Neil Asher Silberman to be undertaking an important historiographical task.[62] Though the work of these particular scholars will not be discussed in detail here, it will be seen in the discussion of texts, below, that minimalists prefer the conclusions of scholars who date composition of the Bible to a late date, namely, one in the Persian or Hellenistic period.

Explanation
Minimalists, like other historians, see explanation as one of history's goals. Thompson said that historians "attempt to explain and describe…fragments of the past."[63] Whitelam, citing Finley, also states that "the historian does not merely describe but attempts to understand and explain."[64] As for types of explanation, Davies draws on rational explanation for some of his ideas. He accepts the label of "positivist," defining a positivist as someone who bases knowledge on "the accumulation of empirical evidence and logical deduction from it."[65] Further, Davies says, historians should employ "a consistent methodology and the controlled use of concepts like probability, confirmation, evidence, and argument" in explanations.[66] Given minimalists' predisposition toward structures and

---

62.   See Van Seters, *Abraham in History and Tradition*; idem, *In Search of History: Historiography in the Ancient World and the Origins of Biblical History* (New Haven: Yale University Press, 1983); idem, *The Pentateuch: A Social-Science Commentary*; Baruch Halpern, *The First Historians: The Hebrew Bible and History* (San Francisco: Harper & Row, 1988); idem, *David's Secret Demons: Messiah, Murderer, Traitor, King* (Grand Rapids: Eerdmans, 2001); David W. Jamieson-Drake, *Scribes and Schools in Monarchic Judah: A Socio-Archeological Approach* (JSOTSup 109; Sheffield: Almond Press, 1991); Marc Zvi Brettler, *The Creation of History in Ancient Israel* (New York: Routledge, 1995); Yairah Amit, *History and Ideology: Introduction to Historiography in the Hebrew Bible* (The Biblical Seminar 60; Sheffield: Sheffield Academic Press, 1999); Israel Finkelstein and Neil Asher Silberman, *The Bible Unearthed: Archaeology's New Vision of Ancient Israel and the Origin of Its Sacred Texts* (New York: Free Press, 2001).

63.   Thompson, "Defining History and Ethnicity," 181.

64.   Keith W. Whitelam, "Sociology or History: Towards a (Human) History of Ancient Palestine?," in *Words Remembered, Texts Renewed: Essays in Honour of John F. A. Sawyer* (ed. Jon Davies, Graham Harvey, and Wilfred G. E. Watson; JSOTSup 195; Sheffield: Sheffield Academic Press, 1995), 149–66 (153). Whitelam perceives his opinion to be contrary to that of Thompson, citing Thompson, *Early History*, 61. There, Thompson argues that the task of the historian is scientific observation of the "observable singular" and states that going beyond this task involves the "theoretical and hypothetical." Cf. Thompson, "A Neo-Albrightean School?," 690: "When we begin to move beyond [hard facts], we begin to guess…in this we are departing from the knowledge we have and entering the realm of not yet acquired knowledge." Thompson does not state, however, that theory or hypotheticals are bad; he appears to be appealing for a more sound methodology of using theory or hypotheticals. Further, Thompson's practice suggests that he believes a historian should attempt to explain. For instance, in *Early History* he writes, "we do not need to look to a breakdown in international trade to explain the collapse of prosperity during the last third of the third-millennium" (p. 179).

65.   Davies, "Method and Madness," 700.

66.   Ibid.

mentalités as subjects of history, however, it is not surprising that they often turn to the social sciences for explanatory theories and models. Davies explains the attraction of the social sciences for historians:

> The premise of a sociological approach is the construction of the human subject as a *social* being, and a prescription to define and explain this being in terms of social consciousness and behaviour... It corresponds in fact very closely to what modern historians call what they do.[67]

Another advantage, Davies suggests, is that sociologists

> have, at least, the freedom to choose sides, and are not compelled ultimately to vindicate the literature because it is Scripture. In a broad sense, then, a sociological approach may also be read as a metaphor for a secular approach.[68]

Whitelam has also advocated the use of social-scientific theory and models for writing the history of ancient Israel. Whitelam says that such models can assist in explaining why the state of Israel developed in Palestine in the Early Iron Age.[69] Overall, Whitelam finds interaction with social-scientific theories and models useful for historians because, reminiscent of Weber, he believes that familiarity with other cultures aids the imagination of the historian by freeing the ancient society from the "straight jacket of the present."[70] He also claims that modeling is a methodologically pure approach to history: "the appeal to social-scientific theories makes explicit, and therefore open to criticism and debate, the models and assumptions being used to explore the social world of the Bible."[71] In fact, Whitelam, along with Robert Coote, authored a study on the emergence of Israel that concentrated on factors in Palestine such as geography, trade, and settlement patterns and used social-scientific studies of Bedouins, along with a conflict model of society, to explain aspects of early Israelite political structure.[72]

Despite Davies' and Whitelam's general endorsements of the use of the social sciences in history writing, minimalists have voiced several concerns about this combination. Davies himself has argued that due to the lack of primary data about Israel and the fact that biblical Israel is a literary construct, "The identity of the society that produced [the Bible] is an open question... biblical studies has bequeathed to sociology the modest task of explicating a society of dubious and untested historical reality."[73] In terms of the comparative method discussed in Chapter 1, then, Davies questions whether enough is known about Israelite society for any comparative work to be valid. Lemche, however, has been the

---

67. Philip R. Davies, "Sociology and the Second Temple," in *Second Temple Studies*. Vol. 1, *Persian Period* (ed. Philip R. Davies; JSOTSup 117; Sheffield: JSOT Press, 1991), 11–19 (12).
68. Ibid., 19.
69. Whitelam, "Sociology or History," 152.
70. Ibid., 154.
71. Keith W. Whitelam, "The Social World of the Bible," in *The Cambridge Companion to Biblical Interpretation* (ed. John Barton; Cambridge Companions to Religion; Cambridge: Cambridge University Press, 1998), 35–49 (45).
72. Robert B. Coote and Keith W. Whitelam, *The Emergence of Early Israel in Historical Perspective* (Sheffield: Almond Press, 1987).
73. Davies, "The Society of Biblical Israel," 25.

most vocal critic of the use of the social sciences in history writing about ancient Israel. He has objected several times to what he perceives as unsophisticated methodology in this interdisciplinary procedure. Sociology, he says, "is a mighty academic discipline with an enormous variety of conflicting schools, opinions, theories and interests."[74] In particular, the sheer number of models available requires a cautious approach.[75] Thus, "It is always a problem when theologians try to introduce the results from other disciplines, since very often they simply do not know what they are dealing with... Even the biblical scholar will have to acquire a broader and more diversified picture of the foreign discipline in question in order to form his own opinions."[76] In this sentiment, then, Lemche echoes some of the concerns expressed in Chapter 1 about the competence of scholars using social-scientific theory.

Lemche identifies two further problems that can result from historians' simplistic interaction with the social sciences. The first is the possibility that historians would mistakenly identify a phenomenon from an outside culture with one from ancient Israel. As an example, Lemche points to what he calls Alt's "eclectic isolation" of the small-cattle nomad as the prime comparative model for the early Israelite.[77] Second, Lemche is skeptical of the value of the covering-law or even limited-law explanations that sociological models offer. He writes, "By using a model the various single phenomena belonging to the object of study are analyzed not on behalf of their own content but on behalf of the content of the model as such."[78] He claims that scholars who create models are very careful to include only facts and aspects of culture that do not contradict each other.[79] In addition, Lemche worries, models can leave out "the human propensity for variation."[80] Similarly, every model has a limited number of variables, and Lemche doubts whether a few variables can correctly categorize any human society.[81] Thus, he argues, the social sciences "cannot act as a *Deus ex machina* providing miraculous and indisputable solutions to any conceivable historical problem."[82]

In light of these concerns, Lemche proposes that when historians use social-scientific material they recognize both the complex nature of human society and the limited value of any model as a heuristic tool. Lemche demonstrates this

74. Lemche, "The Origin of the Israelite State," 56. Sociology can be understood here to include anthropology. Cf. idem, *Early Israel*, xv.
75. Niels Peter Lemche, "On the Use of 'System Theory,' 'Macro Theories,' and 'Evolutionistic Thinking' in Modern Old Testament Research and Biblical Archaeology," *SJOT* 4 (1990): 73–88 (82).
76. Ibid., 87–88.
77. Lemche, *Early Israel*, 82. In Chapter 1, historians' enthusiasm for the Balinese cockfight was offered as an example of this type of uncritical comparison.
78. Lemche, "On the Use of 'System Theory,'" 73.
79. Ibid., 74.
80. Lemche, *Early Israel*, 410. Lemche here is speaking specifically about cultural evolutionism and new archaeology's processual theory. Cf. idem, "On the Use of 'System Theory,'" 81–83.
81. Ibid., 82.
82. Lemche, "The Origin of the Israelite State," 57.

method in *Early Israel*, where he discusses nomadic societies and their possible relationship to early Israelite society. There, Lemche claims that the social sciences describe seventeen different types of nomads. He profiles five types and highlights the significant variations among them. In his analysis, Lemche leaves open the possibility that early Israelite society did not conform to any of these types, noting that it could offer knowledge of an eighteenth type of nomad. A later quote from Lemche sums up his approach: "so long as the sources have the final word to say, models are unharmful."[83]

In short, minimalists' assumptions about and methodology for using social-scientific theories and models to aid historical explanation appear very similar to the principles laid out in Chapter 1. Minimalists appear to agree that historians who use social-scientific models must have a solid knowledge both of the ancient society in question and of the social-scientific theories and data they are using. They also recognize that a society may not fit an existing model perfectly. Differences among minimalists are apparent—while Lemche and Davies have some concerns about historians' use of the social sciences, Whitelam is more optimistic about the possibility and the value of the enterprise.

Minimalists also appear to be aware of some issues of narrative and explanation that were introduced in Chapter 1. As seen in the discussion of historiography, Davies contends that all historiography is narrative.[84] Thompson asserts that the value of narrative in history lies in its capacity for explanation:

Historical narration typically is developed through a descriptive account: from the chronologically precedent to the subsequent. This allows the rationale of causality, what some might call the "story line," to develop unimpeded by alternatives from the divine infinity of possibility.[85]

Thompson's description of narrative appears to be applicable to both event-oriented and non-event-oriented history, as was Ricoeur's, discussed in Chapter 1. On the other hand, minimalists, like most present-day historians, do not value overarching themes or "grand narratives" in history writing. For instance, Davies calls *Heilsgeschichte* (an understanding of the theme of the Bible's historical writing popularized by von Rad) a "virus" that "represented the idea that the eschatological destiny of the entire world lay hidden (or revealed) in [the Bible's] stories."[86] Outside of these few observations, however, discussion of narrative in history writing has tended to surface in minimalists' examinations of

83. Lemche, "On the Use of 'System Theory,'" 82.
84. See also Davies, "This Is What Happens..." 106.
85. Thomas L. Thompson, "From the Stone Age to Israel," in *Proceedings: Eastern Great Lakes and Midwest Biblical Societies* (ed. Terrance Callan; Grand Rapids: Eastern Great Lakes Biblical Society, 1991), 9–32 (9). Grabbe accuses Thompson of wanting to "abandon the narrative format" for Palestinian history (Lester L. Grabbe, "Reflections on the Discussion," in Grabbe, ed., *Can a "History of Israel" Be Written?*, 188–96 [190]). Thompson, however, does not directly suggest that in his article in the same volume ("Defining History and Ethnicity in the South Levant"), but does advocate regional and archaeological histories (p. 183).
86. Philip R. Davies, "The Future of 'Biblical History,'" in *Auguries: The Jubilee Volume of the Sheffield Department of Biblical Studies* (ed. David J. A. Clines and Stephen D. Moore; JSOTSup 269; Sheffield: Sheffield Academic Press, 1998), 126–41 (141).

ancient texts. For instance, the problem of how to distinguish between history writing and fiction has been recognized as pivotal to understanding such texts, as will be seen below. Also, minimalists assert that preconceived tropes borrowed from the Bible unduly direct the shape of historical narrative.

Summary of Minimalists' Views on Subject and Explanation
In summary, minimalists have departed from mid-twentieth-century biblio-centric ideas about ancient Israel and theoretically advocate history that is less focused on individual humans or on Israel as a religious community and more interested in the social structures of the several peoples of the ancient Levant. In order to explicate this subject, minimalists turn to social-scientific theories and models, which they approach with both enthusiasm and caution. Minimalists also consider the explanation of the context and formation of biblical literature an important task of the historian. Many of their assumptions about subject and explanation in history, however, are predicated on presuppositions about ancient texts. Therefore, this analysis will now turn to the assumptions and methodo-logical approaches minimalists bring to the examination of texts, especially the Bible.

Texts

Minimalists, like historians in general, place great value on textual sources as evidence for the past, but some particular convictions separate them from other historians of ancient Israel. Minimalists contend that "the historian who intends to re-create the past should always concentrate on the *acknowledged* contempo-rary sources and delegate all other kind [*sic*] of information to a second place,"[87] a position similar to Finley's (discussed in Chapter 2). They also agree that much of the Hebrew Bible is not an eyewitness account of what it reports, mak-ing it suspect for historical reconstruction.

As for the Bible's date, minimalists frequently cite Jamieson-Drake's study of literacy in Judah, which argues that a state structure and concomitant record keeping could not have existed there before the eighth century BCE.[88] After this point, their opinions diverge. Davies argues that the Hebrew Bible was written and codified in the Persian period by a society of immigrants in Persian Jehud who adopted local traditions about the past and religion and used them as the traditions of their new community.[89] Davies bases this opinion partly on Ernst

87.   Lemche, *The Israelites in History and Tradition*, 22. Lemche claims to be quoting Ranke here but gives no citation for this claim nor any reference to a work by Ranke in his bibliography.
88.   Jamieson-Drake, *Scribes and Schools in Monarchic Judah*. For critiques see Anson F. Rainey, "Stones for Bread: Archaeology versus History," *NEA* 64, no. 3 (2001): 140–49 (142), and Richard S. Hess, "Literacy in Iron Age Israel," in Long, Baker, and Wenham, eds., *Windows Into Old Testament History*, 82–102.
89.   Davies, *In Search of "Ancient Israel"*, especially Chapters 5–7, and idem, *Scribes and Schools: The Canonization of Hebrew Scripture* (Library of Ancient Israel; Louisville, Ky.: Westminster John Knox, 1998).

Axel Knauf's contention that Biblical Hebrew was a late, invented language.[90] Whitelam also locates the Bible in the Second Temple period but admits that "it has become evident that very little is known about the social and historical background of the Second Temple period."[91]

Thompson agrees that the *terminus a quo* for the Hebrew Bible must be the Persian period, noting that external sources for the history of Judaism, such as the Elephantine texts, also date to this time period,[92] and, like Davies, imagines that the Bible was brought together as an aid to community formation. More likely, however, in his opinion, is a Hellenistic date for the Bible:

> It is in the historical context of the Maccabean state that Palestine clearly possesses for the first time both the independent state structures and the national consciousness necessary for the development of a library and a coherent collection of tradition so marked by self-conscious identity.[93]

Thompson also argues that, thematically, the Hebrew Bible betrays a Hellenistic provenance, citing Greek story patterns and worldviews that he finds in the texts.[94] Lemche asserts that the date of biblical books must be arrived at by using the most firm information about when a book existed, namely, the date of the first extant manuscripts.[95] For example, Codex Vaticanus of the fourth century CE is the earliest known full copy of Samuel. From there, Lemche argues, scholars can work backwards and conclude that fragments of Samuel among the Dead Sea scrolls suggest, but do not prove, that the book was written by the Hellenistic period (since the entire book is not extant there). Similarly, one could also argue that Samuel's presence in the Septuagint dates the book to

---

90. Ernst Axel Knauf, "War 'Biblisch-Hebräisch' eine Sprache?," *ZAH* 3 (1990): 11–23. For a critique of Knauf and Davies, see Avi Hurvitz, "The Historical Quest for 'Ancient Israel' and the Linguistic Evidence of the Hebrew Bible: Some Methodological Observations," *VT* 47 (1997): 301–15.

91. Whitelam, "The Social World of the Bible," 40; cf. Davies, "Method and Madness," 702.

92. Thompson, "Defining History and Ethnicity," 183.

93. Thomas L. Thompson, "The Intellectual Matrix of Early Biblical Narrative: Inclusive Monotheism in Persian Period Palestine," in *The Triumph of Elohim: From Yahwisms to Judaisms* (ed. D. V. Edelman; Grand Rapids: Eerdmans, 1996), 107–24 (110). Thompson's comment raises the question of how the Qumran community, i.e., an unofficial, non-state-sponsored community, developed its library and collection of tradition.

94. This argument can be found throughout Thompson's *The Mythic Past*.

95. Niels Peter Lemche, "The Old Testament—A Hellenistic Book?," *SJOT* 7 (1993): 163–93 (169–70). It should be noted that Lemche is careful about his use of terminology in this article. The Hebrew Bible, or the *collection* of certain books in Hebrew, he argues, dates to the second century CE. Lemche prefers the term "Old Testament" to refer to the corpus in general, since this terminology does not neglect the Septuagint. Thompson appears to agree with Lemche's method of dating texts. See Zipora Talshir, "Textual and Literary Criticism of the Bible in Post-Modern Times: The Untimely Demise of Classical Biblical Philology," *Hen* 21 (1999): 235–52 (246–48), where she recalls several personal conversations with Thompson where he claimed that the date of a text is its latest full copy despite earlier attestations. See also Thompson, "Lester Grabbe and Historiography," 152, and idem, *The Mythic Past*, 8, where Thompson notes that the earliest texts of the Bible (attested in the Dead Sea scrolls) date from Hellenistic times and show, in comparison to later recensions, that the form of the text was not yet fixed. As seen in the previous chapter, Albright also made this observation and used it to discredit source criticism.

Hellenistic times.[96] Lemche, like Thompson, also contends that literary patterning in the Bible reflects Hellenistic influence. Thus, Gen 1 has God acting "as if he wished to be in accordance with some ideas current among Greek natural philosophers from the 6th century and onwards."[97] In addition, Lemche asserts, the Bible's historical narratives show the influence of Greek historians such as Herodotus.[98]

Finally, minimalists admit that a late source such as the Bible may include some "surviving fragments from the past,"[99] but these fragments, they claim, are preserved without their original context. Trying to identify and date such fragments is a "futile enterprise" because "the logic invariably will be circular."[100] Whatever early sources may have existed, minimalists also claim that the ancient biblical writer likely used them uncritically.[101] Lemche says, "my intention is to emphasize that the late literary context makes these sources an unlikely starting point for historical analysis so long as we cannot with any certainty decide which tradition is old and which is not."[102] In other words, the issue of the existence of older, perhaps even primary or eyewitness, sources about Israel's past is complicated by the problem of identifying them.

96.   As will be seen, non-minimalists generally do not agree with minimalists' arguments for a late date for the Bible's composition. Lemche has anticipated and answered some criticisms of his dating of the Bible. He admits that his scheme compresses the composition of parts of the Bible considered separate sources, such as those supposedly written by the Yahwist and the Chronicler, into a short amount of time. He also concedes that the language of the Deuteronomistic literature is different from that of Ecclesiastes, and that to most scholars the Hebrew Bible appears to predate the Septuagint. Lemche considers the solutions to these concerns "quite plain" (Lemche, "The Old Testament—A Hellenistic Book?," 188). He proposes "ethno-linguistic as well as socio-economic arguments" as explanations (p. 188). These include the suggestion that differences in social location and ideology could account for different storylines or sources; local dialects of Hebrew, if better researched, could explain differences in the written Hebrew of the Bible; and the argument that Hebrew manuscripts of the Old Testament do not need to predate the Septuagint translation by centuries in order to be its *Vorlage*. For critiques see Hans M. Barstad, "Is the Hebrew Bible a Hellenistic Book? Or: Niels Peter Lemche, Herodotus, and the Persians," *Transeu* 23 (2002): 129–51, which will also be discussed in the next chapter, and Brettler, "The Copenhagen School," 1–22. See also Niels Peter Lemche, "'Because They Have Cast Away The Law of the Lord of Hosts'—or: 'We and the Rest of the World': The Authors Who 'Wrote' The Old Testament," *SJOT* 17 (2003): 268–90, where Lemche argues that a religious elite in Babylon after the exile wrote the Old Testament, and that they subsequently took on "Taleban-like" fervor, moving back to Palestine and establishing their ideas there.

97.   Lemche, "The Old Testament—A Hellenistic Book?," 171.

98.   Niels Peter Lemche, "Good and Bad in History: The Greek Connection," in *Rethinking the Foundations: Historiography in the Ancient World and in the Bible* (ed. Steven L. McKenzie and Thomas Romer; Berlin: de Gruyter, 2000), 127–40.

99.   Thompson, "The Intellectual Matrix of Early Biblical Narrative," 112.

100.   Lemche, "New Perspectives," 53. In his *Early History* (89–96), Thompson presents a summary of the works that led to what he calls "The Systematic Critique of the Comparative Method" of dating biblical texts. Thompson sees his own *Historicity of the Patriarchal Traditions* and Van Seters' *Abraham in History and Tradition* as particularly influential in overturning accepted dating of biblical sources.

101.   Lemche, *The Canaanites in Their Land*, 164.

102.   Ibid.

It is unclear if minimalists share an opinion about whether near-eyewitness sources contain better historical information than secondary sources. Lemche's quote, above, and their general belief that the Bible is unreliable in part because it is late and secondary, appear to indicate that some minimalists would correlate an earlier date with better reliability. On the other hand, Thompson writes, "I…have never made the simplistic argument that what is secondary or late is thereby to be judged unhistorical."[103] Philosopher of history David Henige has offered, in an article praising the minimalist approach, a number of reasons that eyewitness accounts are better than secondary ones. He contends that "Implications do follow from dating, and they are serious."[104] Furthermore, he says that "Transmission is the inexorably fatal enemy of accuracy, as has been demonstrated thousands of times in various tests in psychology, sociology, and other fields, including history."[105] Finally, he argues, the "rules of evidence…do not arrogate [primary evidence] to canonical status; they only note that it is less likely to be unreliable than centuries-later secondary or tertiary sources."[106]

Minimalists' justifications for doubting the Bible's reliability depend on assumptions besides the concern that the Bible is not an early or primary source for Israel's past. Poststructuralist theories of language and narrative have also played a part in their understanding of the Bible, as minimalists recognize that narrative can describe both real and unreal events. Since most of the supposed historical information found in the Bible occurs in the narratives of Genesis–2 Kings and Chronicles, minimalists believe that such information must be treated with suspicion from the outset. For instance, Lemche writes, "the Israelite historians composed a novel, the theme of which was the origin of Israel and its ancient history."[107] Thompson also claims that "at least in ancient history, we haven't learned to tame [the] fictive hearts" of documents that purport to describe the past.[108] He extends this type of analysis to most of the narrative of the Hebrew Bible in his *The Mythic Past*, where he argues that the Bible's historiography is a type of Hellenistic narrative that is not concerned with facts and real happenings, but instead meditates on philosophical–religious problems.

Minimalists find specific evidence of fiction in particular aspects of ancient narrative. Lemche points to recurring themes and apparent similar purposes of Pentateuchal stories as markers of potentially fictive elements there.[109] Thompson argues that the presence of a recurring literary pattern, such as the ascendancy of the younger son, should warn readers that the story's particular details were probably conceived in light of the overarching aim of the document. Furthermore, these patterns, he says, are prevalent because of their plasticity:

103. Thompson, "A Neo-Albrightean School?," 693.
104. David P. Henige, "Deciduous, Perennial or Evergreen? The Choices in the Debate in 'Early Israel'," *JSOT* 27 (2003): 387–412 (399).
105. Ibid.
106. Ibid., 400.
107. Lemche, *The Canaanites in Their Land*, 158.
108. Thompson, "Lester Grabbe and Historiography," 147.
109. Lemche's "New Perspectives on the History of Israel" is an extended discussion of this thesis.

> Words like "motifs" and "metaphors" are rather too abstract for the items I would like
> to define as the smallest units of the tradition of biblical literature that have the ability
> to persist and to be used in variable forms. Like the Lego-block, many of the smallest
> units of our early Bible are quite plastic and easily transferable. They are suitable for
> multiple purposes.[110]

The hypothesis that patterning or stylized presentation may indicate fictional elements within a text has caused minimalists to turn a critical eye to ancient texts other than the Bible, even those that might qualify as eyewitness or near-eyewitness reports of the events they describe. Propagandistic texts, in their view, are especially likely to be fictive. For instance, Lemche posits that the heroic presentation of the Idrimi inscription, which tells the story of this king's life and rise to power, masks the actual circumstances of an usurper's rise to the throne.[111] Thompson contends that style, form, metaphor, and flattering presentations in the Deir 'Alla inscription, the Mesha inscription, the monuments to Sargon and Hammurapi,[112] and the ancient Near Eastern king lists,[113] show that their presentations are fictive, as well.[114] Thus, minimalists believe, many extrabiblical texts that historians have traditionally used when writing the history of Israel are, in their details, no more reliable than the Bible.

Though aspects of poststructuralist literary analysis, such as the notion that literary motifs are detachable from a referent, appear in minimalists' thought, minimalists have not accepted entirely dehistoricized or synchronic readings of the texts, another hallmark of poststructuralism. For instance, though Whitelam does assert that such readings of the Bible have shown that division into sources is not necessary for understanding some of its texts,[115] he is not entirely comfortable with the "domain assumption...that the text is autonomous."[116] Others consider synchronic readings to be fundamentalist and/or fearful Christian responses to historical scholarship that has discounted the Bible's claim to represent past reality.[117] Historical context, they believe, is necessary to understand the Bible, and they have particular ideas about how historical context interacts with a text's content and potential interpretation.

Since minimalists believe that remnants of eyewitness accounts of people and happenings in ancient Israel are difficult to identify in the Bible, and that ancient sources may be rife with literary invention, they consider the most reliable historical information ancient texts provide to be nonintentional information. As

---

110. Thompson, *The Mythic Past*, 277.

111. Lemche, *The Israelites in History and Tradition*, 24–25.

112. Thompson, *The Mythic Past*, 11–15; see also idem, "Problems of Genre and Historicity with Palestine's Inscriptions," in *Congress Volume: Oslo 1998* (ed. A. Lemaire and M. Sæbø; VTSup 80; Leiden: Brill, 2000), 321–26. For criticism of Thompson's analysis of the Moabite stone, see J. A. Emerton, "The Value of the Moabite Stone as an Historical Source," *VT* 41 (2002): 483–92.

113. Thompson, "Lester Grabbe and Historiography," 151.

114. Thompson, "A Neo-Albrightean School?," 693.

115. Whitelam, "Between History and Literature," 63.

116. Ibid., 64.

117. See Thompson, "A Neo-Albrightean School?," 695–96; Lemche, *Prelude to Israel's Past*, 230–31.

Thompson says, *"prima facie* [the biblical] stories are only data, and direct evidence for the intellectual activities of their writers."[118] Citing Wellhausen, he argues that "texts give evidence for what they imply; not for what they say."[119] Or, as Whitelam explains, "the value of [ancient texts that tell about the past] for the historian is not so much in the past they purport to describe but as...an insight."[120] In other words, the value of such texts for historians is not in the content of the story that they tell but in the overall attitudes and assumptions that the texts convey. Particularly germane for socio-historical understanding of the Bible itself, a goal of minimalist history, are indications in the text about conceptions of the past and of the deity held by the authors or community that produced the Bible.[121]

The assumption that the most reliable historical information found in the Bible relates to the time of its composition or compilation, along with the assumption that the Bible's stories are at best secondary historical sources and potentially fictive, characterize minimalists' thoughts about the biblical text. Yet these notions are based on an underlying assumption that minimalists bring to consideration of the Bible as evidence, namely that historians must have a unified, coherent theory of the Bible's composition. This belief is reminiscent of both Alt and Albright, who had firmly stated ideas about the historical development and relationship of the Bible's many parts. Whereas Albright saw poetry as early, and Alt and Noth found communal creeds behind the creation of much of the narrative, minimalists, as seen above, see community formation in the periods of colonization of Palestine by the Persians or Greeks and Romans as the key to understanding the Bible as a whole.

Discussion or justification of this position on a theoretical level is largely absent from the minimalists' scholarship, but glimpses of it appear in reaction to approaches taken by other scholars. For instance, Davies juxtaposes his position with that of Norman Whybray, noting that they both agree that examining the Bible closely and asking questions about its origin and transmission is good historical procedure. Yet Whybray is confident that proposing different explanations for different components of the literature (i.e. source or redaction criticism) is valid, while Davies insists that the final editing or compilation of the text sets the context for its meaning and that no meaning can be considered outside of

118. Thompson, "Lester Grabbe and Historiography," 146. See also idem, *The Mythic Past*, 10, 34, 72, 78–81, 237, and throughout.
119. Ibid., 147; idem, "Defining History and Ethnicity," 187. Cf. idem, "Methods and Results: A Review of Two Recent Publications," *SJOT* 15 (2001): 306–25 (312): "When we consider the implications of the reuse of tradition, the process of identity creation involved in tradition building is itself a product of the narratives reiterated. The meaning-bearing capacity of our texts far exceeds the intentions and the worldview of our authors or even of the intellectual culture they strove to present."
120. Whitelam, "The Social World of the Bible," 41.
121. See, for example, Keith Whitelam, "Recreating the History of Israel," *JSOT* 35 (1986): 45–70 (42–53), and idem, "The Social World of the Bible," 35–49. Lemche's *The Israelites in History and Tradition*, and Thompson's *The Mythic Past* (especially Part Three), are also attempts at interpreting what the Bible says about the society that produced it and what historical insights can be made from this analysis.

this process. Davies concludes that "the important thing is to find explanations for the fiction [i.e. the biblical text]... I have decided for a more systematic explanation. Whybray, if I understand correctly, prefers a more ad hoc one. Whybray prefers systematic accounts in the Old Testament; I prefer systematic explanations."[122] In other words, Davies claims that Whybray breaks the text into sources, an "ad hoc" approach, and from these sources forms a systematic account of the Bible's composition. Davies posits the text as a system whose parts cannot be separated, and thus requires an explanation for the entire system. Similarly, Thompson criticizes William Dever for lacking a "coherent diachronic composition theory"[123] and praises Finkelstein and Silberman for consistently dating the composition of many of the historical narratives in Samuel and Kings to the time between Hezekiah and Josiah (though he disagrees with them).[124] Like their predecessors, then, but with different results, minimalists assume that the Bible can be explained systematically and place much importance on forming coherent hypotheses about the Bible "that will account for its features as fully as possible."[125]

In summary, the conclusions that minimalists reach about the potential uses of the Bible for history are founded on standard historical procedure that is, in principle, the same as most historians', including Alt's and Albright's.[126] Minimalists ask questions about the text's genre, original context, date, transmission history, and representation of reality, and believe that an explanation of the biblical text must precede any historical conclusions that are drawn from it. Minimalists' method is also consistent with reactions to the antirepresentationalism and postmodernism observed in Chapter 2. Minimalists seem to indicate that eyewitness or near-eyewitness sources for Israel's past would be helpful, but they contend that such sources are difficult to find. Minimalists are also extremely careful when using ancient histories or depth-dimensional sources. Consequently, they use the Bible as a source of nonintentional information about cultural structures and *mentalités* of the postexilic period and beyond since texts, including the Bible, bear witness mainly to aspects of the society in which they were written. Given the many potential problems minimalists see for using ancient texts as evidence for Israel's past, they claim that any understanding of ancient Israel or Palestine before approximately the sixth century BCE must be based on artifacts and the findings of archaeology.

Artifacts

Minimalists, like most other historians of ancient Israel, firmly believe that archaeology can provide evidence about the past. Minimalists also claim that artifacts provide more objective and reliable information than do texts: "texts

122. Philip R. Davies, "'Ancient Israel' and History: A Response to Norman Whybray," *ExpTim* 108 (1996): 211–12 (211); cf. idem, "Whose History," 105.
123. Thompson, "Methods and Results," 309.
124. Ibid., 317.
125. McCullagh, "Bias in Historical Description," 60.
126. For a similar assessment of minimalists' use of evidence, see Zevit, "Three Debates," 10.

can and do mislead through the intentions of their authors," but artifacts never mislead "through their own intentions."[127] Minimalists appeal for independent evaluation of archaeological data, and believe that artifacts from ancient Palestine continue to be interpreted in light of the biblical story.[128] For instance, critical evaluation of archaeological artifacts should not involve, claim the minimalists, attempts to locate distinctly Israelite material culture. Lemche has protested that archaeologists studying the Late Bronze and Early Iron ages have looked for "the most minute changes in architecture, pottery, town lay-out, and so forth...to show the presence of new (foreign) elements among the existing population" of Palestine due to the Bible's presentation of Israel as foreign to the land.[129] The Tel Dan stele is another example of an archaeological find that minimalists believe has not been evaluated independently of biblical concerns. Specifically, minimalists claim that scholars who have found the words "House of David" on the stele have been influenced by the Bible and that such a reading is unsupported by epigraphy and philology.[130] In addition, minimalists have expressed concern that

> Any movement in scholarship which appears to cast doubt upon the ability of the biblical story to hold together the ancient relics and what most people nowadays imagine to be the "real" past is a threat to what might be called the "biblical archaeology industry," in which the state of Israel, countless academic institutions in the United States (especially) and several individual scholars have a high stake.[131]

Thus, minimalists see bias in favor of the biblical portrait of Israel as well as economic self-preservation at work in archaeological practice.

In keeping with their call for nonbiblical archaeology, minimalists also advocate freeing the nomenclature and dating of archaeological periods from any biblical references. Davies says, "If the fate of the non-biblical data is to be

127. Davies, "Method and Madness," 702.

128. Thompson claims that Noth's questioning of the existence of external evidence for the Bible was an inspiration for him and others to question and finally put an end to Albrightian biblical archaeology. Nevertheless, Thompson ("Martin Noth and the History of Israel," 85) writes: "Noth's opposition to biblical archaeology and particularly to biblical archaeology's efforts to create a pre-settlement history had nothing to do with critical scholarship. It was drawn rather from the requirements of his amphictyony hypothesis, which was only viable if Israel's unity was a developing characteristic of settlement rather than of an earlier event." In the 1970s, others besides Thompson and Van Seters warned that mixing interpretive frameworks from the Bible and archaeology was methodologically unsound. William Dever is credited with inaugurating and popularizing the practice of nonbiblical Syro-Palestinian archaeology. See, e.g., Dever, "The Impact of the 'New Archaeology' on Syro-Palestinian Archaeology," 15–29. Ironically, Dever has become one of the most vocal critics of the minimalists, as will be seen in Chapter 5.

129. Lemche, *Early Israel*, 387. See also Thompson, *Early History*, 10–26, 77–84, 112–16, 158–70; Lemche, "New Perspectives," 57–60; idem, *The Israelites in History and Tradition*, 72–73.

130. Lemche and Thompson, "Did Biran Kill David?"; Philip R. Davies, " 'House of David' Built on Sand: The Sins of the Biblical Maximizers," *BAR* 20, no. 4 (1994): 54–55; Thompson, "Problems of Genre and Historicity." George Athas, *The Tel Dan Inscription: A Reappraisal and a New Interpretation* (JSOTSup 360; London: Sheffield Academic Press, 2003), supports the minimalists' claims, as well, and will be discussed in Chapter 6.

131. Davies, "Introduction," 14.

made to fit into the remnants of a framework *which they themselves have not sponsored*, then they are not being properly utilized."[132] In other words, minimalists want to let the data suggest their own organization, as do postprocessualists. Thus Lemche, following Israeli archaeologists including Finkelstein, has suggested a specific remedy for one problem in terminology, namely what to call the period between 1200 and 900 BCE. These three centuries traditionally have been divided between the Iron I and Iron II periods, but archaeology has shown only a gradual change in settlement patterns and the continuity of cultural patterns in Palestine during this time frame.[133] Therefore, Lemche believes these years should be called a "transitional period" in order to minimize the influence of the Bible on the interpretation of artifacts from this period.[134]

Among minimalists, new archaeology has been greeted with both enthusiasm and trepidation. Whitelam claims that its "movement away from the investigation of individual sites to more comprehensive regional surveys is a prerequisite for the advancement of our understanding of the history" of Syria–Palestine.[135] On the other hand, Lemche, in line with his general stance on using social-scientific models to explain the past, has serious reservations about the processual theories that new archaeology promotes. It appears that minimalists would welcome some of postprocessualism's tenets, since they advocate allowing artifacts to supply their own framework of interpretation, but no detailed discussion of postprocessualism and its ramifications for the interpretation of specific artifacts or assemblages has been undertaken by a minimalist scholar. In other words, the concern that a probiblical bias often enters into interpretation of artifacts is easier to identify among the minimalists than are general principles pertaining to the use of artifacts as evidence for the past.

Combination of Texts and Artifacts

The discussions of how minimalists evaluate and use texts and artifacts have already disclosed much about how these scholars combine evidence provided by these two sources. In short, minimalists believe that it is "necessary to insist on a

---

132. Davies, "Whose History?," 108 (italics in original).
133. Specifically, 1200 BCE was traditionally considered the terminus of the Late Bronze Age and the approximate date of the Israelite conquest of Palestine. Further traditional divisions of the Iron Age are also based on biblical events. Iron I was said to end in either 1000 BCE, the supposed date of the beginning of the united monarchy under David, or in 925 BCE, the supposed date of Solomon's death and the split of the northern and southern parts of the kingdom. Iron II ended in 586 BCE with the conquest of Jerusalem by the Babylonians. Iron II has also been divided into Iron IIA, which ended in 720 BCE with the Assyrian destruction of the northern kingdom of Israel, and Iron IIB, which extended from 720 BCE to 586 BCE, when the Babylonians destroyed Jerusalem. For a contrasting view of the Iron I–Iron II transition, which advocates disjunction in settlement patterns, see Avraham Faust, "Abandonment, Urbanization, Resettlement and the Formation of the Israelite State," *NEA* 66 (2003): 147–61.
134. Lemche, "The Origin of the Israelite State," 52–53; idem, *The Israelites in History and Tradition*, 65.
135. Whitelam, "Recreating the History of Israel," 56.

methodology of writing the history of the ancient Near East which observes a careful distinction between the types of materials at hand, and which allows historical conclusions to be drawn only after each type of material has been independently examined."[136] Also, they contend that "The study of the history of Israel needs to be released from the constraints imposed on it by the methodological priority accorded to the biblical texts."[137] Put in terms of Halsall's theories, minimalists' insistence on the parity, or even primacy, of archaeological sources vis-à-vis textual ones indicates that they would be opposed to uses of archaeology that could be described as illustrative, justificatory, or for gap filling. Davies sees the consequences of these types of uses of artifacts as particularly unacceptable, since "to assign to non-biblical data the role of 'elucidating,' 'confirming' (or equally, of 'denying') the biblical narrative (or 'biblical record') will mean that the many remaining gaps in our knowledge are occupied by biblical data."[138]

Minimalists do argue, however, that they could more easily accept the picture of the past found in problematic texts such as the Bible if the picture painted by archaeology were similar. They rarely find this to be the case. In Lemche's words: "We started trying to reconcile the biblical imagery with other sources, and the comparison repeatedly led to the conclusion that such a harmonization is impossible."[139] It also should be noted that most minimalists do not claim that history cannot be written without reference to texts, and, in fact, most use texts liberally in the historical studies they produce.

In the absence of explicit discussion on the part of minimalists on how scholars would accomplish independent examination of both artifacts and texts, as well as how they would use the results of these examinations, a brief look at some minimalists' works can illuminate more about their assumptions and practices in this area. Thompson's *Early History of the Israelite People* provides archaeological, geographical, and topographical information about Palestine in general in the Bronze and Iron Ages, but eventually narrows its focus to entities and events important to the Bible such as Benjamin, Judah, and the destructions of Israel and Judah by imperial powers. Lemche's *Prelude to Israel's Past* begins by recounting the "biblical portrait of the period" and then separately presents information gleaned from texts, archaeology, and knowledge of "lifestyle and economy." On the other hand, Lemche's *The Israelites in History and Tradition* concentrates on identifying Israel within the artifactual record and examining how the writers of the Bible understood Israel.[140] As will be seen in

---

136.   Thompson, *The Historicity of the Patriarchal Narratives*, 3.
137.   Whitelam, "Recreating the History of Israel," 59.
138.   Davies, "Whose History?," 107.
139.   Lemche, "Ideology and the History of Ancient Israel," 184.
140.   It should be noted that the two works by Lemche discussed here differ in approach from his earlier history: *Ancient Israel: A New History of Israelite Society* (The Biblical Seminar 5; Sheffield: Sheffield Academic Press, 1988); trans. of *Det Gamle Israel: Det israelitiske samfund fra sammenbruddet af bronzealderkulturen til hellnistisk tid* (Aarhus: ANIS, 1984). In this book, Lemche presents a history of Israel in a very traditional form, with chapters on the premonarchical and monarchical periods, the exile, and the postexilic period, as well as a chapter on Israelite religion.

Chapter 5, this approach of separating, evaluating, and comparing textual and artifactual evidence is not very different from approaches taken by non-minimalists. Again, however, the conclusions that minimalists draw from their practice differ from non-minimalists' conclusions primarily because they minimize the Bible's value as a historical source, both on its own and in helping to interpret artifacts, especially for pre-exilic or pre-Hellenistic times.

Summary of Minimalists and Evidence

Though the current debate between minimalists and non-minimalists can be described as hinging on the value of the Bible as a historical source, this analysis has shown that minimalists come to their opinion about the Bible based on a number of assumptions. The Bible, for minimalists, is not an eyewitness account. Furthermore, minimalists find indications of fiction in the Bible, seek external evidence to cohere with the Bible's account (but do not find it), and believe that the information the Bible can provide about the past relates mainly to the time of its composition, which they date later than conventional opinion holds. Yet the current debate about evidence for Israel's past is not limited to the value of the Bible or other sources *per se*, but has evolved into an epistemological debate. Minimalists and their views on evidence are now at the center of a discussion of how historians come to know what they know about the past.

A quote from Davies, mentioned earlier in this chapter, and repeated in part here, exemplifies minimalists' self-perception of their epistemology: "The label 'sceptic' honours a historian—unless a biblical one, where faith in biblical narratives is expected."[141] Thus, minimalists claim that while skepticism of supposed evidence for the past is a primary responsibility of the historian, historians of ancient Israel, because of a bias in favor of the biblical texts, do not turn an appropriately skeptical eye towards this supposed evidence. In fact, says Davies, biases play a very large role in whether historians consider a source reliable:

> For the modern historian, "reliability" is something that reflects the degree to which an ancient story is internally consistent, and consistent with other data; and also to the extent that it corresponds with our own notions of *what we are inclined to accept*, for whatever reasons.[142]

Minimalists' insistence that potential historical evidence, especially the Bible, be treated with suspicion, their claims that their own attempts at objectivity are sufficient while other scholars are unacceptably biased, and their role as scholars

---

Lemche claims that in this book he takes a "broader socio-historical approach" to the history of Israel (p. 7), but he does not abandon the framework or characters presented in the Bible. In fact, here Lemche appears to accept much of the Bible's narrative as historical, or at least as having kernels of historicity that are able to be analyzed by sociological methods. For instance, he offers insight into why a leader such as Saul may have arisen and what increased state-like centralization would have meant for the inhabitants of Palestine without seriously questioning the overall biblical portrait of this period.

    141. Davies, "Whose History?," 109.

    142. Davies, "This Is What Happens…" 113 (italics in original).

more critical than constructive, have been lauded by scholars outside the discipline. For instance, Henige argues that the Bible must be treated with the utmost caution since:

> It got this way by being believed—and used—far more often that it was disbelieved and disregarded. For this reason alone, the study of its testimony needs, more than most other sources, to be carefully scrutinized, monitored, and, above all, tested. It should be axiomatic that the evidence we most want to believe is the very evidence that we treat the most gingerly, as an antidote to that desideratum. This is not ungenerous treatment of the Bible, but simply a recognition of the manifold effects of its longstanding centrality and scriptural statue.[143]

Henige goes on to imply that historians of ancient Israel have continued to "cycle" through the Bible, looking for evidence in a source that historians of other professions would have discarded long ago.[144] Also, according to Henige, the minimalists' critical bent does not exclude them from making an important contribution to the discipline:

> I would go so far as to argue that even *un*principled suspicion can have a salutary place in scholarly inquiry.[145]

> An "advance in ignorance" can be a very good thing indeed—a clearing of underbrush that can save large chunks of time and effort by making it clear that some spoors lead nowhere. Instead of endlessly recycling slight variations of argument in hopes of squeezing a few "facts" from the sources, certain strategies and goals are treated as—at least provisionally—of no value. Those who expose these hard realities make no less a contribution—and perhaps even a greater one—than those who apply one form of triage after another, only to come up with a case no more or no less persuasive than the status quo ante.[146]

> My impression is not that the minimalists congratulate themselves on "advancing knowledge," but regard their work as sustained and systematic devil's advocacy, and are therefore less interested so much in "winning" than in advancing discussion.[147]

> devils' advocacy...puts all sides of a discussion under pressure and forces them to look more carefully at their own work and also to broaden the optic of their research.[148]

Henige's praise of the minimalists' critical work does ignore the fact that minimalists believe that by choosing the proper subjects and evaluating the evidence critically, some history can be written. Yet minimalists, who appear to have started an epistemological controversy, have not defended themselves in such a

143. Henige, "Deciduous, Perennial or Evergreen?," 389. Henige's comments are made in the context of a response to Iain Provan, whose criticisms of minimalists and opinions about historical method will be discussed in Chapter 5. For a similar defense of minimalists see Jeremy Zwelling, "The Fictions of Biblical History" (review of *The Mythic Past* by Thomas L. Thompson), *History and Theory* 39 (2000): 117–41.
144. Henige, "Deciduous, Perennial or Evergreen?," 411.
145. Ibid., 391 (italics in original).
146. Ibid., 397.
147. Ibid.
148. Ibid., 410. Cf. McCullagh ("Bias in Historical Description," 56) who asserts that peer reviews are an effective check on subjectivity.

spirited manner, and Henige's remarks provide an entrée to the questions of how historians know what they know about the past and the minimalists' contribution to the history of ancient Israel as a discipline. In Chapter 5, other opinions about such matters will be discussed, and Chapter 6 will evaluate both sides of the debate and offer some suggestions.

Truth

As discussed in Chapter 1, most historians adhere to a correspondence theory of truth, which for history requires that true statements correspond to past reality. On the surface, the above description and analysis of several of the minimalists' assumptions and practices indicate that minimalists usually conceive of historical truth in the same way. Their disagreements with other historians of ancient Israel center on what types of evidence can provide the best facts about ancient Israel and the extent to which a history that focuses on Israel reflects the reality of ancient Palestine. Close examination of their assumptions, however, reveals a tension between minimalists' identification of fiction in history and their assertion that their own reconstructions represent ancient reality better than do ones that rely heavily on the Bible. In other words, though minimalists have an appreciation for the role of narrative and invention in constructing coherent plots and explanations within histories, especially ancient ones, minimalists rarely comment on the narrative qualities of their own works and their potential ramifications for interpretation, meaning, and truth. Nevertheless, it appears that minimalists would defend the truth of their narratives by arguing that they would withstand critical inspection of the evidence used in them. This is so because, minimalists claim, they employ critical historical method better than do other historians of ancient Israel, or, more specifically, take a more objective view of the Bible as a historical source than do other scholars.[149]

While theoretical justifications of the truth of minimalists' historical reconstructions are lacking, minimalists have criticized the nature of other scholars' truth claims about ancient Israel. They assert that plausible or probable reconstructions of the past do not measure up to an acceptable level of proof. In the words of Thompson: "there is little historiographic value in 'better' or 'best' analogies, when there is no clear evidence, only uncertain possibilities."[150] The tendency to rely on plausibility, minimalists claim, can be traced to Alt and Albright and other "paraphrasers" of the biblical text.[151] In essence, minimalists here appear to be disputing a type of historical truth that could be classified as truth by coherence. For some scholars, the Bible is considered to be a truth-bearer, and thus it is important to them that historical accounts cohere with the

149. Also, Lemche's claim that it is "almost always the modern historian—and only this person—who is endowed with the methodological remedies to analyze" ancient texts for fictitious or propagandistic elements is reminiscent of Albright (*The Israelites in History and Tradition*, 25).

150. Thompson, *Early History*, 93.

151. See, on the patriarchs, Thompson, *The Historicity of the Patriarchal Narratives*, 4; on Alt's peaceful infiltration model, see Lemche, *Early Israel*, 413.

Bible's claims. Minimalists maintain that in the case of ancient Palestine, such presuppositions allow for uncritical and untrue histories to be written.[152] Robert Carroll has gone so far as to call this type of history "bogus history."[153] Nevertheless, as will be seen, other historians of ancient Israel defend plausibility as a useful, or necessary, criterion of truth in history.

The advent of postmodernism and its ramifications for defining historical truth have been noticed as well, particularly by Davies. As discussed earlier in this chapter, Davies argues that historians should "refuse to tell a story," instead, "identify[ing] the relevant 'sources' and expound[ing] them as ancient cultural explanations of what really happened…expressing, like Picasso, several dimensions at once."[154] In other words, Davies advocates a type of multivalent truth, one where the historian's role is to present a number of voices and self-perceptions of past historical subjects. As seen in Chapter 1, truth in plurality has been promoted by scholars such as Burke but opposed by others such as McCullagh, who believes the historian's responsibility is forming a coherent story from disparate information. Davies does admit that the value of multivoiced history is not yet proven:

> What can a juxtaposition of partial, subjective stories, orphaned of their parent, the Master Narrative, tell us? My argument that "history" subsists now only in narratives that ultimately cannot and should not be reconciled actually rids us of an assured past, a firm base on which to build our present and future. It becomes a game, played with differently-coloured counters of experience, memory, observation and imagination.[155]

In the end, though, Davies seems to return to more traditional notions of historical truth. The "notion of truth or reality as a criterion" must remain, so that "It is possible for us, then, to evaluate human discourse in terms of how far it conveys recognizable images of reality."[156]

Minimalists have also recognized that histories may be considered true under a pragmatic, or instrumentalist, theory of truth. Lemche observes that history, especially in its modern form, "help[s in] establishing a common destiny, i.e. communality, among a certain group of people."[157] Furthermore, some minimalists have claimed that the pragmatic outcome of history should be judged on ethical terms. As seen above, Whitelam's *Invention of Ancient Israel* denounces the role that histories of ancient Israel can play in consolidating modern Israeli/ Jewish identity at the expense of Palestinian identity. In contrast, Whitelam explicitly aims to provide the non-Israelite or non-Jewish inhabitants of ancient Palestine with their own voice so that their modern counterparts can find

---

152. Cf. Henige, "Deciduous, Perennial or Evergreen?," 396, 408.

153. Robert P. Carroll, "Madonna of Silences: Clio and the Bible," in Grabbe, ed., *Can a "History of Israel" Be Written?*, 84–103.

154. Davies, "This Is What Happens…" 114–15.

155. Ibid., 116.

156. Ibid., 117. Ultimately, however, a community's expectations and needs seem to him to be at the root of the need for history to correspond to past reality, since he notes that, "[f]or some reason this matters to us, as it did not matter to the Assyrians or Judaeans" (ibid.).

157. Lemche, "The Origin of the Israelite State," 47.

communal definition in a past community. Truth in correspondence to reality, however, still holds sway over the pragmatic needs of a modern-day community for Lemche, as he is not fond of how some Christians have rejected historical truths about ancient Israel and instead adopted literary or narrative analyses of the Bible in order to maintain the "Bible's legitimacy…as an inspired source of information for themselves as the people of God."[158]

Additionally, some effects of postmodernism can be seen in minimalists' struggle to define the significance of the history of Israel for human communities, as well as for theology or knowledge in general. Whereas Albright clearly believed that his scholarship approached questions of universal importance, and Alt and Noth appear to have concurred, postmodernism has relativized truth claims and has pointed out their potential repressive possibilities. This intellectual milieu seems to be at the root of some questions Thompson poses in *The Mythic Past*: "Why is our understanding of the Bible as fictive considered to undermine its truth and integrity? How does historicizing this literature give it greater legitimacy? Why, in fact, does a literary work as influential as the Bible need further legitimation?"[159] Davies considers the postmodern situation and decides that in order for biblical studies to survive, it will have to abandon the pretense of having "a dominant and authoritative cultural voice" and "lose some introversion and arrogance and realize just how unimportant to most people are the things on which we pride ourselves so much."[160] Similarly, Lemche's *Prelude to Israel's Past* concludes with a chapter on "Theological Vantage" and a section entitled "What Do We Seek in the Bible?" where he argues that despite the fact that the Bible's "claims to absolute authority and undeniable truth cannot stand… [I]ts dialectic importance remains intact inasmuch as it presents ideas and thoughts that are just as valuable to present-day readers as to the audience for which it was originally written."[161] Minimalists thus recognize that history challenges certain religious beliefs that are based on the Bible, but have not made detailed arguments for why negative conclusions about the Bible's historical reliability need not destroy the general importance of the Bible to religious readers, or to others.

To summarize, minimalist historians of ancient Israel appear to have a firm idea of historical truth, and chide others to live up to the ideal that what is written about the past should correspond to past reality. They also appreciate the role history can play in modern communities, but it is unclear what exactly they believe that the truths of the history of ancient Israel can contribute to knowledge or to humanity in general. Davies in particular is probing the idea of a new truth-standard for historians, one that is less dependent on coherent narrative truth but that overtly takes into account different perspectives about the past.

158. Lemche, *Prelude to Israel's Past*, 231.
159. Thompson, *The Mythic Past*, 5.
160. Davies, "The Future of 'Biblical History,'" 141.
161. Lemche, *Prelude to Israel's Past*, 231.

Summary of Assumptions and Practices of
Minimalist Historians of Ancient Israel

The preceding analysis of minimalist historians of ancient Israel has explored a number of their assumptions and practices. An examination of whether a general description for their philosophy of history can be proposed is now in order. As seen in Chapter 3 of this study, Zevit argued that *In Search of "Ancient Israel"* by Davies exemplified a third, or postmodern, paradigm of history, and that Lemche and Thompson could be considered historians of this paradigm, as well.[162] To review, the tenets of Zevit's third paradigm are (quoted here in part):

1. a heightened sensitivity that topics or issues worthy of study may be marginal to the focus of mainline biblical studies and that though data bearing on them may not be directly available, they may be inferred from the biblical text;
2. the selection of "ideological" topics for study;
3. the reading of historiography, both ancient and modern, as narrative fiction, on the one hand, and as a hegemonic instrument of subjugation and power, on the other;
4. the assumption that meaning is produced primarily by contemporary readers; and
5. the claim that any interpretation of a text is as valid as any other.[163]

Minimalists appear to accept some of these tenets some of the time. They do read the Bible as narrative fiction and do recognize that histories have the power to include or silence voices. Minimalists, however, have actually selected few ideological topics for study,[164] though many have suggested that the Israel portrayed in the Bible would be an appropriate topic of this type. While minimalists

---

162. Cf. Talshir, "Textual and Literary Criticism," 235, who calls minimalists postmodernists because for them "scientific skepticism has evolved into total chaos." See also William G. Dever, "Save Us From Postmodern Malarkey," *BAR* 26, no. 2 (2000): 28–35, 68–69; idem, *What Did the Biblical Writers Know and When Did They Know It: What Archaeology Can Tell Us about the Reality of Ancient Israel* (Grand Rapids: Eerdmans, 2001), especially Chapter 2, "The Current School of Revisionists and Their Nonhistories of Ancient Israel."

163. Zevit, *The Religions of Ancient Israel*, 58. Dever's assessment of minimalists as postmodernists is based on characteristics similar to these that Zevit describes, but are more polemical. See, e.g., Dever, *What Did the Biblical Writers Know?*, 52, where he names some principles of postmodernists/minimalists as "Always attack the Establishment on principle...polarize the discussion...celebrate the bizarre...pretend to be scientific," and so on. For a potentially more cynical take on minimalists, see Ferdinand E. Deist, *The Material Culture of the Bible: An Introduction* (The Biblical Seminar 70; Sheffield: Sheffield Academic Press, 2000), 58–61. In a passage that does not name minimalism *per se* but implies it strongly, Deist argues that new theories arise because scholarship always has a need for something more exciting. In particular, he says, scholarship responds to dissatisfaction with the effects, especially political, of the belief system that accompanies it. Also, he claims that scholars are attracted to the possibility of being the harbinger of a new way of thinking that is counterestablishment and has "the potential of capturing the imagination of great numbers of prospective students" (p. 60).

164. One exception is Lemche's *Israelites in History and Tradition*. Thompson's *The Mythic Past* might also qualify as such a study.

may agree that in theory the meaning of a text is produced by its reader, they do not claim that any interpretation of the Bible is as valid as any other, not for historical purposes and not in general. Also, minimalists do not appear to see themselves as writers of fiction or literature that is open to a variety of inter-pretations. They consider themselves to be historians who aspire to describe and explain what actually happened in the past despite the challenges that increased awareness of historiography's literary character has brought to the field.

Taking an opposite view from Zevit, Hans Barstad has claimed that Thompson and Lemche (and by implication other minimalists) are "the first of the last modernists," since, in his opinion, they have not shifted the paradigm of history away from the traditional concern with representation of hard facts.[165] Indeed, minimalists do hold some assumptions in common with Zevit's second-paradigm, modern historians. They are sensitive to the limits of documentary evidence for reconstructing the past, and they recognize that interpretation of texts and artifacts is always subjective to a degree. Minimalists' skepticism of the ability of some scholars, such as religious Christians or Jews or modern Israelis, to write objective history is in line with the second paradigm's require-ment that history be written "with no special pleading" for any single set of conclusions. Their enthusiasm for archaeological data and sociological explana-tions are a continuation of ideas championed by Albright and Alt. Also, their call for a history of Palestine that takes into account long-term social processes is descended from the *Annales* school. Finally, for minimalists, as for most historians, true statements in history should correspond to facts about reality.

In conclusion, it appears that minimalists neither subscribe to full-fledged postmodernism nor to history as it was understood in the early and mid-twenti-eth century.[166] The goals of minimalist historians, which include representation and explanation of the past, are in line with those of traditional historians' goals, though minimalists are cautious about the possibility of representation. Their quest for objectivity, as well as the preferred subjects of their history—cultural structures and *mentalités*—are in fact descended from second-paradigm histori-ans' ideas and practices. Minimalists believe explanation is an important part of history writing and seek rational explanations of historical processes, often guided by social-scientific theory. They also adhere to a correspondence theory of historical truth: a true statement about the past describes what occurred in reality. On the other hand, aspects of history's linguistic turn have persuaded minimalists that the Bible and other ancient texts are better understood as crea-tive works containing fiction rather than as intentionally truthful accounts of

---

165.   Hans M. Barstad, "History and the Hebrew Bible," in Grabbe, ed., *Can a "History of Israel" Be Written?*, 37–64 (51). Cf. Mayer I. Gruber, "The Ancient Israel Debate: A Jewish Postcolonial Perspective," *ANES* 38 (2001): 3–27 (17): "Whitelam reveals again and again that his approach is, in fact, characteristically a 19th century historicism"; and Provan, Long, and Longman, *A Biblical History of Israel*, 32, for a similar assessment of Davies.

166.   For a critique that agrees with this assessment (despite his earlier claims), see Zevit, "Three Debates," 13–14.

what actually happened in the past.[167] Additionally, minimalists oppose historians' tendency to use the Bible to define the objects, subjects, and chronological framework of historiography. Consequences of the minimalist view include a low opinion of the value of the Bible as a historical source for the time periods to which it is not a primary eyewitness, and a corresponding minimization of the importance of Israel, whether biblically or historically conceived, for understanding the past of ancient Palestine. In summary, the minimalist approach to the history of ancient Israel can be said to be a critique, but not yet a revision, of aspects of traditional history. Many non-minimalist scholars have reacted to and incorporated aspects of the minimalists' critiques in their own history writing. These scholars are the topic of the next chapter.

167.   It is not clear, however, that minimalist notions of fiction in the Bible can be attributed to "Deconstruction strategies developed by J. Derrida," as Zevit (ibid., 14) claims.

Chapter 5

NON-MINIMALIST HISTORIANS OF ANCIENT ISRAEL

Introduction: Defining "Non-Minimalists"

In the 1990s, minimalist approaches to the history of ancient Israel became entrenched in the discipline, and historians of ancient Israel at large began to recognize and grapple with the ideas of the minimalists in earnest. Minimalist assumptions and practices brought about a variety of reactions from scholars. Some incorporated ideas of the minimalists into their scholarship, while others solidified their defenses of the positions that the minimalists appeared to be attacking. Whatever their reaction, most historians of ancient Israel held on to core opinions that the Bible can provide reliable information about the past it describes, even for the period prior to the exilic period, and that Israel is an acceptable subject of history, even an Israel akin to what the Bible describes.[1] Since these two assumptions are fundamentally opposed to what this study has described as basic minimalist beliefs, scholars who in general adhere to them will simply be called "non-minimalists" here.

It was seen in the previous chapter that minimalists' arguments about the reliability of the Bible and the proper subjects of history intersect with their beliefs about many other topics, including objectivity, representation, the role of narrative in history (especially in historical writing from the ancient world), the value and use of incidental information, the place of social-scientific theory in history, the classification and use of artifacts, the place of skepticism in historical research, and the nature of the truth claims history makes. Likewise, non-minimalists' responses to minimalists relate to assumptions and practices in history writing. In this chapter, theoretical statements by non-minimalist historians of ancient Israel that explicitly or implicitly address such issues remain the focus of discussion. Of course, every response to the minimalists does not appear in this sample, but it seeks to be representative of both the diversity of and general trends in the assumptions of non-minimalist historians of ancient Israel.

As well as describing non-minimalists' reactions to minimalist challenges, this analysis will also discuss the effects of postmodernism on non-minimalists writing Israel's history. Postmodernism has added new dimensions to discussions of topics such as objectivity, narrative, and truth that, as seen in the previous

---

1. Cf. Zevit, "Three Debates," 16.

chapter, intersect at many points with concerns raised by minimalists. Finally, after consideration of the influence minimalists and postmodernism have had on recent theoretical discussions among historians of ancient Israel, the analysis will seek commonalities among non-minimalist historians in order to ascertain whether a new way of conceiving and writing Israel's history is forming in response to these influences.[2]

Goals of History Writing and Representation of the Past

Traditional ideas about history writing and its goals have been presented several times in this study. In general, it has been observed that historians believe in the existence of a real past, hope to relate what actually happened in that past as well as to explain why, and thereby strive to produce a meaningful account of the past. These assumptions and goals also hold for non-minimalist historians of ancient Israel. Historians in general also agree that the past can be represented somehow, but they differ in their conceptions and descriptions of representation. Some non-minimalist historians have discussed how representation should work in history. For instance, Grabbe reports that at the first meeting of the European Seminar in Historical Methodology, which included non-minimalist scholars as well as Davies, Lemche, and Thompson, the participants agreed that reconstruction is an adequate description of the historian's task if a reconstruction is "simply a way of making sense of the data, is always tentative, and is in the nature of a hypothesis to be tested."[3] V. Philips Long compares the process of representing the past to painting instead of constructing, and recommends that historians "discern the major contours of the subject by, as it were, half-closing their eyes to perceive the big picture."[4] "Simplicity, selectivity, [and] suggestive detail," he says, are the hallmarks of a good historical representation.[5] Despite the different analogies, both Grabbe's group and Long attempt to include indications of the contingencies and imperfections of historical representation in their description of the process.

Most non-minimalists' definitions of history do not differ much from definitions given by historians in general, either. Halpern's definition of history as "the undertaking of rendering an account of a particular, significant, and coherent sequence of past human events," is a typical example.[6] Occasionally,

2.   As Zevit, for example, claims in his discussion of his fourth paradigm of history writing (*Religions of Ancient Israel*, 69–73).

3.   Grabbe, "Reflections," 188.

4.   V. Philips Long, *The Art of Biblical History* (Foundations of Contemporary Interpretation 5; Grand Rapids: Zondervan, 1994), 244.

5.   Ibid.; cf. Provan, Long, and Longman, *A Biblical History of Israel*, 82.

6.   Halpern, *The First Historians*, 6. See also Gösta Ahlström, "The Role of Archaeological and Literary Remains in Reconstructing Israel's History," in Edelman, ed., *The Fabric of History*, 116–41 (116); idem, *The History of Ancient Palestine from the Paleolithic Period to Alexander's Conquest* (JSOTSup 146; Sheffield: JSOT Press, 1993), 19–20; Ferdinand E. Deist, "Contingency, Continuity and Integrity in Historical Understanding: An Old Testament Perspective," *Scriptura* Special Issue 11 (1993): 99–115 (109); Lester L. Grabbe, "Introduction," in Grabbe, ed., *Can a*

however, a non-minimalist's definition of history will indicate engagement with difficult or controversial issues. For instance, Diana Edelman has addressed the problem of formulating a definition of history that theoretically can be universal, that is, one that can apply to both ancient and modern history writing. She proposes using the term "historiography" to define a "broad category" of writing that encompasses many genres whose "subject matter deals with current or past people, events or reality."[7] Given this general definition, Edelman then works on the distinctions between modern and ancient historiography. She claims that each type of historiography has distinguishable characteristics: while ancient historiography may explain occurrences in terms of divine causation as well as human causation, modern historiography "creates meaning by using rational thinking that links data into chains based on cause and event."[8] Writers of history in modern times, she adds, critically evaluate their sources, while ancient authors did not.[9] It follows for Edelman that modern-day historiography has a substantially better capacity to relate what actually happened than did ancient history writing, an opinion she shares with Albright and Lemche.

K. Lawson Younger's definition of history addresses modern and postmodern concerns about objectivity and truth in history writing, as well as the issue of the role of narrative in the formation of a historical account. Younger says that "History writing is not nationalistic or based on an unbiased objectivity... Moreover, history is artistically constructed and does not necessarily follow a strict chronological framework of presentation."[10] He instead defines history as "a committedly true account which imposes form on the actions of men in the past."[11] The postmodern flavor of Younger's "committedly true" history that "imposes" a structure on events of the past is tempered, however, by his traditional belief that human action is the subject of history.

Halpern, like Younger, recognizes that the historian's subjectivity and mode of construction play a part in history writing, and he seeks to incorporate these factors into definitions of history. For instance, he says, "History is the way we organize our understanding of the world as it has been."[12] He also argues that historiographical intention on the part of the author is the crux of history writing. In his words:

"History of Israel" Be Written?, 11–18 (13); Edwin Yamauchi, "The Current State of Old Testament Historiography," in *Faith, Tradition, and History: Old Testament Historiography in Its Near Eastern Context* (ed. Alan Millard, James K. Hoffmeier, and David W. Baker; Winona Lake, Ind.: Eisenbrauns, 1994), 1–36 (1).

7. Diana V. Edelman, "Clio's Dilemma: The Changing Face of History-Writing," in Lemaire and Sæbø, eds., *Congress Volume: Oslo 1998*, 247–55 (253).

8. Ibid.

9. See Edelman's example of the ancient history writer who complied the stories of Saul in "Clio's Dilemma," 253–55. On the other hand, Herodotus did distinguish between "hearsay" and "autopsy."

10. Younger, *Ancient Conquest Accounts*, 35.

11. Ibid., 46.

12. Halpern, *David's Secret Demons*, 111.

> The principal criterion [of history] can only be one: does the work parlay the available
> evidence (sources) into coherent narrative *about* events susceptible to reconstruction
> from the sources? In other words, did the narrator have reason to believe what he or she
> wrote, or did the narrator depart at will from the sources, concocting freely about
> matters concerning which he or she had no, or contradictory, evidence?[13]

Halpern's description of history has repercussions for both ancient and modern history. As will be discussed in the section on texts, below, Halpern insists that the biblical authors, particularly the Deuteronomistic Historian, intended to compose an authentic story about the past, used ancient sources, and wrote a story that is likely reliable in many of its details. General ideas about history can be extrapolated from Halpern's description, as well, including the notions that narrative is history's form, human-driven events are history's subject, and intention is the key to distinguishing history from fiction.

The question of whether history can claim to be a discourse about knowledge and truth seems to underlie J. Maxwell Miller's and Paula McNutt's definitions of history. They call history an ongoing conversation between the past and the present.[14] McNutt explains that the idea of a conversation replaces the idea of history "as what we know or think we know about past events and peoples"[15] with the notion that historians constantly are examining their ideas about the past as well as evidence for the past. By this definition, then, historical conclusions can never be final, but meaningful communication between the past and present can occur.

Just as definitions of history in previous chapters provided an entrée to issues debated by Altians, Albrightians, minimalists, and historians and philosophers in general, so these descriptions of history introduce a range of issues of concern to non-minimalists. For instance, these definitions indicate that non-minimalists pay attention to how modern history writing differs from and is similar to ancient history writing; how language and literary form, particularly narrative, influence the presentation and apprehension of information about the past; what role the modern interpreter of the past plays in representation of the past; and how interpretation of the past can never be completely objective or fixed. Each of these topics will be discussed in this chapter, as will additional adjustments by non-minimalists to traditional notions about history writing and their reactions to minimalists' notions of history. Since objectivity has been at the forefront of modern definitions of history in general and minimalists' claims about Israel's past in particular, the discussion will begin there.

---

13. Halpern, *The First Historians*, 12.

14. J. Maxwell Miller, "Reading the Bible Historically: The Historian's Approach," in *To Each Its Own Meaning: An Introduction to Biblical Criticism and their Application* (ed. Stephen R. Haynes and Steven L. McKenzie; Louisville, Ky.: Westminster John Knox, 1993), 11–28 (12); Paula M. McNutt, *Reconstructing the Society of Ancient Israel* (Library of Ancient Israel; Louisville, Ky.: Westminster John Knox, 1999), 2.

15. McNutt, *Reconstructing the Society of Ancient Israel*, 2.

Objectivity

Most of the historians and philosophers discussed in this study consider objectivity in history to be a regulative ideal rather than an attainable goal. As seen in the previous chapter, objectivity in the history of Israel is a contentious topic, but unfortunately, theoretical examinations of objectivity by current non-minimalist historians of ancient Israel are scattered and limited.[16] Examples of scholars who have addressed objectivity include Knauf, who argues that objective history is possible (as well as morally and politically necessary). Historians produce objective history, he says, by formulating it "in accordance with the principles of objective knowledge,"[17] which include being constantly self-critical and open to dialogue. Historians must remember, however, that objective knowledge is "transient and preliminary."[18] Similarly, Provan asserts that being objective is equivalent to having an open mind rather than being firm in one's preconceived opinions.[19] Brettler, noting that the objectivity of the natural sciences has also come into question, maintains that although historians must negotiate biases to apprehend and interpret data, "the idea that 'all we have is biases' is false."[20]

As for recognizing one's own biases, Provan has suggested that historians should openly admit their biases and allegiances in their work.[21] Thus, in *A Biblical History of Israel*, Provan and coauthors Long and Tremper Longman III discuss at length their "theistic convictions and theological motivations."[22] Gottwald also has included personal information in his *Politics of Ancient Israel*, disclosing, among other things, that he is a democratic, socialist, free-church "christian" who likes some aspects of ancient Israel and doesn't like others.[23] This information, he claims, reminds the reader and himself that his investigation of ancient Israel is carried out in a world that is invested in his conclusions. On the other hand, James Barr has doubts that this "presupposition-alism," which he calls "Freudian, psychoanalytic," and "a fashion of a limited theological current,"[24] can solve any historical or disciplinary problems.

---

16. For an earlier description of historians' practices, which includes a discussion of objectivity, see George W. Ramsey, *The Quest for the Historical Israel* (Louisville, Ky.: Westminster John Knox, 1981), 1–23.

17. Ernst Axel Knauf, "From History to Interpretation," in Edelman, ed., *The Fabric of History*, 26–64 (28); cf. Gottwald, *The Tribes of Yahweh*, xlii.

18. Ibid., 29.

19. Iain W. Provan, "In the Stable with the Dwarves: Testimony, Interpretation, Faith and the History of Israel," in Lemaire and Sæbø, eds., *Congress Volume: Oslo 1998*, 281–319 (303–4).

20. Brettler, *Creation of History*, 10.

21. Provan, "Ideologies, Literary and Critical," 606.

22. Provan, Long, and Longman, *A Biblical History of Israel*, 103–4.

23. Norman K. Gottwald, *The Politics of Ancient Israel* (Library of Ancient Israel; Louisville, Ky.: Westminster John Knox, 2001), 30–31. Gottwald uses the small "c" in "christian" to "renounce any sense of Christian [*sic*] religious superiority or imperialist designs."

24. Barr, *History and Ideology in the Old Testament*, 69 and n. 26.

Non-minimalists' evaluations of minimalists' objectivity, and their reactions to minimalists' accusations of bias, also help clarify some of their ideas about objectivity. For example, Provan, Long, and Longman point out a potential weak spot in Whitelam's call for objectivity. On the one hand, they note, Whitelam seems to claim "that reason and evidence always and inevitably function in the service of an ideology and a set of commitments."[25] How then, they ask, can Whitelam take issue with scholars' commitment to ancient Israel as a historical subject? "[I]s his objection that other scholars simply do not share his particular set of commitments—that they do not support him in the story about Palestine that he wishes to tell?"[26] In this light, Whitelam's argument for Palestinian, instead of Israelite, history, though portrayed as a call for objectivity, has more to do with pragmatics or ethics. Objectivity, imply these scholars, remains equally impossible, or possible, no matter what history's subject. As seen in the previous chapter, minimalists and non-minimalists have also accused each other of being "ideological," which appears to be the preferred pejorative term (rather than "biased") in the debate about objectivity. Gottwald explains that the accusation that a historian is ideological implies that he or she possesses a "dogma or fantasy that obscures and distorts the object of study."[27] Putting Gottwald in McCullagh's terms, ideological historians would be those whose desire for a certain conception of the past to be true clouds their historical judgment.

In summary, despite the lack of theoretical attention paid to the issue of objectivity, non-minimalists appear to be aware of the necessary subjectivity of all history writing and seem to be more at-ease with this subjectivity than minimalists.[28] The consequence of this approach is that non-minimalists keep objectivity as a goal but rarely engage in the kind of sustained critiques of others' objectivity that are characteristic of the minimalists.[29]

Subject and Explanation

While non-minimalist historians of ancient Israel have seldom dealt with the issue of objectivity, they have paid more attention to issues of potential subjects and modes of explanation in history. While minimalists contend that historians have inflated ancient Israel's role in the past, non-minimalists, in contrast, appear to be neither ready nor able to abandon Israel as a potential subject of

25. Provan, Long, and Longman, *A Biblical History of Israel*, 108.
26. Ibid.
27. Gottwald, "Triumphalist Versus Anti-Triumphalist Versions of Early Israel," 26.
28. Non-minimalists also give hints that they believe subjectivity might be beneficial, for example: "Bias can enhance historiography, except where it runs amok, as where a writer repudiates obvious fact (such as the Holocaust), and indulges in fantasy or fraud" (Halpern, *The First Historians*, 11).
29. One exception to this generalization is William Dever. See, e.g., "Revisionist Israel Revisited"; idem, "Save Us From Postmodern Malarkey"; idem, *What Did the Biblical Writers Know?*, 23–52. Provan's "In the Stable with the Dwarves" also included a sustained critique of minimalist ideology. Provan's rhetoric was toned down in Provan, Long, and Longman, *A Biblical History of Israel*, especially pp. 3–9, 62–70.

history. Gottwald notes, for example, that sources for peoples of ancient Palestine are meager, and also questions whether an audience for what he calls an antitriumphalist history of Palestine exists.[30] In a similar vein, Sandra Scham considers the idea of a proper approach to the past to be an idea perpetuated by academic "elites" that does not give credence to the "many contending, and perhaps equally valid, ideologies" of human beings at large.[31] Thus, Scham argues, since interest in Israel's past is tied to religion, "Ultimately, we must ask ourselves if it really makes sense to divorce a scholarly discipline from its primary basis of relevance to the rest of the world."[32] Another objection to minimizing Israel as a historical subject comes from Bob Becking, who agrees with Davies that "'ancient Israel' [is] a product of the mind of biblical scholars," but asserts that Davies "fails to see, however, that what he calls 'historical Israel' is a product of the mind too."[33] In short, these scholars recognize that a concept of "ancient Israel" is problematic but nevertheless believe that it remains a valid starting point for history writing.

Non-minimalists also recognize that historians must choose between writing "the actual history of the peoples/nations, and the history of their self-understanding and religion."[34] In general, they appear to be concerned that human subjects remain part of histories of ancient Israel. As seen in the definitions of history discussed above, Halpern and Younger define history's subject as human events. Deist, however, addresses the phenomenon of suprahuman structures, such as economics, becoming subjects (or nonsubjects) in history, and concludes that "investigations [of] this or that area of human experience...do not constitute history. History has to do with insight into the whole process involved in human decisions."[35] He claims that history must take seriously the human dimension in order to avoid reducing "human beings to mere economic commodities or to slaves of any so-called social law."[36] In addition, Barstad has discounted the applicability of the methods of Braudel and the *Annales* school for writing the history of Israel: "Since biblical historiography is narrative, event oriented and preanalytical, it simply does not provide us with the kind of empirical data the anti event-oriented and anti-narrative analytical scientist Braudel could use."[37]

30. Gottwald, "Triumphalist Versus Anti-Triumphalist Versions of Early Israel," 30–31. The opinion that sources for peoples of ancient Palestine, especially non-Israelites or Judeans, are scarce can implicate both the Bible and extrabiblical sources.

31. Sandra Scham, "The Days of the Judges: When Men and Women Were Animals and Trees Were Kings," *JSOT* 97 (2002): 37–64 (41).

32. Ibid.

33. Bob Becking, "Inscribed Seals as Evidence for Biblical Israel? Jeremiah 40.7–41.15 *Par Example*," in Grabbe, ed., *Can a "History of Israel" Be Written?* 64–83 (68).

34. Ahlström, *The History of Ancient Palestine*, 28. As the title suggests, in this book Ahlström attempts to make Palestine, not Israel, history's subject. However, much of the book is concerned with the community described in the Bible.

35. Deist, "Contingency, Continuity and Integrity in Historical Understanding," 387; cf. Yamauchi, "The Current State of Old Testament Historiography," 1.

36. Deist, "Contingency, Continuity and Integrity in Historical Understanding," 387.

37. Barstad, "History and the Hebrew Bible," 49.

Barstad goes on to say that adding archaeology to the mix does not improve matters much. Human-oriented history of ancient Israel, however, is also limited by the paucity of evidence. The activities and roles of marginalized or oppressed people in ancient Israel, such as women, can be difficult to identify. Thus Provan, for one, has questioned whether histories about such people can be written, saying that evidence for women's religion in ancient Israel, such as Asherah-worship, is nonexistent.[38] On the other hand, Meyers has combined inferences from texts and comparative study of artifacts to demonstrate that women's lives in ancient Israel need not be considered invisible.[39]

Although some non-minimalists limit history's subject to human events, structures continue to appear as subjects in histories of ancient Israel written by non-minimalist historians. For example, the history of Israelite religion is a well-established, and somewhat separate, discipline within biblical studies. In addition, Gottwald's *Politics of Ancient Israel* and Jon Berquist's *Controlling Corporeality: The Body and the Household in Ancient Israel*, are examples of comprehensive studies that focus on structures or *mentalités*.[40] B. S. J. Isserlin's *The Israelites* and Philip King and Lawrence Stager's *Life in Biblical Israel* are also non-narrative histories that describe the land, social structures, material culture, and beliefs of the Israelite community.[41] Rainer Albertz has attempted to write a history of the so-called "exilic period," that combines political and mental aspects of ancient Israel, and he claims that this combination inaugurates a new method of writing history.[42] Also, Dever has defended a historical perspective that includes the *longue durée*.[43] These examples show that, as a group, non-minimalists categorically exclude neither humans and human actions nor structures as potential subjects of Israel's history.

As with minimalist historians, discussion of explanation in history among non-minimalists has focused mainly on explanations that the social sciences can provide. The recognition of potential benefits of using the social sciences in history writing is not appreciably different among non-minimalist historians of ancient Israel than among other historians, including minimalists. For instance,

38.   Iain W. Provan, "The Historical Books of the Old Testament," in Barstad, ed., *The Cambridge Companion to Biblical Interpretation*, 198–211 (205).

39.   Meyers, *Discovering Eve*; see also idem, "Engendering Syro-Palestinian Archaeology: Reasons and Resources," *NEA* 66 (2003): 185–97; Phyllis A. Bird, *Missing Persons and Mistaken Identities: Women and Gender in Ancient Israel* (OBT; Minneapolis: Fortress, 1997); and Susan Ackerman, "Digging Up Deborah: Recent Hebrew Bible Scholarship on Gender and the Contribution of Archaeology," *NEA* 66 (2003): 172–84.

40.   Gottwald, *The Politics of Ancient Israel*; Jon L. Berquist, *Controlling Corporeality: The Body and the Household in Ancient Israel* (New Brunswick, N.J.: Rutgers University Press, 2002).

41.   B. S. J. Isserlin, *The Israelites* (London: Thames & Hudson, 1998); Philip J. King and Lawrence E. Stager, *Life in Biblical Israel* (Library of Ancient Israel; Louisville, Ky.: Westminster John Knox, 2001).

42.   Rainer Albertz, *Die Exilszeit: 6 Jahrhundert v. Chr.* (BE 7; Stuttgart: Kohlhammer, 2001), 7; published in English as *Israel in Exile: The History and Literature of the Sixth Century B.C.E* (Studies in Biblical Literature 3; Atlanta: Society of Biblical Literature, 2003).

43.   William G. Dever, *Who Were the Early Israelites and Where Did They Come From?* (Grand Rapids: Eerdmans, 2003), 153.

Charles Carter describes social-scientific methodology in history as fundamentally comparative, and says that it functions to provide an interpretive framework for or heuristic model of the past, focusing on similarities and differences.[44] McNutt also asserts that the social sciences help historians consider social structures and processes in Israel by "comparing how the organization and development of complex systems of meaning and practice relate to the contexts of political domination and economic relations."[45]

Reservations about the use of social-scientific modeling and theory among non-minimalists often echo those expressed by Lemche, namely, that models are in danger of being both reductionistic and deterministic, and that scholars not educated about their basic assumptions and conditions risk drawing untenable conclusions.[46] Scham is particularly harsh:

> At this point, no one has produced anything more than rhetoric about a multi-cultural, ethnographically derived history of ancient Palestine—but we are all in serious danger of being subjected to one in the near future. There is no inherent scholarly risk these days in replacing the "mythic" but nonetheless engaging, biblical epic with vapid cultural analogies based upon ethnographic observations of modern Near Eastern cultures.[47]

Edelman is also concerned about social-scientific laws and models in history. The two disciplines differ, she says, because while the social sciences employ general laws, in history, "there will be no conscious and systematic application of a specific theory or model to the evidence."[48] Edelman does, however, endorse what were called limited laws in Chapter 1, saying that "historians can and often regularly do employ closed generalizations, which consist of time-conditioned, culturally relative but enduring regularities in human behavior."[49]

Other criticisms of social-scientific methodology come from historians who are concerned that the text, not a theoretical model, should take priority in history writing. Halpern charges that historians sometimes employ social-scientific

---

44.   Charles E. Carter, "A Discipline in Transition: The Contributions of the Social Sciences to the Study of the Hebrew Bible," in *Community, Identity, and Ideology: Social Science Approaches to the Hebrew Bible* (ed. Charles E. Carter and Carol Meyers; Sources for Biblical and Theological Study 6; Winona Lake, Ind.: Eisenbrauns, 1996), 3–36.

45.   McNutt, *Reconstructing the Society of Ancient Israel*, 15.

46.   For such critiques see Gary A. Herion, "The Impact of Modern and Social Science Assumptions on the Reconstruction of Israelite History," *JSOT* 34 (1986): 3–33; Deist, "Contingency, Continuity and Integrity in Historical Understanding," 102–6; Yamauchi, "The Current State of Old Testament Historiography," 31; Carter, "A Discipline in Transition," 23–26; McNutt, *Reconstructing the Society of Ancient Israel*, 25–31; and Daniel M. Master, "State Formation Theory and the Kingdom of Ancient Israel," *JNES* 60 (2001): 117–31. See also Gottwald, *The Tribes of Yahweh*, xliii. Here, Gottwald critiques his previous work, saying that "[*Tribes'*] predominant modernist stance is most evident in its claim that social science theory and method can comfortably appropriate and subsume the results of other critical practices without dissonance and without leaving 'loose ends' of any significance." This position, he now believes, was too optimistic.

47.   Scham, "The Days of the Judges," 40.

48.   Diana V. Edelman, "Doing History in Biblical Studies," in Edelman, ed., *The Fabric of History*, 13–25 (19).

49.   Ibid., 20.

models in a "scramble to make an end run around interpreting text."[50] Long believes that social-scientific models devalue the actions of individuals and consequently also the texts, such as the Bible, that tell of those actions.[51] Some historians also remain skeptical of the benefits of historians' forays into the social sciences. Miller has remarked that "it can hardly be said that the multi-disciplinary approach has produced any notable breakthroughs or compelling clarifications."[52] Even Gottwald has admitted that no social-scientific model applied to Israel has been able to explain fully the inception or persistence of the Israelite and Judean states.[53]

On the positive side, Carter has suggested some "remedies" for the potential pitfalls associated with interdisciplinary cooperation. He advocates taking a neutral view of primitive societies (so as not to have an oversimplified preconceived notion of them) and having an increased sensitivity to the complexity of social processes.[54] Carter concludes that "the most effective way to avoid overly reductionistic or deterministic analyses of Israelite society and culture is to adopt a methodology that is rigorous and self-critical,"[55] a proposition that can be understood as a call to incorporate aspects of objectivity into comparative research.

Outside of the discussion of social-scientific models in history, non-minimalists have little to say about other aspects of historical explanation. Two exceptions are Edelman and Deist.[56] Edelman, as seen above, rejects the place of covering laws, but accepts limited-law explanations for the past. She also argues that historians' creativity and "genius" show up during "conceptual invention," that is, the process of "link[ing] together pieces of evidence to form a coherent pattern of meaning," contending that historians draw on their daily experience to reconstruct the possibilities of the past.[57] Deist agrees that understanding human action requires analogy, which he calls "the product of the intuitive grasp [of the historian], the fertility and power of which depend on the experience and informedness of the individual imagination."[58] He argues that this intuitive process allows the historian to produce better explanations than those arrived at by scientific methods alone. Deist also promotes what he calls the "widely acknowledged scholarly criterion…of accepting *the most elegant* explanation for a series of observations. *Elegant* here means 'the most simple explanation that can, with the aid of the fewest auxiliary hypotheses, account for the maximum

50. Halpern, *The First Historians*, 5.
51. Long, *The Art of Biblical History*, 135–42.
52. Miller, "Reading the Bible Historically," 25.
53. Gottwald, *The Politics of Ancient Israel*, 115.
54. Carter, "A Discipline in Transition," 26–28.
55. Ibid., 28.
56. See also Ramsey, *The Quest for the Historical Israel*, 16–19.
57. Edelman, "Doing History in Biblical Studies," 15; cf. Ramsey, *The Quest for the Historical Israel*, 15–16. As noted in Chapter 3, in biblical studies this idea was promulgated by Ernst Troeltsch.
58. Deist, "Contingency, Continuity and Integrity in Historical Understanding," 109–10.

of observed phenomena.'"[59] Thus, the comments of Edelman and Deist address aspects of rational explanation as well as the degree to which modes of historical explanation completely explain the past.

The several types of historical explanation presented in this study are based on the assumption of past–present correspondence, which is the assumption that natural and human processes in the past occurred within the same boundaries and limitations as they do today. In modern practice, historical explanations also are based on rational thinking, which attributes occurrences to causes identifiable within a scientific, or secular, mindset. Some historians of ancient Israel, however, especially those who overtly operate out of a religious commitment, may at times find either or both of these premises difficult to hold, as they may require that historians separate their religious beliefs from their historical pursuits. For instance, contrary to the notion that events can and should be explained rationally, Long argues that "The historian may believe that God is the 'lord of history' sovereignly at work behind the scenes and intervening on occasion, and still remain a competent historian."[60] He denounces the "unnecessary tendency of the historical-critical method to exclude from the realm of history any notion of direct divine intervention."[61] The idea that historical explanation can leave room for the activity of God, however subconsciously prevalent it may be among historians of ancient Israel, is one that many historians are unlikely to accept. For instance, Provan, Long, and Longman, who, as discussed above, believe that God is active in the world (presumably in the past and in the present), do not claim that particular events in the past can be explained by divine activity.

Non-minimalist historians have also recognized the explanatory role narrative plays in modern history writing. In the words of Provan, Long, and Longman: "If a minimal definition of 'narrative' is '*a representation of a sequence of non-randomly connected events,*' then a minimal definition of 'narrative history' would be 'a representation of a sequence of non-randomly connected, actual events of the past.'"[62] Knauf has called narrative one level of history (the other two being structures and individuals). Through narrative, Knauf claims, "history adopts purpose and intent."[63] He clarifies, however, that the meaning of a historical narrative is different from the meaning of its constituent parts.[64] In other words, Knauf, like White, believes that historical narrative itself is a bearer of meaning. Deist agrees, arguing that selecting and combining events into a

59. Deist, *The Material Culture of the Bible*, 61.

60. Long, *The Art of Biblical History*, 134.

61. Ibid. His main objection, however, is that "This tendency leads to an a priori dismissal of many events recorded in the Bible and, in some cases, to a general skepticism toward the biblical text as a historical source" (p. 135).

62. Provan, Long, and Longman, *A Biblical History of Israel*, 84 (italics in original). The italicized phrase is quoted from Ann Rigney, "Narrativity and Historical Representation," *Poetics Today* 12 (1991): 591–601 (591).

63. Knauf, "From History to Interpretation," 48.

64. Ibid., 48–50.

narrative produces a whole with meaning that cannot be simplified into "detachable conclusions."[65]

Discussion among non-minimalists of the use of narrative for historical explanation and the "conscious act of constructing a picture of the whole"[66] that bears meaning prompts several questions already familiar from this study: Is narrative an ontological category and, therefore, appropriate or necessary for history writing? Do historians of ancient Israel operate with preconceived tropes? How do narrative histories differ from fictional accounts of the past? The first question does not appear to be of great concern to non-minimalist historians, though Provan, Long, and Longman agree with Carr that life has an inherent narrative structure.[67] The issue of tropes in histories of ancient Israel also is rarely addressed, though Gottwald has claimed that some scholars operate with preconceptions about Israel that are not necessarily based on evidence. Specifically, he identifies Dever and Lemche as scholars who have written "triumphalist" and "antitriumphalist" histories of Israel, respectively. In triumphalist histories, Israel emerges as a victor in history, primarily due to the persistence of Israelite beliefs, while in an antitriumphalist history, Israel merges with other cultures and does not have a special or unique destiny.[68] Becking's claim that historical representations are not constructed arbitrarily but that historical method dictates the "rules of the game"[69] is also germane to this topic. This line of thought holds that historical method is a universal procedure that guides the process of history writing, rather than the unconscious or conscious use of preconceived tropes, and shows a preliminary theoretical caution toward seeing literary shaping as the overriding interpretive factor for understanding historical writing.

The impact of the blurring of the distinction between fact and fiction on history has received some attention from non-minimalist scholars. Knauf takes a positive view of the predicament, saying that "Language wisely makes no difference between the textual mode of history and the mode of story: what is no longer real because it is past is told in the same mode as that which is not real because it is imagined."[70] Knauf's acknowledgment of the similarities between history and story, however, fails to address whether the distinction is critical. Barstad would say that it is not, as he has recommended that conventional

65. Deist, "Contingency, Continuity and Integrity in Historical Understanding," 111.

66. Ibid., 109. Deist (p. 108 n. 19) notes that knowledge of the whole may be "limited and only preliminary."

67. Provan, Long, and Longman, *A Biblical History of Israel*, 83–84. Here they also provide ten ways of describing narrative history (ex.: "Narratives may be distinguished from 'annals' or 'chronicles'") derived from Rigney's "Narrativity and Historical Representation."

68. Gottwald, "Triumphalist Versus Anti-Triumphalist Versions of Early Israel."

69. Becking, "Inscribed Seals," 68–69. Becking's "rules of the game" basically recapitulate empirical methodology. Cf. Lester L. Grabbe, "Are Historians of Ancient Palestine Fellow Creatures —or Different Animals?," in Grabbe, ed., *Can a "History of Israel" Be Written?*, 19–36 (21). Grabbe does not give a definition of historical method.

70. Knauf, "From History to Interpretation," 48. For other discussions that paint history's classification as literature in a positive light, see Provan, Long, and Longman, *A Biblical History of Israel*, 81, and Halpern, *The First Historians*, 5, 8.

history be replaced with "narrative history." Narrative history would not be concerned with verifiable truth, as fact and fiction "are equally interesting and equally relevant."[71] Halpern also acknowledges similarities between history and fiction and even calls history a type of fiction, but he does see an important difference between the two. He claims that unlike a writer of fiction, "the historian tries to avoid communicating what was not so."[72] As seen here and discussed above, however, Halpern stresses that historiographical intent on the part of the author delineates history from fictional accounts of the past. Younger draws a clear distinction between history and fiction, arguing that historical writing is "differentiated from fictional by means of its commitment to its subject matter ('real' rather than 'imaginary' events) rather than by form."[73] In other words, like the theorists discussed in Chapter 1, Younger notes that fiction and history have language and structure in common but that history's referent, the real world, ultimately differentiates it from fiction.

This examination of theoretical statements by non-minimalists about subjects and explanation in history shows that non-minimalists as a group generally see humans as valid subjects for Israel's history, while some include structures, as well. Furthermore, non-minimalists, as defined here, do not categorically denounce using Israel as a starting point for discussing the past, even if this Israel is related to the Israel the Bible describes. These assumptions stand in contrast to the minimalists, who theoretically dispose of the possibility of human subjects and the centrality of Israel in history. Like minimalists, however, non-minimalists consider both the advantages and the pitfalls of using social-scientific theory in history writing, and some have begun to address aspects of narrative in history writing. In short, non-minimalists see the enterprise of Israel's history as able to accommodate a number of approaches to subject and explanation. Of course, practices of evidence and evaluation and use form the crux of any attempt to describe or explain the past, and thus these will be considered next.

Evidence

By now it has been asserted several times that historians of ancient Israel turn to artifacts and texts, including texts uncovered by archaeology, as sources for their historical reconstructions. It has also been claimed that the value placed on the

71.   Barstad, "History and the Hebrew Bible," 61. He offers as an example a national history in which much of a community's own story about itself is included whether or not it can be verified. In some ways, Barstad's suggestion is reminiscent of late twentieth-century trends in anthropological history, discussed in Chapter 1, since the subject's self-definition would play an important role in the organization of the historian's presentation of it.

72.   Baruch Halpern, "Erasing History: The Minimalist Assault on Ancient Israel," *BAR* 11, no. 6 (1995): 26–35, 47 (34). Seeking to clarify how Halpern can argue that history is a type of fiction and yet believe that the authors of the Bible were historians who accurately reported events, Long claims that when Halpern speaks of fiction, he "has in mind *form* (i.e. the way the story is told)." Long himself prefers using the term "artistic" to refer to the creative process of writing history in order to distance it from the potentially negative implications of the term "fiction" (*The Art of Biblical History*, 235–36).

73.   Younger, *Ancient Conquest Accounts*, 35.

Bible as a historical source is a fundamental difference between minimalists and both their predecessors and non-minimalists. In the previous chapter, it was observed that minimalist skepticism about the Bible began a debate about practical matters of evidence evaluation and use that evolved into a discussion of epistemology. Therefore, this examination of non-minimalists' use of evidence in writing histories of Israel will include analysis of assumptions as well as practical and epistemological issues.

Texts

Minimalists have made a major break from mainstream twentieth-century historical criticism by reading the Bible as a document from the Persian period or later that primarily can inform us about general perceptions of the past and ideologies at those particular times. Non-minimalists, on the other hand, by and large are reluctant to dismiss the Bible as evidence for reconstructing aspects of the Late Bronze–Early Iron Age transition and the Iron Age in Palestine.[74] These scholars are aware of the problems the biblical account presents for historical reconstruction, and they recognize reasons that the Bible could be distrusted as a historical source. Miller and Hayes identify many of them: the biblical concept that there was a golden age in the past, the Bible's schematic chronology, divine direction of human affairs, the lineal genealogical descent of most of the Bible's major figures, common storyteller's motifs and folk traditions found in the Bible, general improbabilities in the accounts, the composite and contradictory character of the accounts, and theological intentions in the Bible.[75] Provan has also pointed to the Bible's selectivity and apparent intention in reporting, its overall literary character, and its "presumed lateness" as other factors contributing to the doubt historians have about the reliability of the Bible's version of the past.[76]

On the other hand, several assumptions contribute to non-minimalists' cautious optimism toward the using the Bible as evidence for the past. For one, as Miller and Hayes point out, texts are historians' main primary sources, and deciding "how [a text] is to be interpreted and what sort of historical information can be derived from it" is the most important task of historians.[77] It follows that since the Bible is the main potential primary source of evidence for ancient Israel, historians must try to identify evidence in it.[78] Similarly, Halpern has

---

74. Davies, "What Separates a Minimalist from a Maximalist?"

75. Miller and Hayes, *A History of Ancient Israel and Judah*, 58–63.

76. Provan, "Ideologies, Literary and Critical," 595–98. For an earlier exposition of the story-like character of the Bible, see Barr, "Story and History in Biblical Theology."

77. Miller and Hayes, *A History of Ancient Israel and Judah*, 75. Calling texts the only primary sources for history of course relegates artifacts to a secondary position. See the discussion of artifacts and their combination with texts in history writing, below, and J. Maxwell Miller, "Old Testament History and Archaeology," *BA* 50 (1987): 53–63 (58), and idem, "Is It Possible to Write a History of Israel Without Relying on the Hebrew Bible?," in Edelman, ed., *The Fabric of History*, 93–102.

78. Miller and Hayes outline their own approach, which they call a "compromise position" between using the Bible uncritically and ignoring it (Miller and Hayes, eds., *A History of Ancient*

specifically accused minimalists of "abdicating" the historian's responsibility to consider the text carefully for what information it might provide.[79] Furthermore, though non-minimalists concede that the information in the Bible likely was skewed towards literary or theological ends, they assert that these intentions do not necessarily prevent statements that correspond to historical reality from being present in the text. In Barstad's words: "Even if the historiographers of the Hebrew Bible have as their prime aim the production of 'ideology'…this does not imply that these texts do not yield a lot of historical information."[80] Halpern, as seen above, has introduced another assumption that would allow the Bible to be used as evidence, that of authorial intent. He claims that the authors of the Bible "had authentic antiquarian intentions. They meant to furnish fair and accurate representations of Israelite antiquity," and, using ancient sources, did so.[81] On the other hand, Grabbe asserts that "too much has been made of the aim and purpose of the texts," saying that an author's stated intent to write history does not guarantee that the history is reliable, just as the absence of such intent does not necessarily make the product unreliable.[82]

Another marked difference between minimalists and non-minimalists is the latter's tolerance for using the Bible as evidence without a defined theory of the composition of the entirety of the Bible. Thus, where Davies preferred systematic explanations for the biblical books, non-minimalists generally accept attempts to understand the Bible that include what Davies would call ad hoc explanations for the formation of the biblical text. One argument in support of this position has been made by Amit, who examined the Hebrew Bible for its

---

Israel and Judah, 76–79). For another affirmation of a middle-of-the-road approach see Dever, *Who Were the Early Israelites?*, 226.

79. Halpern, "Erasing History," 29. For example, Halpern claims that minimalists dismiss the historicity of the united monarchy because "there is a possibility that cannot be utterly excluded on the basis of the evidence that the whole construct is a lie" (ibid.).

80. Hans M. Barstad, *The Myth of the Empty Land: A Study in the History and Archaeology of Judah During the "Exilic" Period* (Symbolae Osolenses Fasciculi Suppletorii; Oslo: Scandinavian University Press, 1996), 36 n. 18. Cf., e.g., Rainer Albertz's study of New Babylonian royal inscriptions ("Die Exilszeit als Ernstfall für eine historische Rekonstruktion ohne biblische Texte: Die neubabylonischen Königsinschriften als 'Primarquelle,'" in *Leading Captivity Captive: "The Exile" as Historiography and Ideology* [ed. Lester L. Grabbe; JSOTSup 278; Sheffield: Sheffield Academic Press, 1998], 22–39 [36]), where he argues that although ideological presentation was typical of such inscriptions, that "es [ist] falsch, aus dem stark theologischen und tendenziösen Charakter einer Geschichtsschreibung deren Unhistorizität zu folgern."

81. Halpern, *The First Historians*, 3. In this opinion, Halpern (pp. 29–32) claims to be following Martin Noth and his thesis that the Deuteronomic Historian faithfully used his sources. Nicolai Winther-Nielsen ("Fact, Fiction, and Language Use: Can Modern Pragmatics Improve on Halpern's Case for History in Judges?," in Long, Baker, and Wenham, eds., *Windows Into Old Testament History*, 44–81) claims that a pragmatic theory of communication can also lend support to Halpern's claim that the Bible's authors intended to give factual reports.

82. Grabbe, "Fellow Creatures—or Different Animals?," 32. In addition, Grabbe has argued that the genre of historical fiction, in which there are "fictional characters and plot but…attention to authenticity of historical context" is not attested in antiquity (p. 27). This argument, however, would be hard to defend even within the biblical text, considering modern (and ancient) interpretations of books such as Daniel, Jonah, Esther, and Ruth.

ideological and historical elements. She determined that the two must be considered separately and that scholars "should avoid general statements and assumptions with regard to any of the books."[83] Additionally, many scholars have disputed the minimalists' notion that the Hebrew Bible was written primarily in the Persian period or later, a central thesis of explanations that consider the entire process of the Bible's composition and formation to be late. For example, Avi Hurvitz has argued that Biblical Hebrew is a language that shows chronological development (contra Knauf and Davies), providing several examples to support his argument.[84] Furthermore, Barr points out that more research on Old Persian literature and language must be done before Davies' hypothesis of a Persian-period origin for the Bible can be accepted.[85]

Other important critiques of the minimalists' theory of a systematic, late composition process for the Bible come from Grabbe, who has questioned Thompson's association of certain motifs and writing practices with the Hellenistic world,[86] and Barstad, who has undertaken a similar critique of Lemche.[87] Also, Zechariah Kallai contends that the argument for the Bible's late date and intentional composition "inevitably presupposes an extremely compressed literary process, which does not allow sufficient time" for the development of the types, patterns, and motifs found in the literature.[88] Scholars have also asked why late writers would have invented the particular personalities and social structures found in the Bible, arguing that the best explanation for their appearance in the text is that they were real.[89]

As discussed in Chapter 2, hypothesizing about a text's origin and transmission history, that is, explaining the process of the formation of the text, does not always help historians determine what is factual in a text. Few non-minimalist historians have commented on the relationship of a text's date to its reliability. Besides Grabbe's opinion that intent and reliability do not necessarily coincide, Barstad has also observed that the question of a text's date is separate from "the greater question of the reliability of the biblical traditions for historical reconstructions in general."[90] Halpern, however, apparently does see a connection between date and reliability, as he argues that 2 Samuel provides some reliable

---

83.   Amit, *History and Ideology*, 104.

84.   Hurvitz, "The Historical Quest for 'Ancient Israel' and the Linguistic Evidence," 301–15. For an interesting philosophical discussion of finding history in language itself, see Revathi Krishnaswamy, "History in Language, Language in History," *Clio* 34 (2004): 1–18.

85.   Barr, *History and Ideology in the Old Testament*, 91.

86.   Lester L. Grabbe, "Hat die Bibel doch Recht? A Review of T. L. Thompson's *The Bible in History*," *SJOT* 14 (2000): 117–39. (*The Bible in History* is the British title of Thompson's *The Mythic Past*.)

87.   Barstad, "Is the Hebrew Bible a Hellenistic Book?," 129–51.

88.   Zecharia Kallai, "Biblical Historiography and Literary History: A Programmatic Survey," *VT* 49 (1999): 338–50 (339–40); cf. Ernest Nicholson, "Current 'Revisionism' and the Literature of the Old Testament," in Day, ed. *In Search of Pre-Exilic Israel*, 1–22.

89.   E.g. Ahlström, *The History of Ancient Palestine*, 36; Gottwald, *The Politics of Ancient Israel*, 22–23.

90.   Barstad, "Is the Hebrew Bible a Hellenistic Book?," 131.

facts about David because it dates to the end of the ninth century BCE at the latest (and possibly to the late tenth century).[91]

Although for the most part non-minimalist scholars generally are content to rely on ad hoc explanations for the biblical text and apparently have reached no theoretical consensus about the association between a text's date and its historical reliability, Provan stands out as a dissenter on both counts. Provan, a vocal critic of the minimalists, also criticizes what he sees as theoretical and methodological uncertainty among most historians of ancient Israel. He argues that no historians of ancient Israel have fully engaged the problems associated with using ancient texts as historical sources. He presents his concern as epistemological rather than methodological, contending that rational critical inquiry requires questioning history's preconceptions about how historians should draw conclusions from evidence.

Provan laid out his position in a number of articles,[92] and continued this line of argument in detail in *A Biblical History of Israel* (writing with Long and Longman). There he charges that selective use of the biblical text for history, that is, the practice of including the Bible's information about some biblical figures and events in histories but not others, starts historians of ancient Israel down a slippery slope that inevitably leads to the radical skepticism of texts characteristic of the minimalists. The book specifically takes issue with Miller and Hayes and Soggin, who consider the biblical account a potentially reliable source for the past beginning with the Judges and with David, respectively. The claim of Provan and his coauthors is that, from a literary standpoint, aspects of these stories, and of stories describing later periods, are equally as fantastic, romantic, and legendary as are the Bible's stories that describe earlier periods.[93] Thus, scholars should not exclude stories of Israel's early history on the basis of such considerations alone. Their approach, however logical it sounds, ignores Miller and Hayes' and Soggin's reasons for beginning to use the Bible when they do, which are based on external evidence found in archaeology and other texts.[94] Nevertheless, the assumption behind Provan, Long, and Longman's method is that ancient texts such as the Bible should be given the benefit of the doubt.[95] Thus, they propose to use almost all of the biblical texts, beginning with the stories of the patriarchs, in their history of Israel.

91.   Halpern, *David's Secret Demons*, 57–72. Similar claims about the reliability of parts of the story of the exodus, especially details in the Song of the Sea, appear in his "Eyewitness Testimony." See also Nadav Na'aman, "In Search of Reality Behind the Account of David's Wars with Israel's Neighbors," *IEJ* 52 (2002): 200–24 (220–24), and Yamauchi, "The Current State of Old Testament Historiography," 26.

92.   Provan, "In the Stable with the Dwarves"; idem, "Ideologies, Literary and Critical."

93.   Provan, Long, and Longman, *A Biblical History of Israel*, 9–18.

94.   Provan's opinions on the value of such evidence for verification of the Bible's claims will be discussed below, but it can be noted here that he would not find the presence of correlations between external evidence and the Bible necessary for using the Bible as evidence.

95.   Cf. Anthony J. Frendo, "Back to Basics: A Holistic Approach to the Problem of the Emergence of Ancient Israel," in Day, ed., *In Search of Pre-Exilic Israel*, 41–64.

Provan also challenges the assumption that relates a text's date to its reliability by arguing that historians' preferences for eyewitness or near-eyewitness accounts, nonideological accounts, and "accounts which fit our preconceptions about what is normal, possible, and so on" ought to be reexamined.[96] The issue is pursued in detail in *A Biblical History of Israel*:

> No good reason at all exists to believe that those claiming to be eyewitnesses are not (like the later reporters of events) interpreters of those events, nor is there any reason to assume on principle that their testimony is going to be more or less trustworthy. There is, indeed, no reason to believe that earlier accounts are generally more reliable than later accounts. No necessary correlation at all, in fact, exists between the sort of interaction that "witnesses" have with events and the quality of access to events provided to others through them.[97]

This claim contradicts generally accepted notions of the reliability of historical evidence (and many legal traditions that generally do not allow second-hand testimony, or hearsay, in court). In addition, Provan adds to this point a challenge to the assumption, held by many minimalists, that texts are "relevant in the first instance to their own times" and only secondarily to the period they describe "precarious," and asks why historians should accept it.[98] It should be noted that Provan and his colleagues do not advocate a complete change in historical method, as they too ask basic questions about a text's origin, provenance, and so on. They are, however, urging historians to examine more closely the assumptions they bring to this process and the conclusions they draw from the answers they give. The discussion of issues relating to the primacy of eyewitness sources for history writing, the relationship of a text's date to its reliability, and ad hoc use of the texts for history writing that Provan has instigated has not yet worked its way through the discipline. Perhaps the next decade will bring firmer theoretical support for certain practices, and non-minimalists will become more clearly differentiated on these matters. Chapter 6 of this study will consider these issues and offer some new opinions on them, as well.

In summary, non-minimalists, like minimalists, recognize that ancient textual sources, especially the Bible, may be ideologically biased. In the case of non-minimalists, however, this observation does not preclude factual information being identified in such texts. Non-minimalists' ease with theories of the Bible's composition that do not comprehensively explain the entire process also

96. Provan, "In the Stable with the Dwarves," 296–97.

97. Provan, Long, and Longman, *A Biblical History of Israel*, 57. Also, they argue that oral tradition may have provided reliable information for the biblical writers since, they claim, many societies place strict controls on oral storytelling that keep the account essentially the same through multiple retellings. Unfortunately, they give no examples to support this claim (pp. 57–58). Henige ("Deciduous, Perennial or Evergreen?," 399) gives a few examples that critique this assumption (though he is responding to comments made by Provan in previous articles).

98. Provan, "In the Stable with the Dwarves," 292 n. 24. Similarly, Gruber ("The Ancient Israel Debate," 11) takes issue with what she sees as a trend in which "To this day books and articles written in the tradition of modern biblical criticism employ the terms 'exilic,' 'post-exilic,' and 'close to the exile' as code words for 'unauthoritative.'"

distinguish them from minimalists. Non-minimalists' approaches to texts, particularly the Bible, have several practical applications. First, the assumptions non-minimalists bring to texts as evidence allow for many different types of information to be found in them. Unlike minimalists, non-minimalists do not rule out the possibility that reliable specific information about individuals, particularly ones living in pre-exilic times, could be identified in the Bible. This position is expedient since, as seen above, non-minimalists in general want to include human subjects in histories of ancient Israel. Second, leaving open the possibility that late or ideologically biased sources could preserve reliable information allows the Bible to potentially provide data for the reconstruction of the formation of the monarchy in Israel and even events farther back in time. Of course, historians themselves make the final judgment calls about whether textual sources are reliable for writing about Israel's past.[99] Also, like other historians, non-minimalists seek all possible sources of evidence for their historical reconstructions, and thus base their reconstructions on assumptions about how artifacts can be used and how interpretations of them relate to texts.

Artifacts and the Combination of Texts and Artifacts

The archaeology of Syria–Palestine has been linked to interest in the Bible since the discipline's inception in the late nineteenth century. As seen above, minimalists have argued that Syro-Palestinian archaeology should separate itself from biblically influenced presuppositions and frameworks. They have not been alone in this opinion, nor did they invent it. The most prominent early opponent of biblical archaeology was Dever, who in 1981 reviewed how the archaeology of Syria–Palestine had changed under the influence of new archaeology. Dever thought the changes were beneficial, and contended that Syro-Palestinian archaeology should continue to move toward a social-scientific, theory-based modeling approach.[100] Seven years later, Dever claimed that this new approach had helped early or "proto-" Israel come to light, elucidated the culture of the Philistines, and shown aspects of urbanization and centralization in Palestine in the Iron Age.[101] Archaeology conceived outside of the goals of history, Dever claimed, had indeed contributed to historical understanding.

---

99. Two ends of the spectrum of non-minimalists' opinions about the reliability of the Bible can be seen in Grabbe, "Fellow Creatures—or Different Animals?," and V. Philips Long, "How Reliable are Biblical Reports? Repeating Lester Grabbe's Comparative Experiment," *VT* 41 (2002): 367–84, discussed in more detail in the next chapter.

100. Dever, "The Impact of the 'New Archaeology' on Syro-Palestinian Archaeology," 21. See also Øystein S. LaBianca, "Sociocultural Anthropology and Syro-Palestinian Archaeology," in *Benchmarks in Time and Culture: An Introduction to Palestinian Archaeology* (ed. Joel F. Drinkard, Gerald L. Mattingly, and J. Maxwell Miller; Archaeology and Biblical Studies; Atlanta: Scholars Press, 1988), 369–87. For a recent discussion of biblical archaeology, see Zevit, "Three Debates," 6–9.

101. William G. Dever, "Impact of the 'New Archaeology'," in Drinkard, Mattingly, and Miller, eds., *Benchmarks in Time and Culture*, 337–52.

Despite Dever's enthusiasm, historians of ancient Israel have questioned the feasibility of independent interpretation of artifacts. Some believe that artifacts are "mute" and doubt that they could be meaningfully interpreted without the help of texts. Proponents of autonomous archaeology counter that archaeologists use their own theoretical framework to interpret the artifacts and that historians' inability to appreciate this is due to the heavy weight they give textual sources.[102] In turn, the possibility of forming frameworks for the interpretation of artifacts from Iron Age Palestine without using concepts from the Bible has also been called into question, notably by Miller, who points out that "Simply to use the name 'Israel' in association with the Iron Age means to draw on written sources."[103] Another objection to using archaeology independently to reconstruct the past revolves around its use of what Dever called "timeless laws of the cultural process."[104] For instance, Edelman, as seen above, claims that sociological models do not suffice to explain the past, but that historians are ultimately better equipped than archaeologists to synthesize many different types of data into a historical reconstruction.[105]

Non-minimalists also have varying ideas about how archaeology and artifacts should be used in history. Miller espouses a traditional view, arguing that archaeology's findings should be subordinate to the conclusions drawn from texts. While acknowledging that sometimes archaeology can drastically alter the historian's conception of the past, Miller asserts that using archaeology illustratively is the "most appropriate" practice for the historian.[106] Similarly, Long writes "archaeology's greatest potential [for historical study] is in the delineation of the general milieu (cultural, material, etc.) within which specific events may have taken place."[107] In history, Long contends, the text always retains priority; archaeology must not "supplant" the written sources.[108] Some scholars, however, appear to hope to recover more from artifacts than an illustration of the biblical text. Theoretical statements to this effect are difficult to locate, but some recent publications can be used to show how non-minimalists use artifacts as independent sources of evidence in history writing.

Isserlin states at the beginning of his *The Israelites* that correlation of specific artifacts with certain events or people described in the Bible is almost impossible, and argues that archaeology should not be put to this use.[109] Thus, archaeology can only offer broad insights into Israelite culture. On the other hand, he claims that the biblical text, as well as other ancient texts, are also incomplete

102. E.g. Knauf, "From History to Interpretation," 41.

103. Miller, "Is It Possible to Write a History of Israel Without Relying on the Hebrew Bible?," 94; see also his "Old Testament History and Archaeology," 51–62.

104. Dever, "The Impact of the 'New Archaeology' on Syro-Palestinian Archaeology," 21.

105. Edelman, "Doing History in Biblical Studies," 22–23. Or, as Binford put it ("Archaeological Perspectives," 11), "an accurate and meaningful history is more than a generalized narrative of the changes in composition of the archeological record through time."

106. Miller, "Old Testament History and Archaeology," 60.

107. Long, *The Art of Biblical History*, 145.

108. Ibid., 148.

109. As did Noth, see Chapter 3.

and selective sources of evidence for ancient Israel, and that the two must be combined in order to present a comprehensive view of Israelite culture.[110] The structure of Isserlin's book is topical, with archaeology and texts each providing information on subjects such as agriculture and religion.[111] Merging of artifacts and information derived independently from texts can also occur on a smaller scale, such as in Jeffrey Blakely's study that argues that Halpern's map of David and Solomon's kingdom, derived from the Bible, coincides with evidence from archaeology.[112]

A contrasting approach to combining artifacts and texts in a theoretically equal manner is using artifacts to verify textual claims. Artifacts used in this manner include nonbiblical texts, such as inscriptions, annals, chronicles, and other records from the ancient Near East uncovered by archaeology. This approach can be seen in *The Bible Unearthed* by Finkelstein and Silberman. These authors believe artifacts provide independent and different information from texts, and state that the goal of their study is "reconstruct[ing] the history of ancient Israel on the basis of archaeological evidence—the only source of information on the biblical period that was not extensively emended, edited, or censored by many generations of biblical scribes."[113] Based on these assumptions, they use artifacts to ask questions about the Bible's veracity.[114] On the other hand, Dever has published two comprehensive studies that claim that the Bible accurately represents many aspects of ancient material culture and that, reciprocally, artifacts can help illuminate and even verify parts of the Bible.[115]

110. Isserlin, *The Israelites*, 10–20.

111. Keel and Uehlinger take a similar approach in their history of Israelite religion, relying heavily on artifacts as sources separate from, but relatable to, the biblical text. See Othmar Keel and Christoph Uehlinger, *Gods, Goddesses and Images of God in Ancient Israel* (Minneapolis: Fortress, 1998); trans. of *Göttinnen, Götter und Gottessymbole* (QD 134; Fribourg: Herder, 1992). Their approach is discussed in more detail in Chapter 6.

112. Jeffrey A. Blakely, "Reconciling Two Maps: Archaeological Evidence for the Kingdoms of David and Solomon," *BASOR* 327 (2002): 49–54.

113. Finkelstein and Silberman, *The Bible Unearthed*, 23.

114. Though Finkelstein and Silberman's method is akin to methods proposed and used by minimalists, they are not minimalists since they do not shy away from making ancient Israel the center of their historical investigation. Dever ("Excavating the Hebrew Bible, or Burying It Again?" [review of Israel Finkelstein and Neil Asher Silberman, *The Bible Unearthed: Archaeology's New Vision of Ancient Israel and the Origin of Its Sacred Texts*], *BASOR* 322 (2001): 67–77 [69]) expresses frustration that Finkelstein and Silberman do not address the impact of their method and conclusions for the current debate in the discipline: "whether they like it or not, the publication of this provocative book will propel its authors right into the thick of the battle... [A]lthough Finkelstein and Silberman are moderates, the biblical revisionists will try to co-opt them and will then try to use their archaeological exposition to vindicate their own extremist positions." See also Thompson's review of *The Bible Unearthed* ("Methods and Results"), where he both praises and criticizes Finkelstein and Silberman.

115. Dever, *What Did the Biblical Writers Know?*; idem, *Who Were the Early Israelites?* Central to Dever's thesis are the Merneptah Stele, the hundreds of Late Bronze Age and early Iron Age villages founded in the central hill-country of Palestine on virgin soil, and the continuity with Canaanite culture evidenced both by the material record (such as pottery) and textual record (such as language and religion). Cf. Provan, Long, and Longman, *A Biblical History of Israel*, 100: "if we

Most non-minimalists seem to keep to the middle of the road on the issue of whether texts and artifacts can be used to substantiate each other's claims. Ahlström has articulated the moderate position, claiming that "harmonization" of texts and artifacts for writing about Israel's past cannot and should not always be done. Problems Ahlström names include texts steering the interpretation of artifacts (especially since he sees the text as biased in favor of a Jerusalem-centered version of history), and the possibility of conflicts between artifacts and claims of the text. On the other hand, he notes, archaeology has significantly broadened our knowledge about ancient Israel and the background of the Bible.[116]

Provan has added another dimension to the discussion by directly questioning the assumption that the claims of a text such as the Bible need to be doubted until verified by external evidence such as artifacts. He asks:

> Why should verification be a prerequisite for our acceptance of a tradition as valuable in respect of historical reality? Why should not ancient historical texts rather be given the benefit of the doubt in regard to their statements about the past unless there are compelling reasons to consider them unreliable in these statements and with due regard (of course) to their literary and ideological features?[117]

In addition, the first part of *A Biblical History of Israel* includes an extended discussion of this question, one that again reaches into epistemology. Human knowledge, claim Provan, Long, and Longman, is always based on testimony. Put another way, in order to know anything, humans must have faith in others' testimony. The authors point out that in everyday life people willingly believe many things others tell them without skepticism. Why, then, should the same credence not be applied to the biblical testimony about the past?[118]

It is important to understand that Provan, Long, and Longman's claim that texts such as the Bible should be given the benefit of the doubt is made solely on the basis of the notion of faith in testimony; arguments such as Halpern's for a text's reliability due to the author's historiographic intentions provide only secondary support. Furthermore, they blame the current evidentiary crisis in the discipline on misguided dependence on science as a model for history writing, and place themselves in what they see as a long line of dissent from this idea that has developed over the course of the twentieth century.[119] Provan and his

have understood our biblical texts properly, and if they are testifying truly about the past, then we should expect convergence between the biblical testimony and the interpretations of the archaeological data."

116. Ahlström, "The Role of Archaeological and Literary Remains."

117. Provan, "In the Stable with the Dwarves," 291–92.

118. Similarly, Younger (*Ancient Conquest Accounts*, 337) has argued that "The reader of a historical text must curb his skepticism in order not to misconstrue the obvious... He must willingly suspend his disbelief in order to 'participate' in the world of the text." Cf. also Alan Millard, "Story, History, and Theology," in Millard, Hoffmeier, and Baker, eds., *Faith, Tradition, and History*, 37–64 (64): "the historian and the commentator are obliged to treat the reports [of divinely influenced events] as factual evidence of ancient events."

119. Provan, Long, and Longman, *A Biblical History of Israel*, 39–43. The positions that Provan, Long, and Longman see as dissenting from scientific history, however, could also be seen as accommodations to scientific history that retained important aspects of empirical methodology.

colleagues' challenge of skepticism's place in empirical history opens the possibility for discussing a number of fundamental questions: Should the history of ancient Israel be considered a scientific enterprise? What role does skepticism play in history, scientific or not? As in the cases of Provan's other epistemological questions about evidence, it appears that historians of ancient Israel have not yet had time to digest or respond to his arguments.[120] Therefore, some preliminary responses to Provan and some suggestions for further discussion will be made in Chapter 6.

In summary, whereas minimalists are in general agreement that (1) artifacts take precedence over texts as evidence for historians and (2) artifacts do not support the reliability of the biblical text, non-minimalists show a range of views about the relationship of artifacts to texts. Some let artifacts take precedence over texts, some place both types of evidence side-by-side, and some claim that in order for artifacts to be interpreted texts must be used. Also, some non-minimalist historians use artifacts to illustrate the world of the Bible, whereas others use artifacts to strengthen, or weaken, the text's claims about the past. Going further, Provan is willing to let claims from ancient texts such as the Bible potentially stand without any reference to other types of evidence. Thus, while minimalist and non-minimalist historians of ancient Israel have been seen to generally agree on methodological procedures to be applied to texts but to differ in assumptions and conclusions about them, in the case of artifacts there exists a variety of assumptions, methods, and conclusions. Yet on the whole, the attention both minimalists and non-minimalists pay to artifacts show that the enthusiasm for the information artifacts can provide about the past still exists among historians of ancient Israel.

Truth

This study has claimed that historians, including minimalists, usually adhere to a correspondence theory of truth. Consequently, for most scholars, a true history relates what actually happened in the past. Discussions of truth among non-minimalist historians of ancient Israel, however, demonstrate that a new conception of history's truth is emerging in the discipline. One aspect of this modified understanding of historical truth is the realization that historical representation is an imperfect and complicated task. Brettler notes that historians "must remember the tentative nature of their reconstructions."[121] Barstad also says that history "does not want to tell *any* story about the past, it wants to tell the *most likely* story, to account for the reality of what happened in the past."[122] Barstad's comment implies that although history "wants" to tell what really happened, it may not be able to. It follows that non-minimalists accept that sometimes historical conclusions can at best be called probable or

---

120. With the notable exception of Henige, from outside the discipline.
121. Brettler, *Creation of History*, 142.
122. Barstad, "History and the Hebrew Bible," 44.

likely.[123] For instance, McNutt suggests that "history is not so much what 'really' happened in the past as it is what historians can convince us 'probably' happened."[124] Becking has gone as far as providing a ratings scale that indicates the likelihood of certain historical conclusions, demonstrating it by evaluating evidence provided by inscribed seals and the Bible.[125]

The professions by non-minimalists that history writing always gives an incomplete picture of the past and that probable reconstructions are sometimes the best the historian can offer are at home in twentieth-century modernist and postmodernist understandings of history. As Zevit points out, the relativity and uncertainty of historical reconstruction formed a core assumption of history as it was practiced by most historians in the twentieth century (Zevit's second paradigm).[126] Also, postmodernism has emphasized that the inherent biases of the historian, the historian's mental construction of the past, and the process of constructing a narrative prevent the past from being objectively and completely represented. It has been shown that non-minimalists are aware of these issues. In addition, historians of ancient Israel since Albright, like historians of the late twentieth century in general, have largely refrained from including grand narratives or overt indications of a substantive philosophy of history in their works.[127] On the other hand, consideration of other postmodernist ideas of history, such as the suggestion that the authoritative voice should be completely removed from history, and Lyotard's contention that historians should construct small narratives, do not seem to inspire much theoretical reflection among non-minimalist historians of ancient Israel at this time.

Gottwald has described how he thinks historical truth should be envisioned in light of poststructuralism and postmodernism. He champions a type of historical truth that he calls "relational, inferential, hypothetical, and constructivist."[128] In other words, modern and ancient histories can be understood as constructions, "each alleging possible or probable 'correspondence'" with reality.[129] He also

---

123. Grabbe ("Reflections," 188) notes that in the first meeting of the European Seminar on Historical Methodology, participants generally agreed that "probable" could be defined as the "degree to which something is likely to happen based on common experience." Minimalists, as seen in the previous chapter, believe that using probability as an historical criterion permits historians to assert the past reality of things for which there is very little evidence.

124. McNutt, *Reconstructing the Society of Ancient Israel*, 7.

125. Becking, "Inscribed Seals," 75–83.

126. Zevit, *Religions of Ancient Israel*, 39–48.

127. See, e.g., the discussion Provan, Long, and Longman, *A Biblical History of Israel*, 103–4. McNutt is an example of a scholar who eschews any semblance of an overarching plan, preferring to collect and evaluate different ideas about Israelite society: "Each perspective is worth considering, and reconsidering, as we engage in the task of constructing and reconstructing histories of ancient Israel" (*Reconstructing the Society of Ancient Israel*, 9). On the other hand, a substantive philosophy of history, although not overt, may be implied in histories of ancient Israel, as will be discussed in detail in Chapter 6.

128. Gottwald, *The Tribes of Yahweh*, xxxvii.

129. Ibid., xli. Gottwald goes on to discuss how at the time *The Tribes of Yahweh* originally was written, he believed its reconstruction to correspond to, or mirror, reality but now realizes the impossibility of that goal.

writes that "the textuality of all history and the inevitably constructed nature of every reading of the past" should not lead scholars "to forgo historical reconstructions but to offer them with greater self-awareness as to their hypothetical character, and to acknowledge that multiple readings of past history are in principle as tenable as multiple readings of present history."[130] This constructivist understanding of history, Gottwald claims, allows historians to free themselves from the search for the most objectively true reconstruction and to ask themselves "how thoroughly we have attended to the full range of data relevant to our constructions and how carefully we have assessed the role of ideology in our own constructions in active dialogue with other ideologically shaped constructions."[131] The history of Israel, Gottwald argues, could greatly benefit from such an understanding of historical truth since knowing what actually occurred in ancient Israel is extremely difficult.[132]

In a similar vein, Deist has argued that the relative, nonobjective status of the historian can actually assist in the search for truth. Following Kant, he opines:

> If…parties would accept the *relativity* of their observational perspectives, an opportunity [could be] created for them to argue about the better observational position, to formulate *hypotheses* on the shape of the perceived object, or to accept their views to be complementary. It is therefore possible wholeheartedly to endorse the relativity of observation *without* giving up the search for validity… Such a debate probably will not and cannot lead to the discovery or formulation of a "universal truth," but it may, at the very least, allow for a *better argued option*.[133]

Proposing that history writing be judged by a constructivist, hypothetical mode of truth is not necessarily antithetical to the quest to determine what actually happened in the past. It can be seen, rather, as an attempt to retain aspects of truth by correspondence within the postmodern context that recognizes the relativity and mediacy of all statements about the past.

Since historians traditionally have been overwhelmingly partial to the correspondence theory of truth, it is not surprising that few historians of ancient Israel appear to champion a coherence theory of truth. Some scholars, however, come close to doing so by arguing that a history of ancient Israel must share some features with the biblical accounts. For instance, the essays in *Faith, Tradition, and History* (ed. Millard, Hoffmeier, and Baker) revisit a number of the biblical texts that minimalist, and sometimes mainstream, historians no longer use as historical evidence in order to argue for their historical worth. Put another way, the essays in this book seek to demonstrate that true statements about ancient Israel in many cases do cohere with the biblical report. Provan, Long, and Longman's *A Biblical History of Israel* exhibits a similar opinion. They write: "Even a 'paraphrase of the biblical text' would likely be a surer guide to the real past, in our view, than the replacement story offered by those

130. Gottwald, *The Politics of Ancient Israel*, 4.
131. Gottwald, *The Tribes of Yahweh*, xlii.
132. The alternative, remaining with a correspondence theory, "seems to leave only the options of despairing subjectivity or willful dogmatism" (ibid., xli.).
133. Deist, *The Material Culture of the Bible*, 42 (italics in original).

who systematically avoid the biblical text in seeking to speak about that past."[134] Of course, scholars arguing that Israel's history should cohere with the Bible defend such claims using arguments that support the Bible's value as evidence. Thus, the reasoning and assumptions behind claims that history can and should cohere at points with the Bible is intertwined with assumptions about the evaluation and use of evidence.

As for pragmatic or instrumental truth in history, Halpern recognizes that history provides communities with an aid to cohesion,[135] and Gottwald has examined "The Legacy of Israelite Politics" in the epilogue to his *The Politics of Ancient Israel*.[136] With modern Israel in mind, Mayer Gruber argues that claims that the patriarchs, exodus, and united monarchy never happened are problematic for so-called "secular Israelis" because they (unknowingly) have "adopted Wellhausen's view that the authentic basis for the life of the new Israel was the Israelite heritage of the pre-exilic, i.e., the pre-586 BCE era."[137] She suggests that for Israelite history to be beneficial to society, historians must actively further "truth and liberation" for all people[138] and "cease...to see the post-exilic era in the history of Israel/Judaism as an abyss of no interest to either religion or history."[139] The majority of non-minimalists, however, have not rushed to examine openly the potential consequences of their historical conclusions for modern-day political or religious communities, perhaps because correspondent, not pragmatic, ideas of truth still hold sway for most of these historians.

While some non-minimalist historians have attempted to understand historical truth by combining aspects of correspondent truth with postmodern ideas, others have attempted to define historical truth in a way that combines aspects of correspondence, coherence, and instrumentalist theories of truth. For example, Long writes, "we might say that historical reconstructions that are *coherent* with all that we now know about a subject may be deemed reliable guides to the past, and may be assumed (barring discovery of conflicting evidence) to *correspond* to the past in a manner similar to the way in which a representational painting corresponds to its subject."[140] Deist also contends that truth has several components, or, more specifically, that several factors contribute to the judgment that a

134. Provan, Long, and Longman, *A Biblical History of Israel*, 99.

135. Halpern, *David's Secret Demons*, 111.

136. Gottwald, *The Politics of Ancient Israel*, 249–52; see also idem, *The Hebrew Bible in its Social World and in Ours* (Atlanta: Scholars Press, 1993), 237–383 (a compilation of articles by Gottwald on the relationship of Israel's past to modern theological and social theories). See also Elmer A. Martens, "The Oscillating Fortunes of 'History' within Old Testament Theology," in Millard, Hoffmeier, and Baker, eds., *Faith, Tradition, and History*, 312–40 (340). Barr (*History and Ideology in the Old Testament*, 9–10) also notes that the general public is still quite interested in what actually occurred in ancient Israel.

137. Gruber, "The Ancient Israel Debate," 11. Of course, Wellhausen did not have the modern-day state of Israel in mind, but Gruber contends that his polarization of pre-exilic and postexilic Israel has affected modern Israelis' ideas about themselves nevertheless.

138. Ibid., 21.

139. Ibid., 23.

140. Long, *The Art of Biblical History*, 192 (italics in original).

statement is valid.[141] One factor is plausibility; when a statement is considered plausible, he argues, it usually agrees with a locally achieved consensus (i.e. coheres with other authorities),[142] corresponds to the evidence, and conforms to other various agreed-upon criteria. A true statement, says Deist, also has pragmatic aspects: it is effective because the rhetoric and aesthetics of its argument are convincing. Finally, Deist claims, a true statement has genuineness, which "indicates the more ethical side of the presentation involving good old honesty (as compared to deceitfulness)."[143]

In conclusion, non-minimalist historians have contributed many new ideas to the discussion of truth in the history of ancient Israel by attempting to negotiate the tension between the modernist, traditional view of historical truth and challenges brought on by postmodernism and the minimalists. Some have accepted relativity and probability in historical reconstructions as unavoidable aspects of history writing. Furthermore, some, like Deist and Gottwald, are even optimistic that the recognition of the relativity of all positions can contribute to the historical enterprise. Non-minimalists also appear to be aware of the effects history can have in modern communities, though this has not been as much of a concern to these historians as some minimalists would like it to be. Furthermore, whereas minimalists are critical of histories that cohere with the Bible, non-minimalists in general hold open the possibility that present-day histories of ancient Israel can share both structure and details with the Bible. Finally, truth by correspondence appears to operate as a regulative ideal among non-minimalists, though they are not as dogmatic about promoting it as are the minimalists.

Summary of Non-Minimalist Historians of Ancient Israel

The defining characteristics of the non-minimalist historians discussed in this chapter are an open attitude toward the possibility that historical information, especially about early Israel, can be found in the biblical text and general agreement that "Israel," even if it is based partly on biblical Israel, can be a proper subject of history. These two opinions stand in contrast to the minimalist approach described in the previous chapter. Also, non-minimalists assume that they do not necessarily need external evidence to support a text's claims, that texts (particularly the Bible) that contain ideological or even fictional elements can still provide some reliable historical information, and that operating without what Thompson called a "coherent diachronic composition theory" is acceptable.[144] Because of these views, non-minimalists have been accused of departing from generally accepted principles of evidence evaluation and use. For instance, Brettler has charged that "biblical histories show so little agreement with the

---

141. Deist, *The Material Culture of the Bible*, 42–43.

142. Contra Thompson, "Lester Grabbe and Historiography: An Apologia," 149: "We don't wish to give unwonted weight to scholarly expertise or consensus. The tendency to do so discourages thought and discipline."

143. Deist, *The Material Culture of the Bible*, 42.

144. Thompson, "Methods and Results," 309.

canons of modern historiography, especially concerning the use of evidence, specifically the evaluation of source material before using it for reconstructing the past."[145] As seen here, however, non-minimalist historians advocate understanding the provenance of textual sources and evaluating them critically before using them to write history—a method that follows the general principles for evaluating texts set out in Chapter 1.[146] The assumptions that go into evidence evaluation and the conclusions that follow differ from those of minimalists and some other historians, but the differences in outcome cannot be blamed on non-minimalists' abandonment of historical method.

In short, while minimalists are firm in their convictions, non-minimalists appear to be in the process of exploring and coming to terms with many of the philosophical and methodological issues raised by the minimalists and by postmodernism. Non-minimalists are aware that ideas about representation, objectivity, subject, explanation, narrative, and truth in history are changing, and they are discussing and negotiating these issues while continuing to write history. They believe that as historians they have the ability to critically evaluate and represent the past but are aware that representation of the past is complicated by a number of factors, including bias. They recognize that the choice of subject and explanatory mode greatly affects the type of history that is written and they seek to make responsible choices. Furthermore, they acknowledge the constructed nature of historical narratives and truth but nevertheless continue to seek ways to improve their historical reconstructions. In addition, non-minimalist historians of ancient Israel are at the forefront of the struggle to understand and use ancient texts in history writing and to integrate conclusions drawn from them with information provided by artifacts. Their engagement with these issues and their unwillingness to make general statements about many of these topics stand in contrast to the decidedness of the minimalists on many issues.

On the other hand, it is too early to identify or name an overall philosophical or methodological movement or trend in current non-minimalist historical scholarship about ancient Israel. Non-minimalists' greatest commonalities lie in their cautious reactions to and incorporations of postmodernism in history writing and their budding appreciation of theory and method. Non-minimalists also are beginning to be self-critical by both defensively and proactively examining some of the presuppositions and practices they bring to writing about Israel's past. Though minimalists exhibit some of these traits as well, serious disagreements exist between the two sides. The next chapter will examine comprehensively the topics and disagreements identified in these five chapters, making specific suggestions about how some of the contentious issues can be further discussed and possibly resolved.

---

145. Brettler, *Creation of History*, 141.

146. See, further, Edelman, "Doing History in Biblical Studies," 15–16; Ahlström, *The History of Ancient Palestine*, 26; Grabbe, "Fellow Creatures—or Different Animals?," 30–35; McNutt, *Reconstructing the Society of Ancient Israel*, 5. Cf. also Ramsey, *The Quest for the Historical Israel*, 6–10, and Kenneth A. Kitchen, "The Controlling Role of External Evidence in Assessing the Historical Status of the Israelite United Monarchy," in Long, Baker, and Wenham, eds., *Windows Into Old Testament History*, 111–30 (128).

Chapter 6

SUMMARY AND CONCLUSIONS

Introduction

The previous chapters of this study have set forth and analyzed many assumptions and practices relevant to writing history. Specific topics discussed include the definition and goals of history; empiricism; objectivity; subject; explanation, including the roles of narrative and the social sciences in history; the type of truth history seeks to convey; how historians evaluate and use evidence, including texts and artifacts; and how they combine the two. Chapters 1 and 2 introduced these topics and offered a general picture of theoretical discussions about them among historians and philosophers of history. It was seen that over the past century, ideas about each of these topics have changed. Objectivity has moved from a goal that historians strive to achieve to an ideal that historians use to guide their endeavors. Subjects of history have expanded from political events and powerful persons to include marginalized or oppressed people, as well as suprahuman structures ranging from economics to *mentalités* about human experiences such as sexuality or death. Explanation in history has followed suit, with historians giving much attention to explanations from the social sciences and also examining narrative's role in explaining and constructing the past. New methods of interpreting evidence, influenced by poststructuralist readings of texts and processual and postprocessual archaeology, have also appeared. All of these developments, of course, have ramifications for notions of historical truth.

Using the framework from the first two chapters, Chapters 3, 4, and 5 explored assumptions and practices of historians of ancient Israel, separating them into three categories. Chapter 3 focused on the two most influential schools of thought about ancient Israel in the mid-twentieth century, those of William F. Albright and Albrecht Alt. Though Albrightians and Altians disagreed on methods of evaluating and using texts and artifacts, they set the program for studying Israel's past by valuing objectivity, seeking ways of finding reliable information about the past in the Bible, and defining and explaining Israel largely in terms of its religion. Both the presuppositions and the conclusions of these schools set the stage for critiques of history writing about ancient Israel that evolved into minimalism, discussed in Chapter 4. Minimalism, in which both the Bible's value as a historical source and Israel's importance as a historical subject are minimized, has inspired years of contentious debate among historians of ancient Israel. Claims of the minimalists that have been particularly controversial include minimalists' reading of much of the Bible as ideological and "late," and therefore not historically reliable, their need for external evidence to verify the Bible's claims, and their assertion that biases, especially religious and national, have interfered with the production of accurate reconstructions of Israel's past. As noted by Zevit, however, "The launch point for minimalist positions is determined by their answers to questions that all (good) historians are trained to ask about any written documents."[1] In short, minimalists' positions have arisen out of the assumptions they bring to and conclusions they draw from historical methodology, not a new methodology altogether.

Most scholars have not adopted minimalist presuppositions *in toto* and thus have been labeled "non-minimalist" for purposes of this study. Nevertheless, many have reacted to and incorporated some minimalist ideas into their scholarship. The ways and extent to which non-minimalist scholars have responded to the minimalists were analyzed in Chapter 5, as were their responses to other developments in the discipline. While non-minimalists are not unanimous on many issues, they generally are more open than minimalists to looser standards or even indecision about questions of objectivity, subject, explanation, the roles of ancient texts and artifacts as evidence, and the kind of truth history should convey. Put another way, whereas minimalists appear to be firm on many of these issues, non-minimalists are engaged in an unresolved, but progressive, conversation about many aspects of history writing.

In the separate treatments of Albrightians, Altians, minimalists, and non-minimalists, scholars largely have been allowed to speak for themselves. This chapter will comprehensively analyze assumptions and practices of the historians of ancient Israel reviewed in this study. As in the preceding chapters, the analysis will be organized topically. This approach will allow important differences and agreements among scholars to be identified. It will also point to philosophical and methodological topics that could benefit from further discussion among historians of ancient Israel, and suggest possibilities for the resolution of some problematic issues.

History Defined:
An Achievable Goal or a Regulative Ideal?

As seen throughout this study, definitions of history provide a glimpse into assumptions historians hold about their work. Awareness of developments in ideas about history in the twentieth century can be seen in the ways historians of ancient Israel often define history by stating history's traditional goals with qualifications. For instance, it has been shown that minimalists prefer the term "historiography" to "history," as historiography points to the interpretive activity of the historian.[2] Also, K. Lawson Younger says that history is a

---

1. Zevit, "Three Debates," 10.
2. Nevertheless, it appears that minimalists fervently advocate that history should describe "what actually happened" in the past with minimal subjective interpretation.

"committedly true account,"[3] and J. Maxwell Miller and Paula McNutt call history a conversation between the past and the present. These examples stop short of claiming that history can represent the past completely, can explain the past fully, or can even be true in a traditional sense. A comprehensive look at how historians of ancient Israel approach objectivity will begin to reveal some of the commonalities and differences in, and reasoning behind, assumptions that play into such notions of history.

Objectivity is Dead, Long Live Objectivity

Objectivity is the basis of empirical history, which appears still to be the standard for historians of ancient Israel. It was seen in Chapter 3 that the question of objectivity in treating Israel's past has been discussed among historians of ancient Israel since at least the mid-twentieth century. At that time, prominent historians such as Albright, Bright, Alt, and Noth believed empirical epistemology and methodology could be applied to learning about the past and were confident that scientific-like objectivity was possible in history. Bias, in their eyes, resulted from deviations from scientific method. As time went on, however, awareness of the inevitability of a certain degree of nonobjectivity or subjectivity in history increased, especially as postmodernism began to blur distinctions between subject and object, fact and value, and history and fiction. These changes also produced a more critical discussion of how researchers' perceptions of the past and their ability to apprehend and judge information about it can be value-laden and, especially in the case of ancient Israel, influenced by religious beliefs. Minimalists picked up on these trends, charging that other historians of ancient Israel are predisposed to certain approaches and conclusions due to religious or national interests. Minimalists have in turn been called "ideological" and have been accused of approaching Israel's past with too much skepticism. Consequently, much of the acrimonious debate about other topics, such as the evaluation and use of evidence and the choice of subject in the history of ancient Israel, has been cast in terms of objectivity.

Ziony Zevit has argued that, in general, historians operating in the postmodern intellectual climate have given up on objectivity and have accepted the idea that scholars "only act as if their conclusions are objective."[4] Yet minimalists, who Thomas Thompson says "strive to be objective scholars,"[5] appear to share in their predecessors' optimism about the possibility of objectivity. Though minimalists certainly are aware that all history writing entails subjectivity, they have been particularly strident in asserting that religious, national, and political biases should be eliminated from the study of Israel's past. This assertion is problematic for a number of reasons. First, minimalists have said little about how scholars who attempt to curtail their biases would write "detached,

---

3. Younger, *Ancient Conquest Accounts*, 46.
4. Zevit, *The Religions of Ancient Israel*, 71.
5. Thompson, "A Neo-Albrightean School?," 693.

positivistic history."[6] Also, minimalists need to demonstrate the benefits of the maximally objective history that they promote. Non-minimalists have not spoken clearly about the need for or possibility of achieving objectivity in the history of ancient Israel, either. Axel Knauf, Iain Provan, and Norman Gottwald have openly suggested and, particularly in the case of Provan and Gottwald, practiced self-criticism by disclosing possible biases in their own works. Yet, as James Barr has pointed out, recognizing, disclosing, and openly battling one's dispositions and prejudices does not necessarily make one's history objective.[7]

Though objectivity is an ideal that is impossible to achieve fully, it is an ideal that should be retained in history writing. As an ideal, objectivity is an appropriate concept for the study of the past since the past existed independently of our perception of it. In other words, as discussed in Chapter 1, an observer of the past theoretically can be independent from the past itself. Even more compelling as a justification for objectivity is the inherent second-hand nature of historical evidence and its need for interpretation by the historian, since objectivity can provide ground rules or common expectations for interpretations.[8] In the case of writing about Israel's past, however, no such hypothetical rules exist, and thus criteria for the maximal achievement of objectivity must be formulated if objectivity is to be made a methodological priority in the discipline.

It has been shown that the predominant approach to objectivity among current historians of ancient Israel has centered on critical evaluation of one's own, or others', biases. Though this process is an important element in reducing subjectivity or achieving some form of objectivity, it is not the complete solution. Objectivity in history writing about ancient Israel will be strengthened when discussion moves beyond the mere recognition of the roots of bias to identifying and remedying bias' manifestations. C. Behan McCullagh's discussion of objectivity in history, presented in Chapter 1, can provide historians of ancient Israel with a basis for formulating criteria for objective history. McCullagh has pointed to four ways that bias manifests itself in history: the misinterpretation of evidence, the omission of significant evidence, false implications about the past, and failure to mention all the important causes of an event.[9] Some additions can be made to McCullagh's description. First, objective historians must be clear about which historical statements correspond closely to evidence and which are interpretations. In doing so, historians need to provide enough information for readers, especially peers (who provide important checks on subjectivity) to evaluate their sense of what constitutes evidence, their interpretations of evidence, and their explanations for events. Similarly, inferences, interpretations, or explanations that arise from the historian's own experiences or conjectures about the evidence should be determined as far as possible and

6. Lemche, "The Origin of the Israelite State," 50.
7. Barr, *History and Ideology in the Old Testament*, 69.
8. Of course, in empirical or scientific research, first-hand observation also should be conducted objectively, or as objectively as possible.
9. McCullagh, "Bias in Historical Description," 40.

acknowledged as such, and any social-scientific or other theory that enters into historical reconstruction should be acknowledged and explained.

An explicit description of how historians employ objectivity as part of historical method would provide historians both with a guide for their own work and for evaluating the work of others. Niels Peter Lemche's interpretation of the Idrimi inscription, discussed in Chapter 4, can be used as an example of how use of the criteria for objectivity suggested here could improve history writing. In both *The Israelites in History and Tradition* and *Prelude to Israel's Past*, Lemche describes the Idrimi inscription as a "fairy tale" without a factual basis that legitimates the ascension of Idrimi, whom he considers a usurper to the throne of Aleppo. In both works, Lemche uses his interpretation of the Idrimi inscription as evidence that some of the biblical traditions, like the inscription, are highly stylized, propagandistic, and fictional. In *The Israelites in History and Tradition*, however, Lemche makes no detailed argument for and provides no detailed discussion of this interpretation of the genre and factuality of the inscription.[10] Without specific information or significant facts about what the Idrimi inscription says and why Lemche believes it must be considered fictional, readers cannot make an informed critique of his thesis. A more responsible and helpful approach can be found in *Prelude to Israel's Past*, where Lemche makes many observations about the inscription and traditional folk literature as support for his opinion about the truth-value of the Bible.[11] In this case, readers have the opportunity to evaluate the merits of his comparison of the Idrimi inscription to the Bible, and Lemche's conclusions appear be more informative and less polemical.

A discussion of criteria for objective history among historians of ancient Israel would also define boundaries for evaluating the objectivity or subjectivity of others' historical accounts. For instance, accusations by historians that others are "ideological" and therefore give priority to the biblical account or ignore it would not suffice to disqualify historical reconstructions; misrepresentation of known facts would have to be shown to substantiate a claim of undue subjectivity. An example of a critique along these lines can be found in V. Philips Long's comparison of information about ancient Israel found in ancient Near Eastern inscriptions and in the Bible.[12] Long re-examines evidence that led Lester Grabbe to conclude that the framework of the biblical stories about the Israelite and Judean kings were accurate but that the details were "sometimes... demonstrably misleading or wholly inaccurate and perhaps even completely invented."[13] Looking at the same texts, Long determines that "Grabbe drew a sweeping conclusion that appears to be unsupported by the evidence."[14] Though

10. Lemche, *The Israelites in History and Tradition*, 24–25.
11. These include claiming that the inscription reflects popular ancient Near Eastern literary patterns and offering other stories of the ascendancy of the younger son and adventure stories as comparative examples. See Lemche, *Prelude to Israel's Past*, 162–65.
12. Long, "How Reliable are Biblical Reports?"
13. Grabbe, "Fellow Creatures—Or Different Animals," 26.
14. Long, "How Reliable are Biblical Reports?," 382.

Long wonders if Grabbe "approached the evidence with certain preconceived notions of what would be found,"[15] his critique rests not on this accusation but on a re-examination of the same evidence.[16] Indeed, Long's examination is more detailed than Grabbe's and gives more comparative examples for the reader to consider, and thus appears both more objective and more accurate.

In addition to formulating criteria for approaching objectivity, historians could advance our understanding of objectivity, as well as the discipline of history, by attempting to write maximally objective comprehensive historical works. Looking back to the 1970s, 1980s, and early 1990s, there can be found some objectively undertaken, comprehensive, or partially comprehensive, studies by minimalists and non-minimalists. Works by minimalists (before they had fully adopted the minimalist approach) include Thompson's *The Historicity of the Patriarchal Narratives* (1974), which formulated and defended an answer to a historical question by presenting and rigorously reviewing information from the Bible, ancient Near Eastern texts, and archaeology. Lemche's *Early Israel* (1985) also addressed historical problems by using these sources as well as social-scientific theory. It offered a new portrait of the early Israelites formulated while critiquing the methods and conclusions of Gottwald's *The Tribes of Yahweh* (1979).[17] As the minimalist position was coalescing, Thompson authored his *Early History of the Israelite People* (1992), which also was a comprehensive work that clearly identified sources, evidence, and interpretations.

In recent years, however, Lemche and Thompson have written less comprehensive history and have instead focused on persuasive theoretical and methodological prolegomena to history. Lemche's *Prelude to Israel's Past* and *The Israelites in History and Tradition* (both 1998) provide information about Bronze Age Palestine and discuss the difficulty of locating ancient Israel in historical sources, yet include little about what happened in Iron Age Israel or Palestine. A history of Persian or Hellenistic Palestine that utilizes the information that minimalists believe the Bible provides about those time periods has also not been produced. Thompson's *Mythic Past* (2000), his most recent monograph, deals with Hellenism, but is mainly a treatise on Greek literary and philosophical influences on the Bible. In it Thompson does not attempt to integrate archaeology or other texts into a historical portrait of Hellenistic Palestine in a systematic way.

The other two prominent minimalists, Philip Davies and Keith Whitelam, also mainly have contributed prolegomena to history rather than full treatments of the past. Davies has been primarily concerned with the Bible and its relevance for history rather than what actually happened in the past. For instance, his *In*

15. Ibid., 384.
16. Long also admits that his "more positive experiences of the reliability of biblical reports" first prompted his examination of Grabbe's claims (ibid., 383).
17. In a 1995 reprint of his earlier comprehensive work, *Ancient Israel*, Lemche notes that he now considers *Early Israel* to be "a kind of introduction to renewed debate on these topics, rather than…a definitive synthesis," and suggests that in light of developments in the field since its original publication, a "totally new version" might be needed (p. 8).

Search of "Ancient Israel" (1992) offered observations on the discipline and its relationship to the biblical text but offered few historical conclusions. His contributions to a textbook entitled *The Old Testament World* (1989)[18] use archaeology and biblical and nonbiblical texts to describe Israel's neighbors from the Bronze Age to Hellenistic times and Israel in the Persian period, but how he would formulate a history of Iron Age Palestine remains unknown and difficult to imagine. Whitelam's major historical contribution, *The Emergence of Early Israel in Historical Perspective* (with Robert Coote, 1987) ignores the Bible entirely and makes historical reconstructions based on archaeological evidence and social-scientific models.

In short, a demonstration of what minimalists believe objectively executed historical method to be and a submission of defended conclusions undertaken with this method would be both informative and enlightening. Such a work would demonstrate how minimalists' evaluation of the Bible as late, which they claim to be more objective than others' evaluations, would provide historically useful information and result in an objectively written history of Palestine, especially one about the Persian and Hellenistic periods.

Among non-minimalists, changes in the approach to Israel's history are beginning to appear, and the influence of the many issues discussed in this study are becoming evident. In the 1980s and 1990s, histories such as *A History of Ancient Israel and Judah* by J. Maxwell Miller and John H. Hayes (1986), *The History of Ancient Palestine from the Palaeolithic Period to Alexander's Conquest* by Gösta Ahlström (1992), and *An Introduction to the History of Israel and Judah* by Alberto Soggin (1983; revised 1993 and 1998) relied rather heavily on the Bible for evidence. Although at the time of their publications these histories appeared methodologically cautious, their methodology would now need more defense in light of the growing skepticism about the Bible as a source for information about Israel's past.

The few works that have followed these three have reacted to skepticism about the Bible's value as evidence in different ways. Taking a conservative, and even defensive, approach, Iain Provan, V. Philips Long, and Tremper Longman's *A Biblical History of Israel* (2003) values almost all of the Hebrew Bible as a potential historical source and challenges those who seek to disregard parts or all of it.[19] Victor Matthews' *A Brief History of Ancient Israel* (2002) is similar in some ways, as it seeks to place Israel in a context that takes into account biblical prehistory such as "The Ancestral Narratives."[20] Matthews, however, unlike Provan, Long, and Longman, discusses nonbiblical evidence for Judah in the postexilic period and recognizes the current desire of some scholars to research the lives of the Judeans left there.[21] On the other hand, K. L. Noll's

18.   John W. Rogerson and Philip R. Davies, *The Old Testament World* (Englewood Cliffs: Prentice–Hall, 1989), 63–114, 58–94.
19.   Discussed in Chapter 5.
20.   Victor Matthews, *A Brief History of Ancient Israel* (Louisville, Ky.: Westminster John Knox, 2002). "The Ancestral Narratives" is the title of Matthews' first chapter.
21.   Ibid., 104–5. Cf. the biblically based treatment of "Those Who Remained" in Provan, Long, and Longman, *A Biblical History of Israel*, 283–84.

Canaan and Israel in Antiquity: An Introduction (2001), seeks to place Israel in its immediate environment without losing Israel to a general ancient Palestine, and also to deal with questions of history as it is understood now and as it was understood by the ancients.[22] In other words, Noll remains a non-minimalist, but incorporates and addresses many current concerns of history, including those brought to light by the minimalists

Compilations such as the *European Seminar in Historical Methodology* series (edited by Grabbe), *Israel's Past in Present Research* (edited by Long; 1999), and *The Fabric of History* (edited by Diana Edelman; 1991) are now common. In these publications, a variety of scholars voice methodological and theoretical arguments about Israel's history and present some brief historical vignettes. Again, such discussion is valuable but should be paired with practice. Actually producing a history of Israel would require historians to make choices on a number of theoretical and methodological issues and synthesize small historical portraits into a larger one, thereby demonstrating how an objective historian goes about selecting, presenting, and interpreting historical facts.

In summary, understanding and implementing objectivity requires descriptive statements of how historians should undertake writing maximally objective histories. In addition, examples of history written with objectivity as a goal are needed to demonstrate the advantages, limits, and results of the theoretical discussion about objectivity. To that end, then, it is not necessarily useful for a historian merely to "own up" to his or her own biases when writing history. Such proclamations direct the reader to detect certain biases in the presentation, though these may not be the only, or the most egregious, biases there. Also, historians may believe that announcing one's subjectivity gives one permission to write a historical work with less effort put into objective research and presentation. As noted several times in this study, historians and philosophers accept that subjectivity can never disappear completely from the historical enterprise. Concern about the subjectivity of the individual historian, however, should be subordinated to a resolution to keep objectivity as a workable regulative ideal for historians of ancient Israel.

Some advantages of retaining objectivity as a regulative ideal for Israel's history have been suggested here, such as providing a basis for historians to evaluate one another's historical claims and to reinvigorate the enterprise of representing and explaining Israel's past comprehensively over time. In addition, McCullagh points out that overly subjective histories "cause misunderstanding of the structures and processes involving the things they describe which can result in inappropriate strategies for altering them."[23] It follows that scholars who strive to be bias-free have the potential to be especially sensitive to the potential inferences and interpretations that could be drawn from evidence for the past. Conceptions of the past very likely influence the interpretation of the present as well as actions in the present, and thus readers of history need accurate and objective reconstructions of the past. Historians are in a privileged

---

22. K. L. Noll, *Canaan and Israel in Antiquity: An Introduction* (New York: Continuum, 2001).
23. McCullagh, "Bias in Historical Description," 50.

position, having access to information about the past that is unavailable or opaque to non-historians. Therefore, historians must consider it their duty to compose history in such a way that, ideally, whatever relevant information that is available is made known and nothing potentially relevant is omitted, while keeping the distinction between evidence and interpretation as clear as possible.

Evidence

Evidentiary issues are paramount in the methodological debate among historians of ancient Israel. As discussed in previous chapters, some historians consider ancient sources problematic because many appear to be propagandistic, in service to a moral, theological, or social agenda, or to be portrayals of the past that have been altered so that events fit into a particular, but artificial, theme or pattern. Artifacts, the other main source of information about the past, also require interpretation in order to be used in history writing, which leads to questions about archaeology's ability to explain the past through artifacts and the relationship artifacts and texts should have in reconstructing the past. Finally, in the past few years, minimalists' approaches to evidence for writing Israel's history have spurred discussion of theoretical issues pertaining to both epistemology as well as methodology. This section will re-examine several specific issues pertaining to evidence that are important to the current discussion among historians of ancient Israel and will argue that objectivity can guide the many decisions historians must make when evaluating and using evidence.

Texts

In the previous chapters of this study it was shown that historians of ancient Israel follow the same criteria for preliminary evaluation of potential sources as do historians in general. Albrightians, Altians, minimalists, and non-minimalists all seek knowledge of a text's origins, intention or meaning in original context, and transmission history. Nevertheless, they bring different assumptions to these questions and come to very different conclusions about the significance of texts, especially the biblical text, as sources of evidence for Israel's past. In Chapter 1, it was also argued that historians favor certain qualities in texts they may use as sources of evidence: they prefer texts that are chronologically organized, that appear to have the intention of imparting historical information, and that are coherent with other texts. These several criteria and types of knowledge historians seek in ancient texts provide a framework for comprehensively analyzing the underlying assumptions historians of ancient Israel hold about using texts as sources of evidence. This analysis will clarify the judgments that historians make about texts and point to better and worse assumptions that factor into the process of deciding whether a text contains reliable information about the past.

Genre

The status of the Bible as "history" and the value of this genre for modern historians are prevalent topics of discussion among biblical scholars and historians of ancient Israel. Scholars seek commonalities among literature from many ancient cultures in order to create descriptions and definitions of ancient history writing. They then attempt to decide, on the basis of these definitions and descriptions, whether parts of the Bible can be considered "history" or "historiography." An example of this type of comparative work has been seen already in Lemche's treatment of the Idrimi inscription. Lemche uses this text as an example of an ancient historiographical (albeit fictional) genre to which he compares parts of the Bible. John Van Seters is perhaps the most notable scholar who has approached Israelite historiography from a comparative point of view. He considers Herodotus's *Historia* to be a valid analogy to historiographical writing in the Bible. He describes the process of history writing in ancient times by saying that Herodotus and "any other early Greek prose writer using the conventions of his day would have composed his work in a paratactic fashion with varying degrees of unity."[24] Older material, he argues, was completely reworked into the new document, not simply inserted. Consequently, Van Seters asks, "Why should early Hebrew prose have been different?"[25] and concludes that the compilation of the Hebrew Bible, like Herodotus' *Historia*, was not the result of the accrual of traditional or historical materials over time, but that the process was a condensed, deliberate event.[26]

Comparing the Bible with other ancient historiography allows for various conclusions about the accuracy of the Bible to be made. Lemche, as discussed, claims that the Idrimi inscription is fictional and thus that parts of the Bible that match its style and presentation are also best understood as fictional. On the other hand, James Hoffmeier writes that "Egyptologists, while recognizing the propagandistic nature of [Egyptian war campaign reports], nevertheless ascribe some historical worth to the bombastic claims," and asserts that Israelite historiography should be treated similarly.[27] In addition, the volume *Faith, Tradition, and History* (edited by Millard, Hoffmeier, and Baker) deals with the topic of

24. Van Seters, *In Search of History*, 37.
25. Ibid.
26. For other arguments along these lines, see Jan-Wim Wesselius, *The Origin of the History of Israel: Herodotus's Histories as Blueprint for the First Books of the Bible* (JSOTSup 345; Sheffield: Sheffield Academic Press, 2002), and Gerhard Larsson, "Possible Hellenistic Influences in the Historical Parts of the Old Testament," *SJOT* 18 (2004): 296–311. In *The Origin of the History of Israel*, Wesselius asserts that Herodotus' histories provide not only a comparative model for understanding Israelite historiography, but actually provided the blueprint for the biblical historical books. For an assessment of the relationship between the biblical Primary History and Herodotus' *Historia*, see Sara R. Mandell and David Noel Freedman, *The Relationship Between Herodotus' History and Primary History* (South Florida Studies in the History of Judaism 60; Atlanta: Scholars Press, 1993). Mandell and Freedman see a noncoincidental relationship between the structures of the two and hypothesize that a "mystic" or "popular" paradigm lies behind the similarities (p. 174).
27. James K. Hoffmeier, *Israel in Egypt: The Evidence for the Authenticity of the Exodus Tradition* (New York: Oxford University Press, 1997), 42.

historical reliability in ancient texts, using Hittite, Sumerian, and Babylonian examples. Here, scholars come to various conclusions about the relationship of facts about the past to propaganda and invention in ancient Near Eastern texts.[28]

These examples suffice to show that no generalizations can be made about the value of historiographical sources from cognate cultures to ancient Israel. They also demonstrate that the comparative approach to historiography in the Hebrew Bible bears only indirectly on the value of biblical texts as evidence for historians. In other words, calling an ancient text "history" or "historiography" on the basis of other ancient texts that have similar features does not determine whether or not factual information can be found in that text.

Other scholars have sought to understand the genre of ostensibly historical biblical texts by taking a more descriptive and analytical, rather than comparative, approach. For instance, they point to the organized and intentional nature of biblical historiography but disagree on whether such a presentation indicates historical reliability. On the one hand, Marc Brettler has argued that literary patterning and ideological factors characterize biblical accounts of the past over, and sometimes against, a desire for accurate reporting.[29] A form of this opinion also can be seen in a principal argument of minimalists, who read the biblical text partly in light of poststructuralist or postmodernist literary criticism. Inspired by these approaches, minimalists argue that the Bible's primary organization benefits the propagandistic intentions of the authors, who disassembled earlier reports of what happened and reconstituted them into new, ideological literature (or even created stories about the past). Thus, claim the minimalists, reliable information about the past is extremely difficult to identify in the biblical account.

On the other hand, Halpern has argued that the very organization of the biblical text attests to the authors' faithful use of sources, making the Bible a product of "authentic antiquarian intentions"[30] and thereby reliable. While Halpern's thesis itself has not been adopted as a consensus, it is in line with historians' general desire that potential textual evidence should be written with the intent of describing the past. While some non-minimalists agree that, in the preliminary analysis, the Bible and other ancient sources should be given the "benefit of the doubt,"[31] most do not profess either positive or negative generalizations about

---

28.   In his essay in this volume, Bill T. Arnold argues that in comparing ancient texts to another, "the similarities serve only to throw into bold contrast the differences," an opinion reminiscent of Weber's ("The Weidner Chronicle and the Idea of History in Israel and Mesopotamia," in Millard, ed., *Faith, Tradition, and History*, 129–48 [148]). The most significant difference Arnold sees between the Bible and other ancient Near Eastern texts has to do with "the significance of this small, seemingly trivial nation of the ancient East [Israel] with its astonishing claims for itself and its God" (ibid.).

29.   Brettler, *The Creation of History in Ancient Israel*, 6.

30.   Halpern, *The First Historians*, 3.

31.   E.g. Provan, "In the Stable with the Dwarves," 292. Of course, Provan is not only talking about the preliminary decision about whether to even consider a text as potential evidence, but is also making an epistemological statement about historians' approach to evidence in general. Provan's epistemological and methodological concerns will be discussed further, below.

the issue of organization, reliability, and intention. Philosopher Paul A. Roth states this notion in more theoretical terms: "The extent to which history respects canons of narrative construction might influence the literary merit of that history. But it hardly seems relevant to determining the conditions under which that history is true."[32] Georg Iggers' summary of the late twentieth-century situation in history nicely describes the situation in the history of ancient Israel, as well: "Although many historians have taken contemporary linguistic, semiotic, and literary theory seriously, they have in practice not accepted the idea that the texts with which they work have no reference to reality."[33]

This discussion of genre and the Hebrew Bible has shown that descriptions and analyses of genres in the Bible and comparison of these with other examples of ancient historiography offer limited help for historians trying to determine a text's value as a source of evidence about the past. Since the reliability of ancient historiography is an open question, analogies between the Bible and such literature can either support the Bible's claims or discount them. Similarly, intention, invention, patterning, and other narrative and literary features may be characteristic of both biblical and nonbiblical historiography, but it is very difficult to ascertain the extent to which these factors occlude or indicate factual reporting in such texts. Thus, while historians seek knowledge about a text's genre in order to understand its intentions and form a judgment about its useful-ness as evidence, in the case of ancient texts, especially the Bible, this knowl-edge helps only in limited ways. Yet historians do not base their judgments about texts on genre considerations alone. Another characteristic that historians seek in their possible sources is correlation of a text with other texts, or coherence between textual sources. This criterion requires some additional clarification, especially in the case of the Bible.

Coherence with Other Texts
What texts could potentially make claims about the past similar to the Bible's claims? Outside of the corpus of biblical literature, written sources from Iron Age Palestine are limited to scattered epigraphic remains. While these may provide small slices of information about Israel's past, they cannot substantiate the many historical scenarios in the Bible.[34] On the other hand, records of military activity and imperial administration from the Egyptian, Assyrian, Babylonian, Persian, and Greek empires can potentially cohere with the Bible in places.[35] For instance, the Assyrian invasion of Palestine in 701 BCE and the failure to capture Jerusalem is reported in the Bible and Assyrian annals, though

32. Roth, "Narrative Explanations," 2.
33. Iggers, *Historiography in the Twentieth Century*, 145.
34. See, e.g., André Lemaire, "Hebrew and West Semitic Inscriptions and Pre-exilic Israel," in Day, ed., *In Search of Pre-Exilic Israel*, 366–85, and Lawrence J. Mykytiuk, *Identifying Biblical Persons in Northwest Semitic Inscriptions of 1200–539 B.C.E.* (Society of Biblical Literature Academia Biblica 12; Atlanta: Society of Biblical Literature; Leiden: Brill, 2004).
35. See, e.g., Simon Parker, *Stories in Scripture and Inscriptions: Comparative Studies on Narratives in Northwest Semitic Inscriptions and the Hebrew Bible* (New York: Oxford University Press, 1997).

naturally with differing slants. Rarely, however, are ancient Near Eastern sources and the Bible identifiably talking about exactly the same event, as events important in one type of source usually do not show up in the other. In the case of the Persian period, for example, Achamenid imperial records can be compared to Ezra, Nehemiah, and Chronicles for general information, but no records of Persian administration exist for Judea and Samaria in the fifth and fourth centuries BCE.[36] Consequently, the result of the search for extrabiblical texts for the history of Israel is that historians of ancient Israel have very few potential nonbiblical texts to start with, and even fewer whose claims can be directly correlated with a story in the Bible.

Regardless of the problems in finding sources to correlate with the Bible, scholars have tried to compare biblical and nonbiblical texts and have drawn both negative and positive conclusions about the reliability of the Bible from the comparisons that they have made. For instance, the Tell Dan inscription seems to claim that Hazael killed Jehoram and Ahaziah,[37] whereas 2 Kgs 9:24-28 reports that Jehu did this. This apparent disagreement is a primary factor in Shigeo Yamada's claim that the conflict of Ben-Hadad with Ahab and Jehoram described in the Bible is the stuff of prophetic legend.[38] As a more general example, Giovanni Garbini combines his opinions that Israel lacked royal epigraphy and that the monarchy the Bible describes is unlike any known among Israel's neighbors to conclude that "The Old Testament has set out a sacred history of universal value, but it is not very reliable as evidence of a secular history of the kind that the Hebrew people actually experienced... [T]he Bible remains as evidence of what they would have liked, but did not happen."[39] On the other hand, Halpern observes that the Bible and "non-biblical, non-Israelite inscriptions" cohere on many details about the names and reigns of kings of Israel and Judah.[40] He argues that these correlations demonstrate that the biblical writer had accurate knowledge of Israel's past.

---

36. Ephraim Stern, *Archaeology of the Land of the Bible*. Vol. 2, *The Assyrian, Babylonian, and Persian Periods, 732–332 BCE* (ABRL; New York: Doubleday, 2001), 578.

37. According to Avraham Biran and Joseph Naveh. They claim that, although Hazael is not mentioned in the pieces of the stele recovered so far, he was its author. See their "An Aramaic Stele Fragment from Tel Dan," *IEJ* 43 (1993): 81–98, and "The Tel Dan Inscription: A New Fragment," *IEJ* 45 (1995): 17–18. This interpretation has been challenged in Athas, *The Tel Dan Inscription*. Athas postulates the author as Bar-Hadad II. The evidence Athas brings to this hypothesis, however, includes a very controversial reading of *bytdwd* in Fragment A, based on suggestions from F. H. Cryer, Davies and Thompson (pp. 217–26). Athas also contests Biran and Naveh's identification of the names Jehoram and Ahaziah in fragment B (pp. 237–44). Athas's adoption of minimalists' readings of the words on the stele, coupled with his interpretation that favors a minimalist view of the events described by the stele (i.e. that the stele does not make reference to biblical characters) has drawn some questions about his objectivity and method. See, e.g., William M. Schniedewind, review of George Athas, *The Tel Dan Inscription: A Reappraisal and a New Interpretation*. No pages. Published 5 October 2003. Online: http://www.bookreviews.org/pdf/3275_3685.pdf.

38. Shigeo Yamada, "Aram–Israel Relations as Reflected in the Aramaic Inscription from Tel Dan," *UF* 27 (1995): 611–25.

39. Garbini, *History and Ideology in Ancient Israel*, 18–19.

40. Halpern, "Erasing History," 30. For a more general argument about coherence in the style of Israelite and ancient Near Eastern chronicles, see idem, *The First Historians*, 213–18. Cf. also the

Halpern's logic does involve a leap of faith; the apparent factuality of Ahab, for instance, does not prove the existence of Jezebel, a conflict between worshippers of Yahweh and worshippers of Baal, or any other aspect of the biblical story about Ahab. Nevertheless, Halpern's argument must be seriously considered. At the very least, it makes summary dismissal of the Bible's account appear unwise and suggests that historians who believe information in the Bible about these kings to be untrustworthy should defend their opinions. In other words, these correlations between biblical and nonbiblical texts, while not enough to commend everything in the books of Kings for historical reconstruction, do support the possibility that the text includes genuine information about the past. Put more generally, coherence with other texts does not substantiate the factuality of many or most of the events reported in the Bible, and likewise apparent contradiction between biblical and nonbiblical texts or inscriptions does not automatically insubstantiate the entirety of either account. Thus, using information found in nonbiblical ancient texts for blanket substantiation or insubstantiation is unacceptable. Such information, however, can be used to evaluate and use specific information in the biblical text as evidence.

Provenance
The origins and transmission history of a text are other pieces of knowledge that historians seek in order to help determine a text's reliability as a historical source. As seen in this study, historians from Finley to the minimalists have claimed that primary sources or near-eyewitness accounts of the past are the best sources for historical reconstruction. Of course, such accounts are notoriously hard to identify in the Bible. Lemche and Thompson, for instance, have eschewed source criticism altogether, claiming that the earliest known date of a text corresponds to the date of its earliest extant copy.[41] Other historians, such as Albright and Alt, were optimistic about their attempts to date parts of the Bible, and though they may not have considered the Bible's oldest sources to be primary sources, they did work with the assumption that older sources provide better evidence than later ones. Scholars have also tried to understand the social context of the Bible's composition in order to evaluate the truth of its reporting. Social context is then used to explain propagandistic or other overarching themes in the text's composition. In many cases, this type of speculation is a circular enterprise—almost everything a scholar can infer about the potential meaning of the text in its original context must be taken from the text itself, or from comparison with other texts assumed to have the same context.

When claims about the date of a text or the society that produced the text cannot be independently verified, determinations about a text's origin and context boil down to better defended and more plausible scenarios. Yet knowing, or

---

analysis of the similar material in Grabbe, "Fellow Creatures—or Different Animals?," and Long, "How Reliable are Biblical Reports?," discussed above.

41. Lemche, "The Old Testament—A Hellenistic Book?," 169–70; Thompson, "Lester Grabbe and Historiography," 152.

supposing, where, when, and why a text originated takes historians only so far. Even if minimalists' late dating of the Hebrew Bible is assumed to be correct, the historian's task does not change significantly. Indeed, a late date may very well disqualify much in the Bible from being a primary source about Israel's most ancient past, but Finley's notion that primary sources are the only reliable sources of evidence about the past appears overcautious and impractical. Most historians of ancient Israel continue to attempt to understand if certain texts in the Bible date to a time near the events they describe, but they also work with information that they do not consider primary, eyewitness, or near-eyewitness. Objectivity is crucial to navigating the problem of provenance's relationship to reliability, as well as to the other issues pertaining to the reliability of texts as evidence discussed here.

Using Objectivity to Evaluate and Clarify Approaches to Texts as Evidence in the History of Ancient Israel
The date of a text's original composition, its original social context, and its transmission history, along with its genre and its coherence with other texts, are factors that historians research and weigh when judging a text's usefulness as evidence for history writing. As seen here, however, attempting to discern these types of information about a text leads historians to other questions such as: How does calling an ancient work "history" help modern historians? How can questions of origins and context be addressed without using circular logic? and, What do apparent correlations of biblical reports with nonbiblical texts indicate about the reliability of the Bible in general? Even if a general consensus about these questions were to be reached, the most important question historians ask of a document remains unchanged: Did the events that the text describes happen as it describes them? No method or formula can resolve this dilemma, and Younger's observation that "systematic methods and categories of analysis through which questions of the validity of referents in historical narrative could be approached are virtually nonexistent"[42] is directly on point.

In the absence of a method or formula, principles of objectivity, such as the ones discussed above, can guide scholars who are making admittedly subjective decisions about a text. Also, objectivity requires that criticisms of history be leveled at the rationale of evidence and explanations in a reconstruction, so using principles of objectivity allows minimalist and non-minimalist approaches to texts as evidence to be evaluated. Such a critique demonstrates that minimalists currently provide a weaker rationale for their decision to minimize the Bible in history writing than do non-minimalists, who continue to try to use it as a historical source.

Much of the success the minimalists have had in stirring up debate about the Bible's reliability as a historical source rests on overinflation of the correlation between understanding a text's origins and evaluating a text for reliable historical information. As discussed in Chapter 4, minimalists advocate systematic

42. Younger, *Ancient Conquest Accounts*, 37.

explanations for the Bible. Systematic explanations of texts, however, allow for systematic evaluations of their reliability that can result in either summary dismissal of texts that have apparently fictional elements or simplistic appropriation of texts that have some plausible elements. Furthermore, this method is essentially the same method as the Albrightians' "diagnostic-detail" approach (discussed in Chapter 3). Whereas Albright and his students validated entire biblical stories on the basis of plausible details, minimalists such as Davies would invalidate them based on the implausibility of details. Systematic evaluation and use of the Bible is also advocated by Provan. He claims that ad hoc use of a text allows historians to pick and choose details at will, and, refusing to do so, decides to consider most of the Bible reliable. Nevertheless, ad hoc evaluation of the text is a better method for historians of ancient Israel; it allows more potential evidence to be considered, and case-by-case examinations can be undertaken objectively, as long as historians make clear how they form conclusions about and from the text.[43]

Another flaw in the minimalists' rationale is the claim that texts must be dated to their earliest possible documentation. It does not require a huge leap in logic to surmise that written copies of many of the biblical books existed before their first certain attestation in the Dead Sea scrolls, for instance, as variations within attested texts in the scrolls appear to stem from a common *Vorlage*. Starting the transmission history of texts in the second century BCE (or later) because their provenance cannot be firmly known prior to that time disregards the difficult questions of their origin and implies that their genesis was in this later time. This move, in fact, violates another prescription of objectivity, namely, that no false implications should be made. Furthermore, whatever point Lemche and Thompson are trying to make by observing that manuscript copies of many ancient texts do not appear until centuries after their supposed composition, their assertions are of no value to serious historians who are quite aware of such matters but hope to understand what the text's original compositional setting might have been.

Minimalists name the Second Temple period as the time of the origin of the Bible, in contrast to the prevailing loose consensus that places the compilation of the Pentateuch and the historical books in, around, or before the sixth century BCE.[44] As discussed in Chapter 4, Davies proposes the Persian period as the time of the Hebrew Bible's composition, and Lemche and Thompson have suggested a Hellenistic provenance. Other scholars, however, have not been persuaded by the minimalists' hypotheses. For instance, Barstad has concluded that Lemche's arguments are speculative and based on uncritical examination of the evidence he uses as proof for his thesis.[45] Hurvitz refutes another cornerstone of the

43. Ironically, in *The Historicity of the Patriarchal Narratives* Thompson used ad hoc consideration of the Bible in order to clarify its description of the patriarchs and to contrast the details of the biblical presentation with generalizations about these stories that had been made in order to argue that the patriarchs were historical figures.
44. This theory was expressed most fully in Noth, *Überlieferungsgeschichtliche Studien I*.
45. Barstad, "Is the Hebrew Bible a Hellenistic Book?," 129–51.

minimalists' argument for postexilic composition of the Bible, namely the claim that Biblical Hebrew is a literary language constructed at this time.[46] Hurvitz's argument in particular is devastating to the minimalists' claims, since he attacks Davies on "the degree to which previous scholarly research in the linguistic realm of [Biblical Hebrew] is taken into account" and "the extent to which evidence of the extrabiblical written sources is used."[47] Hurvitz's critiques can be understood as challenges to Davies' objectivity, since Davies does not appear to have considered all the available evidence for understanding linguistic issues. Also, of the minimalists, only Davies has attempted to explain how and why Persian-era Palestinian people would adopt parts of an earlier community's traditions and value them so highly.[48] Certainly arguments for the Bible's value as a unifying factor in the Persian (or Hellenistic) period can be made, but these do not eliminate other time periods and societies as potential contexts for much of the text's origin. Thus, though a pre-exilic Israelite and/or Judean provenance for Samuel and Kings, for instance, cannot be proven, at this point it seems at least as plausible, and at most points better defended, than scenarios placing the origin of the Bible in the Persian or Hellenistic period.

Additionally, minimalists' assumption that the propagandistic, moralistic, literary, or constructed nature of much of the Bible likely precludes its factuality is difficult to defend. As discussed above, both non-minimalists and philosophers of history, such as Roth and Iggers, claim that the perception that ancient writers felt free to rearrange or rewrite in order to make a point does not automatically disqualify their texts from containing reliable information. Indeed, scholars of other ancient Near Eastern cultures regularly look for facts underneath fantastic presentations.[49] Finally, striving for objectivity requires that all information relevant to a topic be considered. Thus, the Bible, a significant source of information about many aspects of ancient Israel (to paraphrase McCullagh), must be consulted and used in history writing. It should also be noted here that minimalists' claims about the historical value of the Bible, such as Lemche's assertion that minimalists should actually be called "maximalists"

46. Hurvitz, "The Historical Quest for 'Ancient Israel' and the Linguistic Evidence"; cf. Zevit, "Three Debates," 18–19, where Zevit claims that Lemche has not defended minimalists' credentials as scholars of ancient Near Eastern languages, cultures, societies, and archaeology.

47. Hurvitz, "The Historical Quest for 'Ancient Israel' and the Linguistic Evidence," 305. On the first point, Hurvitz simply claims that Davies has ignored a wealth of information about the potential chronological development of Biblical Hebrew that already exists. On the second, Hurvitz reviews external, mainly inscriptional, evidence, for "classical" and "postclassical" Biblical Hebrew and argues that such evidence does support a notion of linguistic development. He then offers a case study of the words for "letter" (i.e. correspondence) in the Hebrew Bible and concludes that the shift from *seper* to *'iggeret* is best explained as a chronological development.

48. Davies (*In Search of "Ancient Israel"*, 89) admits that to do so he must "deploy a little imagination." For datings of the Pentateuch to the Persian period that do hypothesize about political and sociological movements behind the compilation, see Jon L. Berquist, *Judaism in Persia's Shadow: A Social and Historical Approach* (Minneapolis: Fortress, 1995), and James W. Watts, ed., *Persia and Torah: The Theory of Imperial Authorization of the Pentateuch* (Atlanta: Scholars Press, 2001).

49. E.g. Millard, "History and Legend in Early Babylonia," 103–10.

(because they seek to get as much information as possible from the Bible)[50] are problematic. Minimalists have yet to demonstrate how their dating of the text and opinions about what information it contains about the past can be used to provide a reconstruction of any time period or any cultural unit.

In comparison to minimalists, non-minimalists, who as seen in this study are not yet ready to abandon the use of many parts of the Bible for history writing, stand on firmer ground with regard to objectivity. To borrow from Miller and Hayes and Halpern, making efforts to use the Bible and other ancient texts judiciously and objectively is one of the primary responsibilities of historians. Also, objective consideration of *all* of the information known about a text must combine with objective attempts to ascertain what is not known in order that conclusions that are maximally fair to the evidence at hand can be made. The discussion in Chapter 5 of non-minimalists resisting systematic methods for explaining the biblical text and considering its merits on a case-by-case basis demonstrate that non-minimalists have been more responsible in these areas than minimalists. That said, non-minimalists are guilty of too much equivocation on the value of the biblical text for history. Non-minimalists sometimes show caution in using the biblical text, while at other times they seem to choose to employ the Bible with no apparent reservations. Often they are inconsistent in their method.[51] In large part, theoretical justifications for their positions are lacking.

Ultimately, understandings of the Bible's genres, organization, intention, origin, context, and connections to other texts will provide the basis, but not the justification, for historians' opinions about the factuality of the events the Bible reports. Conclusions about these matters will be formulated in the historian's mind based on a mix of rational thought about these factors and subjective judgment. Only an attempt at objectivity can keep subjectivity in check and prevent it from overriding, substituting for, or replacing conclusions drawn from rational thought.

Artifacts

Historians of ancient Israel appear to share more assumptions about the potential evidence that artifacts can provide for history writing than they do about the process of garnering historical information from ancient texts. For instance, while using the Bible in history writing now needs theoretical justification, historians almost universally accept artifacts and archaeology as sources of

50. Shanks, "Face to Face," 28.
51. For instance, in *The History of Ancient Palestine*, Ahlström appears to find specific and detailed information in the Bible about Saul and an early monarchical period in Israel, including the names of federations, chiefdoms, and kingdoms (p. 421) and the size of Saul's first army, 3000 men (p. 437). On the other hand, Ahlström discounts information about the Queen of Sheba, because in the Solomon and Sheba story, Ahlström sees "personalities...portrayed in categories usually found in a saga" (p. 518). Though he speculates that Solomon's control of intercontinental trade might have affected other kingdoms, perhaps forcing someone such as the queen to call on Solomon, he leaves open the possibility that the entire encounter is fictional.

evidence about ancient Israel. Minimalists' claim that artifacts should be evaluated independently from biblical-based chronologies and frameworks also has not met with much opposition.[52] Disagreements about how historians of ancient Israel use artifacts and archaeology mainly occur when historians try to integrate information from these sources with information from the Bible.[53] Since the effort to be objective in history demands that all potential sources of information be taken into account, undertaking this task is another primary responsibility of historians.

Combining texts and archaeology is a comparative enterprise, and therefore the types of information available from each source and their potential compatibility must be considered at the outset. Artifacts, unless they contain writing, are very unlikely providers of information about specific persons or events of the past. Thanks to stratigraphy, archaeology may be able to approximate the date of an assemblage, potentially allowing artifacts to be correlated to events described in other sources.[54] By and large, however, artifacts are examined for indications of historical processes, general social and environmental patterns, clues to ancient symbol systems, and the like. In order for artifacts to yield this type of information, archaeological theory must be employed. As seen in Chapter 2, processual and postprocessual archaeology offer different ways of interpreting artifacts. While processual archaeology seeks patterns and their causes, or laws, in the artifactual record and emphasizes human adaptation to the environment, postprocessual archaeology focuses more on meanings of artifacts —particularly symbolic meanings—in their context.

Though it seems that most historians of ancient Israel strive to respect archaeology as an independent discipline and attempt not to make information from artifacts subordinate to texts, more discussion about archaeology's role in history and the potential contributions of the different types of archaeology would be beneficial. Historians of ancient Israel often appear neither to recognize the different types of information texts and artifacts provide nor to relate the different data in a maximally productive way. Instead, they use artifacts for illustrative or justificatory purposes or to fill in gaps in knowledge. Of course, some current scholars find the subordination of archaeology necessary for history: Miller has argued specifically for illustrative uses of artifacts,[55] and Edelman has argued that history, not archaeology, should describe the development of cultures over time.[56] Yet the outcome of the subordination of archaeology to texts is an understanding of the past that is deficient in a number of

---

52.   Although the feasibility of this trend has been challenged by Miller in "Is It Possible to Write a History of Israel Without Relying on the Hebrew Bible?"

53.   See also Lilian Krawitz, "Separating Mythos from Logos in Biblical Archaeology," *OTE* 16 (2003): 34–46.

54.   In this way, for instance, the destruction of Stratum III at Lachish has been identified with Sennacherib's conquest of the city. See, e.g., David Ussishkin, *The Conquest of Lachish by Sennacherib* (Tel Aviv: Tel Aviv University Institute of Archaeology Press, 1982).

55.   Miller, "Old Testament History and Archaeology," 60–63.

56.   Edelman, "Doing History in Biblical Studies," 19–20.

ways. First, it allows historians to use archaeology in a piecemeal manner, look-ing at specific artifacts without considering the context or potential of entire assemblages. For instance, Miller and Hayes include a picture of a small bronze bull statue in order to show "how Jeroboam's calves may have looked."[57] While Miller and Hayes's illustration may be correct, a more complete history would take into account many such religious artifacts in order to "describe the nature of the religious symbols by which a culture oriented itself,"[58] in this case, the culture at the time of Jeroboam.

Using artifacts to describe "the religious symbols by which a culture oriented itself," assumes that history's subject reaches beyond events and includes suprahuman structures, an assumption that will be discussed further below. Nevertheless, for the time being, if this assumption is granted and structures such as religion become part of history's subject, it becomes evident that artifacts can do more in history than illuminate the background to texts. For instance, Othmar Keel and Christoph Uehlinger argue that artifacts can contribute to understanding ancient Israel's religion by assuming first that "even those objects from a material culture that serve a purely functional role can be or at least might be an expression of certain religious concepts and elements of faith."[59] In other words, many types of artifacts potentially provide information about ancient religious or symbolic systems. Then, they claim, information from artifacts can be combined with epigraphic and textual sources to write a dia-chronic history of Israel's religion.[60] Additionally, Keel and Uehlinger undertake their work with a sense of its importance, recognizing that the comprehensive study of artifacts and pictorial evidence for Israel's religion resonates with debates such as those about women's roles in ancient Israel as well as in the present-day church and synagogue.[61]

There are benefits to letting artifacts play a larger role in history writing other than those demonstrated by Keel and Uehlinger's approach. Processual archaeology and its methods for gathering evidence about daily life and people's relationship to the environment, for example, have made some specific contribu-tions to the understanding of ancient Israel. Lawrence Stager's description of village and family life and the adaptations to the environment evident in the archaeological record is an example of such a contribution that has found

57. Miller and Hayes, *A History of Ancient Israel and Judah*, 242. For a more complete treatment of this artifact in a general work, see Amihai Mazar, *Archaeology of the Land of the Bible 10,000–586 B.C.E.* (ABRL; New York: Doubleday, 1990), 350–52.
58. Keel and Uehlinger, *Gods, Goddesses and Images of God*.
59. Ibid., 10.
60. Keel and Uehlinger, however, recognize that their effort at such a combination is pre-liminary, particularly with respect to potential parallels to and information about symbols that can be found in the Hebrew Bible (ibid., 396). Their work also includes some polemic against ignorance of artifactual evidence about Israel's past: "Anyone who prefers to work exclusively with texts (e.g., to reconstruct 'Canaanite' religion using nothing but textual sources from Ugarit) ought to get little or no hearing" (p. 11); "those who pay little attention to iconography are, generally speaking, less aware of their ignorance than those who are unable to read" (p. 395).
61. Ibid., 1.

general acceptance among historians.[62] Also, claiming that archaeology must be subordinate to history in illuminating the past shows no awareness of post-processual archaeology and the potential it has for history. This deficiency is even apparent among the minimalists, who, like postprocessual archaeologists, assert that artifactual evidence should be treated as equal to textual evidence. Thompson's focus on the ethnicity of ancient Palestine in *Early History* is one example of a discussion that could potentially benefit from postprocessual interpretations of artifacts.[63] Most of the archaeological evidence Thompson brings to bear on his discussion of ethnicity comes from geographical surveys or overall site descriptions. This includes information about public and private architecture, a site's relationship to geographical features, and evidence for agri-cultural practices—all details important to processual archaeologists who are trying to understand the adaptations of a population to its physical surroundings. Postprocessual archaeology, however, would consider shared understandings of culture and its concomitant symbols to be an important part of ethnic identity. In *Early History*, Thompson hardly discusses these aspects of ethnicity, and when he does broach these topics, the primary piece of evidence he uses is the Bible, not artifacts.

Recently, some scholars have used aspects of postprocessualism to address questions about Israel's past, including some that pertain to ethnicity. For example, Shlomo Bunimovitz and Avraham Faust argue that the four-room house, the predominant dwelling in Iron Age Palestine, was uniquely suited to the purity concerns of ancient Israel (as described in the Bible).[64] This study, though written for a general audience, is nevertheless intriguing and should at least prompt discussion of whether purity concerns exhibited in the biblical texts are symbolized in artifacts, as well.[65] Sandra Scham's article examining the symbolic nature of central hill country artifacts associated with "early Israel" alongside texts from Judges associated with the same context, also demonstrates how postprocessualism might be used in writing about Israel's past and some benefits of this approach.[66] Scham explores what can be known about the

---

62. Lawrence E. Stager, "The Archaeology of the Family in Ancient Israel," *BASOR* 260 (1985): 1–35.

63. See especially the subsections "'Israel' as a National Identity" and "The Intellectual Matrix of Biblical Tradition" in Thompson, *Early History*, 412–23.

64. Shlomo Bunimovitz and Avraham Faust, "Ideology in Stone: Understanding the Four-Room House," *BAR* 28, no. 4 (2002): 33–41, 59–60. See also J. David Schloen, *The House of the Father as Fact and Symbol: Patrimonialism in Ugarit and the Ancient Near East* (Studies in the Archaeology of the Levant 2; Winona Lake, Ind.: Eisenbrauns; Boston: Harvard Semitic Museum, 2001).

65. On the other hand, Elizabeth Bloch-Smith ("Israelite Ethnicity in Iron I: Archaeology Preserves What is Remembered and What is Forgotten in Israel's History," *JBL* 122 [2003]: 401–25 [407]) contends that "The silence of the texts regarding the significance of house plans…favors an economic or functional rather than an ethnic impetus and no subsequent importance."

66. Scham, "The Days of the Judges." Dever is also aware of postprocessualism. See, e.g., *What Did the Biblical Writers Know?*, 65–66, 79–95. Here, Dever, however, uses artifactual evi-dence to explore the Bible's reliability on a number of specific historical questions such as city

"lifeways" of people in the hill country of Palestine in the Late Bronze and Early Iron Ages and finds craft specialization,[67] "agricultural expertise,"[68] and an apparent "urban–rural dichotomy in the hills" of Ephraim at this time.[69]

Whereas most historians of ancient Israel would stop with these conclusions drawn from terraces, cisterns, and site layouts, Scham continues with a close look at imagery found on individual artifacts such as a cult stand and a krater. In these she sees both further evidence for the development of "urban crafts," as well as symbolic value placed on domesticated animals such as the bull and the ram and nondomesticated animals such as the ibex.[70] Conceding that "it is difficult to speculate on the basis of only a few images," she nonetheless concludes that "the material culture speaks of a coexistence between agricultural and urban crafts as well as wild and domesticated animal exploitation."[71] She sees this dichotomy borne out in the biblical story of Deborah, Barak, and Jael (in Ephraim), as well, because in these stories images, names, and plots indicate both positive and negative associations with urbanism and technology, as well as with untamed nature.[72] Scham's article ends with a discussion of "Israelite plots" in which she uses Ian Hodder's conception of cultural narratives to characterize her conclusions about each of these geographical units and to argue that cultural differences between them were apparent and important.[73]

Scham's approach is similar to that recommended by Gary Halsall (discussed in Chapter 2).[74] In typical postprocessualist fashion, Scham attempts to put evidence drawn from artifacts on an even footing with evidence drawn from texts,[75] and believes that postprocessual archaeology can assist in the integration of observations from both types of evidence into conclusions. Scham explains: "As a discipline that bridges the sciences and the humanities, archaeology must also provide a bridge between the abstract (interpretation) and the concrete (material culture)."[76] The conclusions Scham makes, however, do not provide

building and the nature of the Israelite cult rather than as an independent source of information about *mentalités* or cultural patterns.

67.   Scham, "The Days of the Judges," 48.

68.   Ibid., 49.

69.   Ibid., 50.

70.   Ibid.

71.   Ibid.

72.   Similar correlations between what Scham calls the "lifeworld of ancient Palestine" and stories in Judges are found for the territories of Manasseh, Benjamin, and Judah.

73.   Ibid., 62–64.

74.   Summed up in Halsall, "Archaeology and Historiography," 822.

75.   "[A]n actual text is a part of the material culture examined but there is no real difference in the analytical tools used for interpreting any artifacts" (Scham, "The Days of the Judges" 44); cf. Dever, *What Did the Biblical Writers Know?*, 67.

76.   Scham, "The Days of the Judges," 41. Whereas Scham conceives of postprocessual archaeology as "a bridge between the sciences and the humanities," Albright saw history filling this role. It seems that both disciplines could help the sciences and the humanities communicate, especially if the relationship of history and archaeology to each other continues to be more clearly defined and useful. Albright, however, also believed that humans channeled their most profound thoughts into religion, whereas postprocessual archaeologists see humans' search for meaning in

reconstructions of particular events and people; rather, they give insight into *mentalités* and lifeways of people that are remembered as the ancestors of Israel and Judah. While historians may decry the lack of human-oriented information in Scham's article, this absence is due not to her method but to the evidence available. In fact, the postprocessual approach allows Scham to say more about this time and place than most recent historians have felt confident saying. Furthermore, Scham's analysis contributes not only to an understanding of Iron Age Palestinian culture, it is also relevant to understanding the Bible itself (which the minimalists advocate as an important task), as Scham states that the "separate cultural strands" evidenced by the various plots in Judges "had a pivotal role in the formation of the variegated cultural sensibilities that came to be known as Israelite."[77] In other words, Scham argues that the book of Judges likely preserved stories that accurately reflected aspects of the symbol systems of various groups in Late Bronze/Early Iron Age hill country Palestine.

Postprocessual archaeology's theories allow for artifacts to be considered for their symbolic and context-laden meaning, and procedures of postprocessual archaeology can guide historians on how to stand independently analyzed texts and artifacts side-by-side in historical reconstruction. Scham's example further shows that by using these methods and procedures, new conclusions about Israel's past can be drawn. Along with the benefits of using archaeology, including postprocessual archaeology, in writing a history of ancient Israel, however, some complications arise. First, historians are rarely trained archaeologists. Thus, historians often encounter artifactual data outside of a theoretical framework. It is necessary, then, that historians become familiar with both the material record of ancient Israel and its various interpretations in the hands of archaeologists. While historians are primarily arbiters of textual information, they need to be able to seek new evidence from archaeology and use the questions asked by archaeology to reframe the questions they are asking of their texts.[78] For instance, Scham's contribution could prompt historians to ask if there is other information in ancient texts relevant to understanding relationships between urban areas possessing technology and rural areas in the Late Bronze or Early Iron Age.

---

culture in general, which includes but is not limited to religion. Postprocessual archaeology's conception appears to be more appropriate for secular societies and even for present-day religious societies, as all are coping with globalization, a phenomenon with symbolic aspects that transcend religion. For a discussion of theological vs. secular frameworks for meaning, see Dever, *What Did the Biblical Writers Know?*, 286–90. For a discussion of how interpretive frameworks in biblical studies since Albright have paralleled those in archaeology, see idem, "On Listening to the Text—and the Artifacts," in *The Echoes of Many Texts: Reflections on Jewish and Christian Traditions Essays in Honor of Lou H. Silberman* (ed. William G. Dever and J. Edward Wright; Atlanta: Scholars Press, 1997), 1–23.

77. Scham, "The Days of the Judges," 63.

78. Archaeologists could, of course, use texts in a similar manner. See, e.g., Dever, *What Did the Biblical Writers Know?*, especially Chapter 3, "What Archaeology Is and What It Can Contribute to Biblical Studies," and Keel and Uehlinger, *Gods, Goddesses and Images of God*, 396.

Another factor complicating the relationship of artifacts to texts in history writing is again that method cannot specify the judgments historians will make about which textual and artifactual evidence to believe and how to relate one to the other. Objectivity can, however, guide these judgments. As was argued above for texts, objectivity can help by ensuring that all potential information is taken into account and by offering guidelines for evaluation of others' judgments. More generally, having objectivity as a goal in history writing would require that no type of evidence about the past is ever privileged from the outset, but that only after investigation and attempts to understand sources as much as possible can some sources or types of sources be understood as better-suited for the historical investigation at hand.

One way of conceiving the relationship of history to archaeology is to see it as analogous to the relationship of electrical engineering to physics or chemistry. Electrical circuits cannot be designed without knowledge of the chemical and physical properties of the materials involved, but electrical engineering has its own purposes and goals (as do chemistry and physics). Likewise, Syro-Palestinian archaeology can exist independently of history, but to write history, archaeology is needed. Archaeology can provide information to be used at points in history's story and may even offer some explanations of change, but history must tell a story that includes events and people about which there may be no tangible remains other than a mention in a text. Thus, while Scham's postprocessual analysis of Late Bronze and Early Iron Age Israel can stop with observations about the perceptions of the physical and symbolic lifeworlds, history must incorporate such observations, using them to attempt to tell a comprehensive story over time.

New Questions About Assumptions Brought to Evidence Evaluation by Historians of Ancient Israel

Discussions of how historians judge whether texts and artifacts convey reliable historical information are fundamental to understanding how historians work. As seen in Chapters 4 and 5, however, recent discussions about evidence for Israel's past have added some additional theoretical questions to the mix. For instance, the position that eyewitness or near-eyewitness accounts are far superior to secondary, depth-dimensional, or otherwise non-eyewitness accounts for history writing is found among historians in general (e.g. Finley) and among minimalist historians of ancient Israel (where Henige has defended it). On the other hand, non-minimalists in general have operated with the assumption that non-eyewitness sources, such as the Bible, can and must be used in history writing, and Provan has asked specifically whether the emphasis placed on primary sources is reasonable or necessary. Minimalists and Henige also assert that sources as contentious as the Bible need to be verified by other, more reliable evidence (such as epigraphic or archaeological finds), while Provan opposes this notion.

At this juncture, objectivity again can help frame the issues and give perspective to the contentious debate. Since all sources should at least be considered, an objectively oriented approach to history cannot support the position that nonprimary sources are worthless or of little use from the outset. As seen above, objectivity can provide criteria for evaluating all types of evidence, and, since the final judgments about evidence are made by historians themselves, also criteria for evaluating the conclusions of peers. Thus, a defined notion of objectivity as a regulative ideal would provide non-minimalists with some of the ammunition they need to lead a louder challenge to primacy of eyewitness sources as evidence for history writing, or at least require a better justification of this position on the part of those who advocate it.

On another level, the debate about primary sources and verification of information in the Bible has been framed in terms of faith and skepticism in epistemology (mainly by Provan and Henige). A faith-based epistemology is one in which historians fundamentally believe, or desire to believe, potential evidence, and is justified by appeals to everyday experience—we believe many things that we have no way to verify independently, and could not operate otherwise.[79] Under a skeptical epistemology, historians are critical of all potential evidence about the past. Scholars justify such skepticism in history by appeals to accepted historical method and examples of historical reconstructions that too naively trusted evidence and turned out to be faulty.

Objectivity cannot navigate between epistemologies of faith and epistemologies of skepticism, but it seems obvious that neither epistemology can or should dominate the thoughts of historians or humans in general. Whenever possible, rigorous examination of evidence for a claim should take place. Skepticism does not underlie this procedure, but rather empiricism and proper scientific historical method (as discussed in Chapter 1). In the absence of potential verification or other proof that evidence is likely reliable, neither automatic skepticism nor faith is appropriate. Rather, some of both is needed, measured out as conclusions are drawn from further investigation of the evidence at hand. For instance, research into the Bible's origins and composition provides some instructive, though not determinative, information relating to its reliability. Comparative analysis of texts from other cultures may not offer proof of any specific features of the events described in the Bible, but can nevertheless lend an air of credibility or incredibility to the evidence that can point historians toward skepticism or faith as they progress in their investigation.[80]

In short, historians cannot choose between faith and skepticism—it is not an either–or proposition, but indeed a false dichotomy that oversimplifies naturally complex philosophical and psychological processes. Perhaps such polarization is to be expected in the early stages of the debate, and the questions brought about by the writings of Henige, Provan, and others will likely be pursued with vigor

---

79.   Also pointed out by Atkinson (see Chapter 1).

80.   Meier's *A Marginal Jew*, vol. 1, especially Chapter 1, provides an example of specific criteria formulated to address the problem of the historical Jesus along these lines.

over the next several years. Nevertheless, instead of positioning themselves on one side or the other of this manufactured divide, historians should continue to pursue questions of evidence using objectivity as a regulative ideal, gaining the most information about their sources as possible, and remaining open to dialogue with other scholars about new methods and conclusions that affect the evaluation and use of evidence for Israel's past.

Subject

How historians choose a subject for history depends on both practical and philosophical considerations. The choice of history's subject is related to evidence, since historians must have information about their subject in order to tell its story. Since the nineteenth century, however, some ideas about proper subjects for history have changed for reasons not related to evidence. At that time, humans, mainly powerful ones (who primarily have been men) were traditionally the subjects of history. Structures such as politics, law, or religion potentially were also part of the story of the past, but usually these demonstrated the backgrounds or consequences of human actions and were not considered subjects of history in and of themselves. Structuralism, arising in the mid-twentieth century, helped move social structures to the forefront of history in general, and poststructuralism continued this trend. As formerly powerless groups came to power, history from below also became an accepted trajectory in the discipline. Thus, by the end of the twentieth century, the discipline of history included chronological stories of *mentalités*, suprahuman social structures, and other subjects that cannot be considered agents in their own development, as well as human beings of many types.

Historians of ancient Israel have reflected the general trends of the twentieth century. Albrightians and Altians focused on events and human action as well as on some structures such as law, religion, and politics. Interest in structures, especially the political structures that constituted the early Israelite state, continued into the late twentieth century. By then, historians of ancient Israel, like historians in general, had also begun to ask questions about humans normally given short shrift in the Bible and modern histories of Israel, particularly women. Though trends in subjects in the history of Israel paralleled larger trends in the historical discipline, during this time the emergence of serious doubts about the Bible's portrayal of Israel's past challenged long-held assumptions that Israel could be identified by some combination—largely derived from the Bible—of geography, religion, ethnicity, and/or culture. Thus, the most pressing issue about history's subject for historians of ancient Israel became the question of how to define the subject of Israel's history in general, that is, how to identify the entity within which human-driven actions and events as well as social structures in Israel's past could be examined.

In response to the evidentiary questions that related to defining Israel's subject, some trends began to emerge among historians of ancient Israel. Minimalism's assertion that the biblical text is full of invented information about ancient Israel, combined with increased attention to literary structures and constructions in the Bible, allowed them to understand Israel as an imaginary construct. Therefore, minimalists suggested potential subjects for history such as the origin, development, and purposes of the idea of Israel, the small political entities of the House of Omri and Judah in ancient Palestine (as attested outside of the Bible), and the origin, development, purpose, and sociology of the Bible itself. Some minimalists even produced sociological histories of Palestinian culture that avoided traditional conceptions of Israel as history's subject. For instance, Coote and Whitelam's *Emergence of Early Israel* reconstructed an Israel without reference to the Bible. On the other hand, as seen in Chapter 5, most historians continued to allow the Bible to help them define their subject. These non-minimalists consider the Bible's portrayal factual in parts of its outline as well as in some of its details. Furthermore, whereas minimalists have advocated sociologically based histories of structures in ancient Palestine, non-minimalists have not reached a consensus about the role of structures or subject-less histories in the reconstruction of Israel's past. Deist, for instance, has explicitly stated that human subjects are necessary to history: "History is…not about generalities but exactly about the human factor in the course of events."[81] Gottwald, on the other hand, has written *The Tribes of Yahweh* and *The Politics of Ancient Israel*, both examinations of structures that organized Israelite society.

In order to clarify the current discussion of acceptable subjects for histories of ancient Israel, evidentiary and philosophical matters must be considered together. First, though objectivity requires that the Bible be given careful consideration as a potential source of evidence for ancient Israel, this argument does not legitimate naive adoption of biblical Israel as a historical subject. The Pentateuch, Deuteronomistic History, prophets, and Chronicles (as well as the New Testament) all portray Israel differently. Thus, on a fundamental level Davies and the minimalists are correct: ancient Israel is a modern scholarly construction. Yet the history of Israel need not be equivalent to the chronological story of differing conceptions of Israel. Rather, what the Bible says about Israel is an indication of what certain members of this community saw as important defining traits of their culture. Culture, including self-conceptions of culture, can provide a basis for defining a subject or subjects for histories of ancient Israel. Specifically, Albright's definition of the culture-unit, which he saw as the proper subject of history, can be used to create a working profile of a culture-unit relevant to the study of Israel's past.

Albright defined a culture-unit as "a geographically and chronologically limited horizon, in which there is a real homogeneity about the aspect of any element or factor, which ceases as soon as we cross these boundaries of space and time."[82] Certainly the idea that a "real homogeneity" can be identified in a group of people, especially ancient people, is problematic. Likewise, Albright's

---

81. Deist, "Contingency, Continuity and Integrity in Historical Understanding," 104.
82. Albright, *From the Stone Age to Christianity*, 84–85.

notion that a group's defining characteristics are so unique that they disappear when space–time boundaries are crossed appears more romantic than scholarly.[83] Postprocessualism furthers the notion that culture is fluid and that trying to restrict a culture to certain traits or time periods is an artificial undertaking. Historians, however, must accept some of the artificiality of defining a culture-unit in order to have an object for study.

Looking at ancient Israel in the biblical account, many potential factors that could explain cultural unity appear diluted. Some examples include Israel's bloodline, which included wandering Arameans, and a Moabite, Ruth, as the ancestress of King David, and language, which, according to the "shibboleth incident" described in Judg 12:6, had noticeable regional differences. Unique aspects of an Israelite culture are equally difficult to find in the artifactual record, as installations common in Iron Age central Palestine, such as four-room houses, collared-rim store jars, lime-slaked cisterns, and terracing, are better understood as general Palestinian rather than Israelite inventions.[84] Albright, of course, found evidence for homogeneity in ancient Israel in these artifacts as well as in the biblical ideal of monotheistic Yahwism.

Despite the difficulty of locating a monolithic Israelite religious tradition, religion does appear to be one good candidate for a unifying, if not entirely homogenous, element in ancient Israel's culture. Certainly the Bible perceives allegiance to Yahweh as greater Israel's primary bond or obligation. Artifactual evidence in the form of inscriptions that include names with a theophoric element of the divine name YHWH indicates that Yahweh-worship was common, and in the Iron II period predominant, among Hebrew speakers in Iron Age Palestine.[85] Such theophoric-YHWH names do not abruptly disappear outside of this temporal–geographical unit, but most later occurrences of these names appear to have their origin in the traditions of Iron Age Palestinian–Israelite culture. On the other hand, identifying Yahweh-worship with early, or incipient, Israel, has been problematic since the time of Albright. For instance, Zevit has

---

83. Of course, the designations used by archaeologists, e.g., "Iron Age," "Bronze Age," etc., imply similar continuity.

84. Schloen, "W. F. Albright and the Origins of Israel," 58; also Bloch-Smith, "Israelite Ethnicity in Iron I," who argues that "not a single feature of [Iron I highland Palestinian settlements] may be conclusively identified as 'Israelite.'" In this analysis she includes four-room houses as well as collared-rim store jars, site location and layout. For a general discussion of the continuity of Israelite culture with Canaanite culture, see Mazar, *Archaeology of the Land of the Bible*, 353–55. For a contrasting opinion see Volkmar Fritz, "Israelites and Canaanites: You *Can* Tell Them Apart," *BAR* 28, no. 4 (2002): 28–31, 63, and Dever, *Who Were the Israelites?*, throughout.

85. Jeffrey H. Tigay, *You Shall Have No Other Gods: Israelite Religion in the Light of Hebrew Inscriptions* (HSS 31; Atlanta: Scholars Press, 1986); Dana Marston Pike, "Israelite Theophoric Personal Names in the Bible and Their Implications for Religious History" (Ph.D. diss., University of Pennsylvania, 1990); Robert Karl Gnuse, *No Other Gods: Emergent Monotheism in Israel* (JSOTSup 241; Sheffield: Sheffield Academic Press, 1997). For an integrated study of the conclusions of Gnuse and Tigay, along with those of others working with this evidence, see Brad Kelle, *Hosea 2: Metaphor and Rhetoric in Historical Perspective* (Academia Biblical 20; Atlanta: Society of Biblical Literature, 2005), Chapter 5. See also Zevit, *The Religions of Ancient Israel*, 439–510, 586–609, 687–90.

argued that Yahweh was but one of many deities venerated by inhabitants of central Palestine in the Iron I period,[86] and even the Bible gives evidence for non-Yahwistic gods and cultic practices. Thus, Israelite culture cannot be defined exclusively by its association with Yahwism. Nevertheless, indications of Yahwistic religion provide a very fruitful entrée into the necessarily artificial process of delineating an Israelite culture-unit for study.

A culture-unit, according to Albright's definition, also requires a "geographically and chronologically limited horizon." Historians of ancient Israel have often posited such horizons based on the biblical material, making Israel geographically conform approximately to the land allotted to the twelve tribes, that is, to an area stretching roughly north to the mountains of Lebanon and south to the border of Egyptian territory. Close reading of the biblical material, however, shows that the majority of the action in the Hebrew Bible occurs near Jerusalem and Samaria, essentially in the modern-day West Bank. Archaeological investigation provides different information about geographical divisions in antiquity. For instance, Israel Finkelstein's work, along with other studies and surveys, has documented new Early Iron Age settlements throughout the central hills and even into the Galilee,[87] and most archaeologists agree that these new settlements have to do with Israel's inception. Research into the Transjordan in the Iron Age still lags behind knowledge of the Cisjordan, but emerging patterns of settlement there appear similar at this time.[88] Archaeology also shows that the Philistines were a powerful force on the coast throughout the Iron Age.[89] Determining ancient Israel's geographical horizon therefore requires an amalgam of both biblical and archaeological information. Placing Israelite culture between the coastal plain to the west and possibly the Jordan River to the east, and in the inhabitable regions north of the desert and south of the Sea of Galilee would be one alternative that, based on both sources of evidence, approximates potentially fluid territorial divisions.

Perhaps the most complex aspect of identifying Israel as a culture-unit is determining its chronological horizon, given the potential evidence. The Bible's story begins with creation, and Abraham is said to have lived centuries before David and any Israelite kingdom. The exodus from Egypt and subsequent entry into Palestine of the Hebrews marks another important era in the biblical story, as do the periods of the judges, the formation of the kingship under Saul and David, and the division of the kingdom after Solomon's death. The destructions of Samaria and Jerusalem close major chapters in the biblical story. Chronological markers of central Palestinian culture used by archaeologists differ from the

86.   Ibid., 604–9 and throughout.

87.   Israel Finkelstein, *The Archaeology of the Israelite Settlement* (Jerusalem: Israel Exploration Society, 1988); Zvi Gal, *Lower Galilee During the Iron Age* (Winona Lake, Ind.: Eisenbrauns, 1992). See also the bibliography in Rudolph Cohen, "Survey of Israel," *OEANE* 5:104–6 (106).

88.   James A. Sauer and Larry G. Herr, "Transjordan in the Bronze and Iron Ages," *OEANE* 5:231–35 (233–34).

89.   See Trude Dothan, "Early Philistines," *OEANE* 4:310–11, and Seymour Gitin, "Late Philistines," *OEANE* 4:311–13.

biblical scheme. They find widespread destruction and indications of cultural change in the form of drastically reduced Egyptian and Anatolian influence in Palestine at the end of the Late Bronze Age. Indications of destructions and population movements in Palestine during the Iron Age can be correlated with Assyrian and Babylonian incursions. On the other hand, the situation in Judah after the Babylonians destroyed Jerusalem is under debate. Scholars agree that Judah's urban centers were destroyed, but some hold that archaeology shows an almost total destruction of the settlements in the Judean countryside, as well.[90] Others argue that the Babylonians retained some rural settlements in Judah, and that archaeology has uncovered indications of these villages.[91] A bias for or against the biblical picture of a postexilic empty land has been alleged as motivation for these archaeological interpretations.

Where to begin Israel's story is the most problematic issue for historians, and different approaches can be seen in historical works from the twentieth century. Albright's *From the Stone Age to Christianity*, Ahlström's *History of Ancient Palestine*, and Thompson's *Mythic Past* begin with Palestine before the Israelites in order to set the stage for them. Miller and Hayes' *History of Ancient Israel and Judah* starts with the conditions leading up to the monarchy, while Soggin's *Introduction to the History of Israel and Judah* claims that history begins with the first extrabiblical indications of Israelite or Judahite political entities, namely, around the ninth century BCE. Abraham Malamat's suggestion that Israel's history begins "when the Israelite tribes crystallized within Canaan," is also a possible starting point, albeit a problematic one, since both the genesis of Israelite tribes and their crystallization are difficult to date.[92] Steven Grosby has argued that the Israelite idea of nationality may have emerged as late as the seventh and sixth centuries BCE. He draws these conclusions only from information about Israel's self-perception found in the Bible,[93] but objectivity requires that all types of evidence, including artifactual evidence that might speak to cultural continuity, be taken into account. Also, Israel's concept of nationality

90. See, e.g., Ephraim Stern, "The Babylonian Gap: The Archaeological Reality," *JSOT* 28 (2004): 273–77.

91. See, e.g., Oded Lipschits, "The Rural Settlement in Judah in the Sixth Century B.C.E.: A Rejoinder," *PEQ* 136 (2004): 99–107.

92. Abraham Malamat, "The Proto-History of Israel: A Study in Method," in *The Word of the Lord Shall Go Forth: Essays in Honor of David Noel Freedman in Celebration of His Sixtieth Birthday* (ed. Carol Meyers and M. O'Connor; Winona Lake, Ind.: Eisenbrauns, 1983), 301–13 (304); repr. in Abraham Malamat, *History of Biblical Israel: Major Problems and Minor Issues* (Culture and History of the Ancient Near East 7; Leiden: Brill, 2001), 3–16. Furthermore, Malamat's assertion that this crystallization correlated with the tribes "becoming the dominant force" in Canaan cannot be accepted (ibid.). The Philistines were at least one dominant force in Canaan for much of the time period of Israel's history, whereas the Judean kingdom, so important to the biblical story, likely was not dominant until after the destruction of Samaria in 721 BCE or Lachish in 701 BCE. In other words, as a chronological marker, the advent of the "dominance" of the Israelite tribes and their successors, the Israelite and Judean kingdoms, is too vague and too problematic.

93. Steven Grosby, *Biblical Ideas of Nationality: Ancient and Modern* (Winona Lake, Ind.: Eisenbrauns, 2002), 68. Grosby's investigation considers religion, territory, and kinship as factors in a nation's self-definition.

may have formed in the time Grosby suggests, but its own account of its nationality, the Bible, includes events that occurred before this time. Thus, Israel as the subject of history cannot begin at the time when the idea of Israel as a nation coalesced, just as American history does not begin with the Declaration of Independence or the constitution.

Though the questions of when to begin Israel's story and how to identify potentially early Israelite unity seem to be hindered by evidentiary considerations at many points, Elizabeth Bloch-Smith has recently made some intriguing suggestions. Rather than understand Israel by what she calls a "Culture Area approach," (such as the one taken here where geography, chronology, and cultural attributes combine in the definition of a historical entity), she advocates a "Tell-Tale" approach. Drawing on ethnographic studies and using comparative practices similar to those espoused by postprocessual archaeologists (and to those demonstrated by Scham), Bloch-Smith takes up the problematic issue of early Israel's self-identity and unity by noting how Israel identifies itself in contrast to the Philistines. She sees "four distinguishing traits of Israelites from their own perspective: circumcision, maintaining a short beard, abstinence from eating pork, and military inferiority."[94] She concludes that "Archaeology makes it possible to date Israelite military conflict with the Philistines plus pork abstinence and wearing a short beard as contextually meaningful practices to the twelfth to eleventh/early tenth centuries B.C.E."[95] She admits that none of these features may have been unique to Israel, but points out that their importance in Israel's self-definition was eventually made permanent in the Bible. Bloch-Smith's approach thus allows for potential evidence for what constituted Israel's early self-definition and the time this notion may have originated to be incorporated into history's early chronological horizon for the Israelites.[96]

On the later end, the Bible sees continuity reaching back from late Persian/ early Hellenistic times until before the exile. Hellenism instigated a new "Israelite" culture, one that can be firmly established as having strong elements of assimilation with a foreign culture quite different religiously and politically from any Israel had experienced up to that time. Therefore, the Hellenistic period would be a justifiable stopping point for ancient Israel's history. Ending Israel's story at the time the Greeks arrive in Palestine, however, need not be combined with any overt or implied judgment on the quality of Israel's religious life after this event.

Since many chronological schemes appear possible for Israel's history, historians again must objectively consider their evidence and justify their conclusions. Objectivity requires that early Israel, so important to the biblical tradition, be given some consideration in determining where a history of Israel begins. Also, objective consideration of Israel's time frame requires that events attested

94.   Bloch-Smith, "Israelite Ethnicity in Iron I," 415.
95.   Ibid., 423.
96.   For an approach to locating early Israel that claims not to use the Bible, see Robert D. Miller II, "Identifying Earliest Israel," *BASOR* 333 (2004): 55–68; for early Israel in general, see Day, ed., *In Search of Pre-Exilic Israel*.

in archaeology but not important to the Bible, such as the destruction of Lachish by the Assyrians, be part of any timeline of significant events in ancient Israel. In the same vein, important biblical events that are difficult to locate in the artifactual record, such as the conquest and the exile, may be used in the time-line but first must be carefully examined. On the other hand, outlining Paleo-lithic, Chalcolithic, and Early and Middle Bronze Age cultures is necessary only if it is shown that languages, religions, patterns of agriculture and survival, or social structures in pre-Israelite cultures may have had some influence on what occurred later in Israel.[97] To borrow from McCullagh, such information would need to be useful for understanding significant facts about or important causes of aspects of ancient Israel; otherwise, it can be omitted.

This brief discussion of culture-units is not sophisticated enough to define ancient Israelite culture fully, but has shown that religion as well as other aspects of Israel's self-portrait found in the Bible and nonbiblical evidence must contribute to considerations of the geographical and chronological horizons as well as the unity of this culture. Furthermore, drawing history's subject from the idea of a culture-unit is beneficial because it allows for events and structures to be included as subjects in history, along with examination of human interaction with structures and the development of structures in response to actions, events, human desires, and needs. In short, using the concept of a culture-unit as a regulative ideal for the subject in the history of Israel takes into account the types of evidence available and allows for humans to be subjects in history, while leaving room for structures of the communities that humans create and inhabit also to be included.[98]

Explanation

As discussed in Chapter 3, Albrightians and Altians believed that religious ideals could explain many aspects of Israel's existence, as well as human actions, resultant events, and cultural structures such as law and kingship in Israel. In addition, Albright and Alt theorized to some extent about explanation in history writing. Albright argued that historians can and should draw on their

---

97. Provan, Long, and Longman, for instance, argue that some tentative correlations between the Bronze Age and the biblical stories of the patriarchs and Moses can be made, which, if convincing, would add an important dimension to understanding Israel's past. Yet though they propose to describe the community of Israel "before the land," their analyses of the biblical stories of the patriarchs and Exodus offer very few historical conclusions. They argue, with many qualifi-cations and without much passion, that "the picture that emerges from the biblical text is analogous to a social pattern attested in the Mari tablets" (Provan, Long, and Longman, *A Biblical History of Israel*, 118), and show potential historical settings for the Joseph story (pp. 123–25) and the exodus (pp. 131–32), as well. Their conclusion to this section, however, does not mention the historical reliability of these stories and any importance that could be attached to that, but rather simply notes that these stories set the stage for the biblical story of Israel's entrance into the land (p. 137).

98. Despite Bloch-Smith's separation of the "Culture Area" and "Tell-Tale" approach, the understanding of a culture-unit proposed in the current study includes room for a culture's "tales" about itself.

own experience for historical explanations, though he did not believe historians should make psychological judgments about why people acted as they did. As for his own method of explanation, Albright claimed to examine aspects of culture separately and as parts of a functioning whole. Albright placed value on finding patterns and laws to explain the past, as well. Alt and Noth, in the tradition of Weber, sanctioned the use of comparative material for explanation, along with hypotheses, scholarly intuition, and the idea of a basic human connection that provided the historian with universal common values and understanding.

Explanation in History, Structures, and the Social Sciences
A major change in explanatory practices of historians of ancient Israel since Alt and Albright has been the increase in the use of social-scientific models and theories. This interdisciplinary undertaking can be successful because, as Natalie Davis noted, social scientists and historians share some interests, including social institutions, processes, and *mentalités*. Historians, however, have also urged that differences between history and the social sciences be recognized, and that difficulties and limits of this combination be addressed. One obvious disconnection between the two disciplines is that social-science theories and models are based on research of modern societies, while historians must base their observations of a society on evidence from the past. Also, the generalizing nature of models has caused concern that facile appropriation of them into historical study could lead to problems. Negative consequences of the combination could include reconstructions of past societies that are based on too little evidence, wrong analogies to social-scientific models, historical details that are obscured in order to make a model fit, and using the model as evidence rather than for comparison.

Historians of ancient Israel have given the topic of explanation using social-scientific theories and models more theoretical attention than any other type of explanation. The discussion of the use of the social sciences in Israel's history in Chapters 4 and 5 showed that many historians of ancient Israel believe the combination is beneficial to understanding the past. Indeed, social-scientific study of ancient Israel is a vital subdiscipline of Israelite history.[99] Scholars who have made explicit statements about the benefits of such cross-disciplinary study include Lemche, who, despite his cautions (discussed in Chapter 4), contends that social-scientific research methods can help identify new patterns or models not already known, and Whitelam, who asserts that social-scientific study of ancient Israel is methodologically pure, since by use of a model many of the researcher's assumptions are made clear. Also, Charles Carter has both advocated interdisciplinary work and laid out a program for its success, urging historians using social-scientific models to be "rigorous and self-critical,"[100] or, in other words, to be as objective as possible.

---

99.   This development traces its roots to Gottwald's *Tribes of Yahweh*. For a compilation of other seminal studies, see Carter and Meyers, eds., *Community, Identity, and Ideology*.
100.   Carter, "A Discipline in Transition," 28.

Not all scholars, however, are enthusiastic about the marriage of the social sciences with historical study for understanding Israel's past. As discussed previously, Scham worries that in social-scientific history there is the potential that meaningful details and culturally unique aspects will be subsumed to "vapid cultural analogies."[101] She argues that ancient cultures often require a "direct historical approach," in which information about the culture is garnered from sources nearer in time and space than modern-day ethnographic information.[102] Also, Miller has questioned whether any valuable insights have been provided by the combination of history and the social sciences.[103]

Though there is disagreement among historians about the value of social-scientific models and theories for explaining Israel's past, such models and theories are useful for history writing. Since the social sciences concern themselves with cultural structures and patterns, social-scientific models and theories are most appropriately used in the history of ancient Israel as sources of comparison that help clarify cultural structures and patterns. As Max Weber advocated, comparison should be used to stimulate not only attention to similarities but also differences. Of course, the many cautions set out here and in the previous chapters also should be taken into consideration. Most importantly, historians need to be educated about the models and theories they employ, and the social sciences and history should participate in a more mutual exchange of ideas.

On the surface, this formulation of the role of the social sciences in historical explanation seems obvious and noncontroversial. Yet, it does not address the decades-old tension between *Annales*-style histories of structures or poststructuralism's histories of nonstructures, and human-action and event-oriented history. In other words, how should historians combine information about structures with information about human actions and events in history? In Chapter 1, it was seen that scholars such as David Hillel Rueben and Mark Bevir argue that explanation ultimately must be based on human agency, while McCullagh claimed that the influence of structures and human behavior on events may not be able to be separated. Furthermore, since this study has asserted that the Bible's conception or conceptions of Israel should be part of the delineation of history's subject, and since the Bible identifies Israel as having a special relationship with Yahweh, consideration of how structures, particularly religious ideas, become part of historical explanations is in order. By and large, historians of ancient Israel have not discussed the relationship of structures to action in theoretical

101. Scham, "The Days of the Judges," 40.
102. Ibid., 42. Some of these ancient sources may be "neither objective nor factual," but are more closely related to the culture under study than other social-scientific data (p. 43).
103. Miller, "Reading the Bible Historically," 25. While it is difficult to know from Miller's comment what types of information about Israel's past he would find valuable, one can point to increased understandings of tribal and clan societies, early state societies, subsistence strategies, prophecy, and dietary laws as a few contributions of the social-scientific study of ancient Israel. Miller, in fact, uses some ideas derived from the social sciences in *A History of Ancient Israel and Judah*. For tribes and clans see pp. 91–93, for subsistence societies see pp. 52–53. Both of these sections are primarily Miller's contribution (see p. 20).

terms.[104] Thus, assumptions about the relationship of structures to human actions in histories of ancient Israel will have to be deduced from examples. For this brief analysis, history writing that seeks to tell a comprehensive story of ancient Israel over time will provide the best case studies. Here, the histories of Soggin, Ahlström, Miller and Hayes, and Thompson will be used.

Alt and Albright placed emphasis on religion as an explanation for ancient Israel. On the other hand, Soggin, Thompson, Miller and Hayes, and Ahlström either ignore religion or place it among other defining and explanatory factors for ancient Israel. Religion is not absent from Miller and Hayes' understanding of Israel's development, but it is not a primary category of explanation, either. For instance, they explain the "Instability of the Northern Kingdom" by the diversity of its population, its economic base, international trade, geographical positioning vis-à-vis other powers at the time, the lack of royal theology there, and "political activism on the part of the Yahwistic prophets."[105] Though, as noted above, ideas derived from social-scientific study appear in their work, they do not discuss models explicitly. Miller and Hayes also present rational explanations for events and human actions.[106] Taking a more materialistic approach, Soggin sets Hezekiah's supposed religious reforms in the context of "restoration of a Davidic empire" that had its motivation in territorial and financial gain at the time of Assyria's rise.[107] Soggin also explains the past by using social-scientific theories of Israel's appearance in Canaan,[108] and occasionally attempts to enter the decision-making process of ancient individuals.[109] Ahlström includes "ideology" and material factors as explanations,[110] as well as rational explanations for human actions,[111] but does not explicitly identify explanatory schemes from the social sciences. Throughout *Early History*, Thompson attributes conditions in central Palestine to geographical and economic–political factors. He devotes an entire chapter to sociological theory,[112] and uses concepts derived from the social sciences throughout the book. Individual human action, and thus any explanation for it, is absent from Thompson's work.

104. Though Max Weber's *Ancient Judaism* does not addresses this relationship in theoretical terms, either, Mayes (*The Old Testament in Sociological Perspective*, 46–48) has deduced Weber's theoretical base as the assumption that a charismatic breakthrough of an individual, such as a prophet, can lead to new structures and beliefs and their rationalization and routinization.

105. Miller and Hayes, *A History of Ancient Israel and Judah*, 234–35.

106. See, e.g., their description of "those who confronted Rehoboam at Shechem" as people with "special reasons for disenchantment with the house of David, beyond Solomon's harsh treatment of his subjects." These reasons include displacement of the house of Saul and deemphasis of cultic places and priests of Ephraim/Israel (p. 230).

107. Soggin, *Introduction to the History of Israel and Judah*, 246–52.

108. Ibid., 159–62. Soggin finds both helpful and unsupportable suggestions in the theories of Mendenhall and Gottwald.

109. Describing Ahaz's decision to call on Assyria for help against Israel and Damascus, he notes "Ahaz and his counsellors seem completely to have lost their heads" (ibid., 240).

110. See, e.g., his description of the reign of Jeroboam (Ahlström, *The History of Ancient Palestine*, 543–58).

111. For example, "Omri's political 'west-orientation' was probably the reason he abandoned Tirzah as the capital of the kingdom" (Ahlström, *The History of Ancient Palestine*, 572).

112. Thompson, *Early History*, 26–76.

The examination of the four histories used as case studies shows that the confidence these scholars have in the Bible as a source of evidence is a major factor in the modes of explanations they see as available to them. Thus, Miller and Hayes and Ahlström, who put some confidence in many aspects of the Bible's description of the past, include religion as part of the explanation for Israel's unity as well as for the actions of individuals. They also find enough information about ideology, economics, class structure, trade, and state formation in the Bible (and in archaeology) to present a picture of ancient Israel that is derived from rational thought about this society's needs and context. For instance, they can explain early Israel without comparing the Bible's description of it to social-scientific models that discuss typical aspects of tribal societies or incipient monarchies.[113] Soggin, who finds reliable evidence for the past scattered throughout the Bible, chooses explanations on an ad hoc basis, as he believes evidence permits. Thompson, who puts little confidence in the Bible's story of early Israel, turns to understandings of the relationship of humans and agricultural economies to the environment to explain the Late Bronze–Early Iron Age transition. He claims that other aspects of early Israelite society that he does not find in the archaeological record, such as religious beliefs and reasons for ethnic self-identification, are "refracted by tradition" from a later time and thus hard to identify.[114]

Rather than provide grounds for general formulations for the types of relationships historians of ancient Israel posit between structures and human actions, or even a generalization of the types of explanations historians of ancient Israel use, this initial look indicates that ideas about evidence for ancient Israel are at the root of ideas about and practices of explanation. Explanations of human behavior that operate on an individual level, such as rational explanation, require evidence of human action, as well as evidence for mitigating factors that may have affected human agents. Such information usually would be found in texts, meaning the Bible in the case of ancient Israel.[115] On the other hand, explanations of structures require information about general patterns in a past culture, some of which could be found in the archaeological record. In the case of religion, however, the scholars discussed in these case studies tend to look for

---

113. See, e.g., the discussions of Solomon's administration in Miller and Hayes, *A History of Ancient Israel and Judah*, 204–17, and Ahlström, *The History of Ancient Palestine*, 501–42.

114. Thompson, *Early History*, 385.

115. Provan, Long, and Longman's *A Biblical History of Israel* would appear to be a recent candidate for reinforcing this assertion since it claims to privilege evidence from the Bible. The authors of this study, however, almost never reach firm conclusions about what actually occurred in ancient Israel and how to explain it. The majority of their chapters that include historical reconstructions, which range from "Before the Land" to "The Exile and After," are devoted to presenting and discussing the biblical pictures of these periods. When considering this evidence, qualifiers such as "if" and "we are told" introduce almost all the Bible's claims (see, e.g., p. 264). Thus, whereas the introductory chapters of the book make a strong case for considering biblical evidence, Provan, Long, and Longman in the end do not use the biblical information with as much confidence as they profess can be done. The result is that they present the occurrence of many specific events, the existence of certain religious ideas, and explanations for them as hypothetical.

evidence in the Bible. Certainly the Bible can provide much information about Israelite religion, but, as argued above, the interpretation of artifacts, especially using ideas from postprocessual archaeology, can illuminate religious beliefs. Thus, artifacts, interpreted properly, can balance out the evidentiary basis on which explanations involving religion are made.

Other Types of Explanation

The prevalence of social-scientific modeling in the practical and theoretical discussion about explanation of Israel's past has led to statements of benefits, cautions, and methods pertaining to the combination. It has also led this study to examine how historians of ancient Israel use information about social structures when explaining human actions, which, as discussed above, many historians of ancient Israel seek to retain as part of history's subject. As seen in Chapters 4 and 5, however, late twentieth-century historians of ancient Israel have not neglected more general considerations of explanation entirely. For instance, Davies has championed "logical deduction" and "controlled probability" as means to historical explanations.[116] Edelman contends that laws have no place in historical reconstructions,[117] and Deist says that explanation begins with the experience of the historian.[118] These statements fall in line with common ideas about rational explanation discussed over the past century, from Troeltsch to Collingwood and beyond. In fact, the relative paucity of such reflection among historians of ancient Israel, combined with rational explanation's persistence in history writing, likely indicates that rational explanation is a practice they take for granted. On the other hand, despite the urgings of openly religious scholars like Long, explanations that involve divine action do not appear to have much support in the academic community.

Conclusion[119]

In summary, explanation in the history of Israel, like explanation in history in general, takes many forms. Rational judgments of historians, sometimes based on personal opinion or experience, appear to be natural contributions to under-standing the past. Models or frameworks of explanation that are based on gen-eral principles or laws are also used. Yet even proponents of the social-scientific study of ancient Israel are careful not to let generalizations eclipse aspects of Israel that may be unique. Finally, as with most other topics examined in this study, the desire of historians of ancient Israel to understand and explain as much about the past as possible is hindered more by evidentiary considerations than by philosophical concerns. Yet as history's subject broadens to include

116. Davies, "Method and Madness," 700.
117. Edelman, "Doing History in Biblical Studies," 19.
118. Deist, "Contingency, Continuity and Integrity in Historical Understanding," 106–7.
119. Narrative, an important vehicle for explanation, has not been mentioned in this review of explanation in writing Israel's history. In order to understand the topic fully and comprehensively, and to consider its importance for history writing about ancient Israel, it will be treated separately below.

elements of culture and society, explanations of many types are needed. Deist's assertion that in general, the "most elegant" explanation for observed phenomena is the best,[120] is a helpful principle to apply, given the broad scope of subjects and explanation common now in history writing. Calling an explanation "elegant" is, of course, subjective, but minimally would require that the explanation be intelligible and relevant to the questions asked and the subjects chosen.

The Nexus of Representation, Language, Narrative, and Truth

Narrative is an exposition of a subject that has a chronological storyline. As discussed in Chapter 1, in history writing narrative has been connected with explanations of human action, though Ricoeur argued that histories lacking human subjects still take on characteristics of narrative. Literary analysis of history writing has raised questions about narrative in history writing that touch on issues of representation and language in history, historians' preconceived notions, selectivity in history, and the impact of a historical presentation on its interpretation. For instance, Wolfgang von Leyden discusses representation and what he called the "mediacy" of language, namely, that in order to represent the past, historians must employ language that can offer only glimpses and interpretations of bygone times. Hayden White argues that historians select the language and the form of their presentations of the past not on the basis of evidence but rather based on preconceived tropes. He also contended that historians' literary style both heavily influences possible interpretations of the past and betrays their belief or nonbelief in what might be called history's telos, grand narrative, or overall direction. Viewed through White's lens, then, historical narrative reveals factors intrinsic to the historian's worldview that in some ways may be too deep-seated and comprehensive to be called merely biases.

Literary criticism of historical writing has also raised the question of whether history is distinct from fiction. Further, deconstruction asks if literature's referent can be identified apart from the construction of the text itself, which, like the history–fiction issue, challenges any special genre or truth status afforded to historical writing. Michel Foucault's claim that truth wields power, and that institutions that claim truth do so for self-preservation, relativizes truth, making truth, including historical truth, a product of the mind of the self-interested reader or writer. Finally, Burke and others have pointed out that the tone the historian chooses—whether an authoritative or a qualified voice—creates a strong impression of how interconnected past events are and the certainty with which they can be understood.

Some reflection on issues of representation and language among historians of ancient Israel can be seen in their general awareness that language can neither completely nor accurately represent the entirety of the past or any part of it. Davies asserts that history is "limited by the boundaries of language," calling

---

120. Deist, *The Material Culture of the Bible*, 61; cf. Cook, *History/Writing*, 6.

histories "literary portraits."[121] As discussed in Chapter 5, Long has urged historians to write history that aims to show a big picture of the past rather than details about it, since representation, he believes, is more reliable and effective when attempted on a broad scale. Historians of ancient Israel have also debated a number of other literary choices historians make, although they may not have understood them as such. For instance, the appropriate subject of history and whether to emplot the events of Israel's past using the major biblical events as chronological markers or by using another framework are partly literary concerns.

On the other hand, historians of ancient Israel rarely have addressed the narrative or literary character of their own work or history's distinction from fiction (though they have applied literary critiques to the biblical text or adopted such ideas from biblical scholars in general). Exceptions include Knauf, Halpern, and Barstad (discussed in Chapter 5) who have defended writing history as a narrative story about the past and have begun to explore the role of language in history, the distinction of history from fiction, and the types of truth claims narrative history makes. Since the mid-twentieth century, historians of ancient Israel also have been largely silent about potential grand narratives in history, the significance of ancient Israel for understanding world history, and the contribution of the discipline to understanding the human condition in general. Albright showed interest in some of these latter topics but, as Zevit noted in his discussion of the third paradigm of history writing, historians in general now decline to consider such overarching matters. In other words, historians no longer find it seemly or necessary to discern patterns that generalize human development in the past and project it into the future, certainly in part due to the democratization of ideas in Western societies and the negative effects ideas of historical evolution had on humanity, as evidenced in modern tragedies associated with colonization and fascism.

Since historians of ancient Israel have only skimmed the surface of issues pertaining to the relationship of representation, language, narrative, and explanation, the remainder of this section will attempt to describe this nexus more fully and to identify trends in and results of literary practices of historians of ancient Israel. A detailed study of tropes, modes of emplotment, argument, and ideological implication used by historians of ancient Israel (along the lines of White's *Metahistory*) is outside the scope of the present study. Nevertheless, some examples can begin to demonstrate the interplay of representation, language, narrative, and, ultimately, truth.

Representation, Language, Narrative, and Truth in Specific Historical Works
As mentioned in Chapter 5, Gottwald has analyzed the frameworks, unstated assumptions, and implications of the scholarship of Dever and Lemche.[122] Though Gottwald does not discuss tropes, modes of emplotment, or modes of argument, like White in *Metahistory* he seeks preconceived metahistorical

---

121. Davies, *In Search of "Ancient Israel"*, 15.
122. Gottwald, "Triumphalist Versus Anti-Triumphalist Versions of Early Israel," 15–42.

frameworks in these authors' works and speculates on how these demonstrate these historians' overall perceptions of the past and the course of human events. Gottwald claims that Dever adheres to a triumphalist picture of Israel, in which an Israel akin to the Israel of the Bible dominates the history of ancient Palestine. This viewpoint, Gottwald claims, is both the result of and a proponent of a worldview that sees "a single teleological line of development from tribal and monarchic Israel onward to later Judaism and Christianity."[123] In contrast, Gottwald finds that Lemche and other minimalists write nontriumphalist histories of Israel. Nontriumphalists consider "biblical" Israel to be a social construct that a Palestinian–Persian or –Hellenistic community invented to explain its past. Thus, Dever's "triumphal" Israel and Lemche's "nontriumphal" Israel represent two potential modes of emplotment and two ends of a spectrum of opinions about the significance of ancient Israel for history and humanity in general. In order to draw conclusions about the relationship of metahistorical frameworks to historical truth in Dever and Lemche's works, Gottwald surveys a range of their scholarship, including articles and books. In order to demonstrate how specific issues of representation, language, narrative, and truth interact within single comprehensive historical works, the histories of Soggin, Ahlström, Miller and Hayes, and Thompson again can be used as case studies.

Soggin's *An Introduction to the History of Israel and Judah* eschews both the biblical-chronological framework and the running narrative readers of histories of ancient Israel may expect. Soggin begins by discussing what he calls "Introductory Problems" in ancient Israelite history and whether a united monarchy existed under David and Solomon. He then examines "The Traditions about the Origins of the People," including the biblical stories of the patriarchs, the exodus, the settlement, and the "Time of the Judges," noting the many difficulties involved in gleaning historical evidence from these texts. The next section, "Divided Kingdoms," begins with the Assyrian movement into Syria–Palestine in the ninth century BCE. Since at this time external evidence begins to parallel the Bible, this is the point at which Soggin believes history can be written about ancient Israel. The remainder of Soggin's book is organized by events prominent in the Bible such as the Babylonian conquest of Jerusalem and the "missions" of Ezra and Nehemiah.

Soggin's work is structured as a series of numbered paragraphs that range from discussions of how a biblical character might have acted to what a modern scholar opines about a certain historical scenario. In the book, Soggin presents some statements with an authoritative voice,[124] while others are qualified.[125] This combination of topical organization and inconsistent tone may be due to

---

123. Ibid., 28.

124. Of Omri's dynasty Soggin (*Introduction to the History of Israel and Judah*, 212) writes, "[it] did not last too long, even if…it rightly remained famous throughout the ancient Near East."

125. For instance, "it only seems logical that the concept of the tribal league should have been taken up again, revised and reformulated [in the postexilic period]. However, in the present state of research we have no information which has even the slightest element of probability about whether such a league ever really existed" (ibid., 176).

Soggin's conception of the book as an introduction and his obvious concern to alert the reader to evidentiary problems. These choices, however, also imply that a more comprehensive and definite portrait of ancient Israel would be difficult to compose. For Soggin, it seems, gaining enough knowledge to represent what happened in ancient Israel is problematic, and for this reason no integrated story can be told.

The histories of Ahlström and Miller and Hayes evidence a more integrated and confident approach to Israel's past. Ahlström's title, *The History of Ancient Palestine from the Palaeolithic Period to Alexander's Conquest*, indicates that it covers a broader geographical area and chronological span than traditional histories of Israel. It further implies that Israel as a religious or political entity will not be the book's primary subject. After an introduction, a geographical overview of Palestine, and a chapter on "Prehistoric Time" (written by Gary O. Rollefson), Ahlström begins his chronological story with the Early Bronze Age—"the period of the formation of written documents"[126] (though at this time written documents are found only in Mesopotamia and Egypt). Reflecting on the overall aim of the book, Ahlström presents the Iron Age as a period of repeated incursions by foreign powers, not as the time when the major biblical events took place. The Transjordan receives slightly more attention than in traditional histories of ancient Israel, as well. The history continues through the Persian period to Alexander's conquest of Palestine. Throughout the book, Ahlström employs an authoritative voice, which produces reconstructions that, though they involve a number of debatable assumptions and interpretations, appear to be certainties.[127] Ahlström's confident use of the Bible for historical information (especially beginning with Saul) and self-assured tone present the reader with a comprehensive picture of Palestine that proceeds unbroken from around 3000 BCE until the fourth century BCE.

A History of Ancient Israel and Judah, by Miller and Hayes, exhibits yet another approach to representation, narrative, and truth claims in the history of Israel. Their subject, "Israel and Judah," basically corresponds to the communities in northern- and southern-central Palestine that the Bible considers greater Israel. Miller and Hayes tell the story of these communities from the pre-monarchical period in the Late Bronze Age until the end of the Persian period. Their history is neither smooth narrative, as is Ahlström's, nor is the book a collection of observations, theory, and hypotheses, as is Soggin's. Rather, in each chapter Miller and Hayes begin by considering the availability of sources for a period, evaluating these sources, and, after this discussion, they proceed to offer an integrated narrative of events that occurred during that time. Miller and Hayes focus on events and characters that appear in the Bible, trying to sort out

126. Ahlström, *The History of Ancient Palestine*, 120.
127. This is particularly evident in some of Ahlström's statements that are based solely on information from the Bible. For example, at the beginning of the chapter entitled "Palestine after Solomon," Ahlström writes, "When Solomon died the kingdom fell apart" (ibid., 543). He also notes that "Religiously and culturally the clans of the north did not feel that they had much in common with the peoples of the south, Judah" (ibid.).

fact from invention and clarify the actual course of events in the Late Bronze and Early Iron Ages.[128] Chapter titles reference important biblical events ("The Era of Assyrian Domination: The End of the Kingdom of Israel," "The Last Years of the Davidic Kingdom," etc.), and almost every subsection of the history is related to the Bible in some way. Miller and Hayes also employ an authoritative voice, but they acknowledge that hypotheses or best-guess scenarios must sometimes be used to fill in gaps in the source material.[129] In short, Miller and Hayes' literary choices and structure produce a history of Israel that is traditional in its efforts to be narratival, comprehensive, and relevant to study of the Bible while also including discussions that allow the reader to see the process by which they arrived at the statements they present as true.

Thompson's *Early History of the Israelite People*, the only comprehensive history written by a minimalist to appear near the time of the three others discussed here, takes a more explicitly methodological approach to issues relating to understanding Israel's past. Over one-third of the book is dedicated to methodological issues, from the documentary hypothesis, to developments in archaeology to the legacy of Alt. After this detailed introductory material, Thompson focuses on selected topics in Israelite history, including "The Origins of the Population" of Iron Age Palestine, information about the transition from the Late Bronze to the Early Iron Age, and the ethnicity of the people of Israel. There is little chronologically organized narrative in the book, but archaeological excavations and surveys along with historical and sociological studies of ancient Israel are extensively cited and discussed. The many studies then function as sources of data from which Thompson formulates evaluative statements and draws a number of historical conclusions.[130] Consequently, the subject of

128. For similar approaches and layout, see the *Biblische Enzykolpädie* series. Each volume treats a specific time period in Israel's history by first presenting literary and archaeological evidence separately and then offering integrated reconstructions. Lemche's *Prelude to Israel's Past* was vol. 1 of this series; also published are Volkmar Fritz, *Die Entstehung Israels im 12. und 11. Jahrhundert v. Chr.* (BE 2; Stuttgart: Kohlhammer, 1996); Walter Dietrich, *Die frühe Königszeit in Israel: 10. Jahrhundert v. Chr.* (BE 3; Stuttgart: Kohlhammer, 1997); Antoon Schoors, *Die Königreiche Israel und Juda im 8. und 7. Jahrhundert v. Chr.: Die assyrische Krise* (BE 5; Stuttgart: Kohlhammer, 1998); Albertz, *Die Exilszeit*; volumes covering the ninth century BCE, the seventh and sixth centuries BCE, the Persian period, the Hellenistic period, and the times of Jesus, Paul, and the early church are planned. For a general description of the methodology of all *Biblische Enzykolpädie* volumes see Dietrich, *Die frühe Königszeit in Israel*, 11.
129. For instance, they argue that though "Jeroboam's cultic moves probably are to be understood as an intentional effort to revive Aaronite traditions and priestly interests in certain of the old northern sanctuaries, especially Bethel, he seems to have passed over the Elide sanctuary at Shiloh." They go on to speculate that "there may have been little left at Shiloh to revive after the Davidic–Solomonic era—although there is no clear evidence, either biblical or archaeological, to conclude that the Shiloh sanctuary had been destroyed during the Philistine wars" (Miller and Hayes, *A History of Ancient Israel and Judah*, 243).
130. See, e.g., *Early History*, 272–78, where Thompson discusses the Egyptian presence in Palestine during the late second millennium BCE. In order to understand the timing of Egyptian withdrawal from the area and the reasons behind it, he reviews theories by G. E. Wright, I. Singer, Ahlström and Edelman, and M. Weinstein, as well as the conclusions of a number of archaeological surveys and excavations.

Early History appears to be the issue of knowledge about ancient Israel rather than ancient Israel itself. On the other hand, while *Early History* contains the opinions of many scholars, it is not left open-ended. Thompson's voice is clear throughout the book, particularly in the final chapter, where he summarizes his understanding of the diversity of the population of Iron Age Palestine and the potential relationship of the Bible to the "Intellectual Matrix" of this period. The lack of a timeline to unify Thompson's observations, however, leaves the reader without a comprehensive view of how he understands the relationship of the information presented to chronological development or change in ancient Israelite society as a whole.

These case studies begin to show how representation, language, narrative, and truth in history writing are related. The authors' choices of tone and literary framework stand out as indicators of the types of truth their histories strive to convey. Ahlström composes a story about Palestine's past and presents it with certainty, indicating to the reader that the past he represents and the connections he makes between people and events over time truthfully correspond to reality. Though Miller and Hayes take a similar approach to Ahlström, by revealing their methodology throughout the book they cannot achieve quite the same illusion of certainty and comprehensiveness as he does. Soggin and Thompson, on the other hand, tell no cohesive story at all, but rather present information from which they draw historical conclusions. Their histories give the impression that representing ancient reality truthfully is quite difficult.

Some additional observations can be made along the lines of Gottwald's notions of triumphalism and antitriumphalism. For instance, both *The History of Ancient Palestine* and *A History of Ancient Israel and Judah* end in the Persian period.[131] Ending Israel's story at this point allows the exile and return to crystallize as the final chronological markers of this community and interrupts any "single teleological line" from early Israel (or before) at this point. Indeed, both archaeology and the Bible report that Israelite culture and religion in Palestine undergo some significant changes at this time, including a new, foreign imperial administration that must sanction the rebuilding of the temple and the reinstitution of worship there in Jerusalem. Yet, as Barstad and others have pointed out, the importance and scope of the exile and return are poorly understood by historians. Furthermore, as seen in Chapter 5, Gruber finds the idea that Israel was more pure before the exile than after prevalent among present-day "secular Israelis," and blames the implications of historical decisions such as these (beginning with Wellhausen) for helping reify this impression. Therefore, at the very least, this choice of an end-point for Israel's history needs to be defended by historians and its potential wider implications examined. This applies especially to Ahlström, who ends his history of all Palestine here without

---

131. John H. Hayes and Sara R. Mandell do continue the narrative in their *The Jewish People in Classical Antiquity: From Alexander to Bar Kochba* (Louisville, Ky.: Westminster John Knox, 1998). According to Professor Hayes (personal communication), this book includes chapters revised from ones originally submitted for, but cut from, Miller and Hayes' *A History of Ancient Israel and Judah.*

clarifying the unique impact of the Persian administration of Palestine on its non-Israelite population.

Neither Soggin's *Introduction* nor Thompson's *Early History* emplot Israel in a biblical-chronological storyline, but the structure of their works may also imply something about the authors' conception of ancient Israel's importance.[132] By focusing on the process of how Israel's past can be known and discovered through a variety of sources, Soggin and Thompson imply that understanding how we construct the past is a more important scholarly undertaking than determining what actually happened in the past. Also, Thompson believes that the actual events in Israel's past cannot be used to justify the attention ancient Israel receives in modern scholarship. Israel's enduring importance in the mind of scholars, he asserts, is a theological construction based on the importance of the Bible, whereas Israel is actually minimally significant for understanding the Iron Age in the Near East and Mediterranean worlds. Thus, whereas the histories of Ahlström and Miller and Hayes may imply that the events of Israel's past are significant because of the Bible (and perhaps by extension, Judaism and Christianity), Soggin and Thompson abstain from indicating whether this past had notable consequences that would be important to modern readers of their histories. One might even conclude that these authors do not see ancient Israel as particularly important in the scope of the human past.[133] In Thompson's case, however, one can see from his ruminations on the topic (discussed in Chapter 5) that he recognizes ancient Israel's importance to Western culture but wonders if its influence, which stems from religion, can be correlated to or justified by historical reality. Thus, his presentation in *Early History* may in fact be indicative of his opinion of Israel's place within a larger worldview.

Recognition of overarching themes, or grand narratives, in particular historical works leads back to the question of evaluation: Which way of telling about Israel's past is best? Given that historians of ancient Israel rarely deal with the existence of tropes or grand narratives in present-day histories, it is not surprising that this question has received little attention from them. Palestinian archaeologist David Schloen has addressed this question, however, arguing that grand narratives are "necessary and unavoidable," and that their "critique and evaluation…must go beyond their rootage in present-day academic politics or ideology…to an appeal to objective data."[134] He also urges historians to avoid evolutionary or Hegelian schemes when reconstructing the past. In other words, as long as evolutionary notions of human development are rejected, Schloen contends, overarching themes in history should be employed and judged based

132. Soggin's discussion includes the Roman period in Palestine, while the latest events discussed in Thompson's *Early History* are the destructions of Israel and Judah in 721 BCE and 587 BCE, respectively.

133. Cf. Gottwald ("Triumphalist Versus Anti-Triumphalist Versions of Early Israel," 38) who claims that minimalists are "rejectionists" or "prophets" who remind historians of ancient Israel that their teleological readings of the Bible have long gone unjustified but who offer no substantive theory about Israel's importance in the world.

134. Schloen, "W. F. Albright and the Origins of Israel," 62.

on the objectivity of their use of the evidence. Schloen's ideas appear to be reasonable as a starting point for thinking about the place of grand narratives in Israel's history, if they are combined with the recognition that some grand narratives that are not evolutionary may also be ethically or morally undesirable.

History's Relationship to Fiction

Another problem for historians that has arisen from history's linguistic turn is the idea that history should be understood as a constructed account that differs little from fiction. Neither the histories discussed here nor other scholarship of Ahlström, Miller and Hayes, or Soggin indicate that these historians are aware of or concerned about this problem. Thompson, however, seems to understand that this critique has been leveled at history. For instance, he says that *The Mythic Past* is "essentially a philosophical and rhetorical discussion opposed to positivist assumptions"[135] that, he implies, provides an example of scholarship about the past that is not concerned with the distinction between actual and "fictional" events. *The Mythic Past*, however, focuses mainly on the fictitious or "mythic" nature of the Bible and historical accounts that use the Bible, rather than on the distinction of fiction from history in general. Furthermore, though Thompson alludes to the subjective nature of historical reconstruction, he appears to hold to the common minimalist assumption, discussed in Chapter 4, that evidence distinguishes history from fiction.[136] Non-minimalists have not addressed the history–fiction issue in much detail either, with the exception of Barstad and Halpern, who have noted similarities between the two types of literature, and Younger, who held that history's real-world referent ensures that present-day history writing about ancient Israel is not equivalent to fiction.

In short, for historians of ancient Israel, the apparent similarities of fiction and history create few problems for their modern histories when responsible use and interpretation of evidence makes the real-world referent of history clear. In general, then, historians of ancient Israel seem to understand history's relationship to fiction in a manner similar to Roger Chartier and Dorrit Cohn, discussed in Chapter 1. Cohn says that history is distinct from fiction because historians draw conclusions from "an ontologically independent and temporally prior data base of disordered, meaningless happenings"[137] using "the eyes of the (forever backward-looking) historian–narrator"[138] rather than those of the omnipotent author of fiction. The historian's imposition of order and meaning on the past, however, does not make history into fiction; the process of organizing events, and using this organization to imply meaning or truth, is an integral part of history.

---

135. Thompson, "Lester Grabbe and Historiography," 141.
136. See especially "Part Two: How Historians Create a Past," in Thompson, *The Mythic Past*, 103–225, and idem, "Defining History and Ethnicity," 181–87.
137. Cohn, *The Distinction of Fiction*, 114.
138. Ibid., 121.

Deconstruction, the Authoritative Voice, and Meaning in History Writing
Deconstruction claims that "languages are generally unreliable in conveying meaning accurately" and that a reader cannot know authorial intent.[139] Though deconstruction is a potent theory in American intellectual life,[140] historians rarely discuss the possibility that communication could be ineffective for these reasons. Indeed, deconstruction presents these assertions as inevitable, and thus historians (and philosophers) can do little, anyway, to combat this problem. An opposite concern is that in history writing one outlook, specifically the historian's outlook, may shape or potentially dominate interpretations of the past. As seen in Chapter 1, the inclusion of multiple perspectives or voices and the construction of small narratives have been suggested as alternatives to comprehensive history written with an authoritative voice. Though no one has yet attempted a history from which aspects of Israelite society are described from many different viewpoints, the publication of historical vignettes rather than large-scale narratives appears to be the current norm in the discipline.[141] These trends, however, seem to be based on uncertainty about evidence for ancient Israel rather on reactions to philosophical concerns.

Conclusions
This brief look at representation, language, narrative, and truth in history shows that the issues involved are varied and far-reaching. For historians of ancient Israel, however, concerns about language, the difficulty of representation, the relationship of narrative story-telling in history to fiction and truth, and the use of an authoritative voice in history have not been as immediately important as the issue of whether there is enough evidence for an attempt at representation of Israel's past to be made at all. Likewise, the four case-studies undertaken here indicate that a historian's perception of available evidence for ancient Israel largely determines how they choose history's subject, types of explanation, the framework for emplotting data, and the voice used to present the past. To summarize these case studies: Miller and Hayes and Ahlström seem sure that there is enough evidence for ancient Israel to be identified, represented, and explained fairly completely. They tell Israel's story over time, and indicate that truthful statements corresponding to the reality of ancient Israel can be made. For scholars such as Soggin and Thompson, however, evidence about ancient Israel is difficult to find and therefore ancient Israel is difficult to represent. Thus, their histories of ancient Israel are not chronologically organized narratives but compilations that indicate throughout that truthful statements in history that correspond to reality are problematic.

Though evidentiary concerns currently overtake literary concerns among historians of ancient Israel, dialogue on these topics could result in more detailed analyses of literary patterning, narrative style, and the like, in present-

139. Zevit, *The Religions of Ancient Israel*, 65.
140. Zevit claims that, on the other hand, most intellectuals in France "ignore the whole discussion" (ibid., 64 n. 95).
141. Discussed above.

day histories of Israel. As Albert Cook has argued, neither the study of literary patterning in history (which he calls "rhetoric"), nor attention only to the evidentiary merits of a historical reconstruction, need dominate the evaluation of history writing.[142] A discussion among historians of ancient Israel that combined the two types of concerns would touch on issues of objectivity, comprehensive history, and truth, and would clarify theoretical understandings of the scope and goals of Israel's history in the context of the current evidentiary debate.[143]

Conclusion:
Truth and Writing History About Ancient Israel

This study has shown that for historians of ancient Israel, philosophical discussion about many of the issues that affect historical truth has been hindered by the pressing question of the relevance of the Bible to the study of Israel's past. Factors that may reflect assumptions about the correspondence of the biblical text's presentation of Israel's past to reality include: the definition of the subject of Israel's history and opinions about the extent to which specific persons, events, *mentalités*, and other structures can and should be included in the description of Israel's past; the possibility of narrative history; and the modes of explanation historians perceive as available to them. It has also been shown that many decisions historians make about using the Bible as evidence require both sound historical methodology and judgment calls. It has been argued that a clear conception of objectivity should guide historians in making many of the judgments history requires of them, including judgments about the extent to which a text's genre, origin, date, and original social context relate to the factuality of the events described in it; the potential that information from the Bible can correspond to information from other texts; and how evidence from artifacts and texts can be combined. This study has also asserted that historians of ancient Israel could benefit from more attempts at comprehensive histories of ancient Israel in order to demonstrate the boundaries within which history's necessary judgment calls can be made and evaluated.

In addition, given the many challenges that traditional notions of history and truth have faced in the late twentieth century, it is not clear how history, particularly the history of ancient Israel, can aspire to truth. The previous chapters showed that historians of ancient Israel, like most modern historians, operate with a general idea that history writing should correspond to past reality. It is evident, however, that historians no longer regard such correspondent truth as an easily definable or attainable goal. Nevertheless, the role language plays in representation, the problems of evidence evaluation and use, and the necessary

142. This is the thesis of Cook, *History/Writing*.

143. It would also give historians of ancient Israel an opportunity to consider if, as Carr suggests, narrative is an ontological category, i.e., whether humans experience life as a linear, meaningful connection of events. The historical books of the Bible would provide an interesting case-study for this discussion. Winther-Nielsen's "Fact, Fiction, and Language Use" is one study in this vein.

incompleteness of explanations for the events of the past need not disqualify efforts to describe what actually happened in the past and why. Furthermore, historians of ancient Israel are increasingly aware that historical portraits both affect the perception of modern communities and are used by them in ways that affect behavior and events in the present. Thus, criteria for truth in history must take into account both the difficulty of recovering the past and writing about it as well as matters relevant to the present.

In response to the need to negotiate these concerns, a new version of truth in Israel's history appears to be emerging, especially among non-minimalists. This type of truth could be called "qualified correspondent truth." Qualified correspondent truth is a practical approach that frees historical truth from the task of portraying past reality with the impression of near-total certainty. It recognizes that history is constructed through language, but strives to create portraits of the past based on solid judgment and attempts at objectivity and correspondence, without surrendering to the notion that history is nothing but a subjective interpretation or a fictional story. To borrow from Deist, qualified correspondent truth recognizes that hoping for "the better argued" reconstruction and explanation of the past is a noble goal. At the same time, qualified correspondent truth operates with the awareness that grand narratives and authoritative voices in history can be both helpful and harmful, since constructions of history wield power and influence ideas about the construction of the present.

Minimalists would no doubt find some of the characteristics of qualified correspondent truth objectionable. They insist that probable or best-guess scenarios are unacceptable for history. Nevertheless, aiming for better, or, put another way, more plausible, reconstructions of the past is a practical way to express history's goal. Striving to make history writing "better argued" also leaves room for new evidence and new methods of interpreting evidence that may further knowledge about the past and improve reconstructions of it. In other words, acknowledging the relativity of plausibility or quality of reconstructions need not and does not correlate to acceptance of naive or simplistic history writing.

In conclusion, qualified correspondent truth seems a particularly appropriate truth-standard for the history of Israel at this time. First, any comprehensive picture of Israel's past must be based on sources in which facts are difficult to identify and confirm, and qualified correspondent truth recognizes the necessary imprecision of evidence evaluation and use. Second, qualified correspondent truth, combined with attempts at objectivity, allows historians to debate each other on the merits and rationale of their reconstructions and arguments while also considering the implications of their reconstructions for theological, political, and other communities with an interest in Israel's past. Finally, qualified correspondent truth opens the door to continued discussion of the importance of Israel's past and the discipline of the history of Israel in the modern and postmodern communities that historians inhabit and to which they speak.

BIBLIOGRAPHY

Ackerman, Susan. "Digging Up Deborah: Recent Hebrew Bible Scholarship on Gender and the Contribution of Archaeology." *NEA* 66 (2003): 172–84.

Adams, John W. "Consensus, Community, and Exoticism." *Journal of Interdisciplinary History* 12 (1981): 253–65.

Ahlström, Gösta. *The History of Ancient Palestine from the Palaeolithic Period to Alexander's Conquest*. Minneapolis: Fortress, 1993.

—"The Role of Archaeological and Literary Remains in Reconstructing Israel's History." Pages 116–41 in Edelman, ed., *The Fabric of History*.

Albertz, Rainer. *Die Exilszeit: 6 Jahrhundert v. Chr.* BE 7. Stuttgart: Kohlhammer, 2001. Published in English as *Israel in Exile: The History and Literature of the Sixth Century B.C.E.* Studies in Biblical Literature 3. Atlanta: Society of Biblical Literature, 2003.

—"Die Exilszeit als Ernstfall für eine historische Rekonstruktion ohne biblische Texte: Die neubabylonischen Königsinschriften als 'Primarquelle.'" Pages 22–39 in *Leading Captivity Captive: "The Exile" as Historiography and Ideology*. Edited by Lester L. Grabbe. JSOTSup 278. Sheffield: Sheffield Academic Press, 1998.

Albright, William F. "Abram the Hebrew: A New Archaeological Interpretation." *BASOR* 163 (1961): 36–54.

—"Albrecht Alt." *JBL* 75 (1956): 169–73.

—"Archaeological Discovery and the Scriptures." *Christianity Today* 12, no. 19 (1968): 3–5.

—*Archaeology and the Religion of Israel: The Ayer Lectures of the Colgate-Rochester Divinity School, 1941*. 5th ed. Baltimore: The Johns Hopkins University Press, 1968.

—*Archaeology, Historical Analogy, and Early Biblical Tradition*. Rockwell Lectures: Rice University. Baton Rouge: Louisiana State University Press, 1966.

—*From the Stone Age to Christianity: Monotheism and the Historical Process*. Baltimore: The Johns Hopkins University Press, 1940. 2d ed. with new introduction. Garden City, N.Y.: Doubleday, 1957.

—*History, Archaeology, and Christian Humanism*. New York: McGraw-Hill, 1964.

—"The Israelite Conquest of Canaan in the Light of Archaeology." *BASOR* 74 (1939): 11–23.

—*Yahweh and the Gods of Canaan: A Historical Analysis of Two Contrasting Faiths*. Garden City, N.Y.: Doubleday, 1968.

Alkier, Stefan and Marcus Witte, eds. *Die Griechen und das antike Israel: Interdisziplinäre Studien zur Kulturgeschichte des Heligien Landes*. OBO 201. Göttingen: Vandenhoeck & Ruprecht, 2004.

Alt, Albrecht. *Essays on Old Testament History and Religion*. Oxford: Blackwell, 1966.

—"The Formation of the Israelite State in Palestine." Pages 171–237 in his *Essays on Old Testament History and Religion*. Translation of *Die Staatenbildung der Israeliten in Palästina*. Reformationsprogramm der Universität Leipzig, 1930.

—"The God of the Fathers." Pages 3–66 in his *Essays on Old Testament History and Religion*. Translation of *Der Gott der Väter*. BWANT 12. Stuttgart: Kohlhammer, 1929.

—"The Monarchy in the Kingdoms of Israel and Judah." Pages 239–59 in his *Essays on Old Testament History and Religion*. Translation of "Das Königtum in den Reichen Israel und Juda," *VT* 1 (1951): 2–22.

—"The Origins of Israelite Law." Pages 79–132 in his *Essays on Old Testament History and Religion*. Translation of *Die Ursprung des israelitischen Rechts*. Berichte über die Verhandlungen der Sächsichen Akademie der Wissenschaften zu Leipzig, Philologisch-historische Klasse 86.1. Leipzig: Hirzel, 1934.

—"The Settlement of the Israelites in Palestine." Pages 133–69 in his *Essays on Old Testament History and Religion*. Translation of *Die Landnahme der Israeliten in Palästina*. Reformationsprogramm der Universität Leipzig, 1925.

Amit, Yairah. *History and Ideology: Introduction to Historiography in the Hebrew Bible*. The Biblical Seminar 60; Sheffield: Sheffield Academic Press, 1999.

Angeles, Peter A., ed. *The HarperCollins Dictionary of Philosophy*. 2d ed. New York: HarperCollins, 1992.

Ankersmit, F. R. "Anthropology and History in the 1980s." *Journal of Interdisciplinary History* 12 (1981): 227–78.

—*Narrative Logic: A Semantic Analysis of the Historian's Language*. Martinus Nijhoff Philosophy Library 7. The Hague: Martinus Nijhoff, 1983.

—"Statements, Texts and Pictures." Pages 212–40 in Ankersmit and Kellner, eds., *A New Philosophy of History*.

Ankersmit, F. R., and Hans Kellner, eds. *A New Philosophy of History*. Chicago: University of Chicago Press, 1995.

Arnold, Bill T. "The Weidner Chronicle and the Idea of History in Israel and Mesopotamia." Pages 129–48 in Millard, Hoffmeier, and Baker, eds., *Faith, Tradition, and History*.

Athas, George. *The Tel Dan Inscription: A Reappraisal and a New Interpretation*. JSOTSup 360. London: Sheffield Academic Press, 2003.

Atkinson, R. F. *Knowledge and Explanation in History: An Introduction to the Philosophy of History*. Ithaca, N.Y.: Cornell University Press, 1978.

Audi, Robert. *The Cambridge Dictionary of Philosophy*. 2d ed. Cambridge: Cambridge University Press, 1999.

Barr, James. *History and Ideology in the Old Testament: Biblical Studies at the End of a Millennium*. The Hensley Henson Lectures for 1997. Oxford: Oxford University Press, 2000.

—"Story and History in Biblical Theology." *JR* 56 (1976): 1–17.

Barstad, Hans M. "History and the Hebrew Bible." Pages 37–64 in Grabbe, ed., *Can a "History of Israel" Be Written?*

—"Is the Hebrew Bible a Hellenistic Book? Or: Niels Peter Lemche, Herodotus, and the Persians." *Transeu* 23 (2002): 129–51.

—*The Myth of the Empty Land: A Study in the History and Archaeology of Judah During the "Exilic" Period*. Symbolae Osolenses Fasciculi Suppletorii. Oslo: Scandinavian University Press, 1996.

Barton, John, ed. *The Cambridge Companion to Biblical Interpretation*. Cambridge Companions to Religion. Cambridge: Cambridge University Press, 1998.

Becking, Bob. "Inscribed Seals as Evidence for Biblical Israel? Jeremiah 40.7–41.15 *Par Example*." Pages 64–83 in Grabbe, ed., *Can a "History of Israel" Be Written?*

Bentley, Michael, ed. *Companion to Historiography*. London: Routledge, 1997.

Berquist, Jon L. *Controlling Corporeality: The Body and the Household in Ancient Israel*. New Brunswick, N.J.: Rutgers University Press, 2002.

—*Judaism in Persia's Shadow: A Social and Historical Approach*. Minneapolis: Fortress, 1995.

Bevir, Mark. "The Subject and Historiography." *Giornale di Metafisica* 22 (2000): 5–28.

Binford, Lewis R. *An Archaeological Perspective*. Studies in Archaeology. New York: Seminar Press, 1972.

—"Archeological Perspectives." Pages 5–32 in *New Perspectives in Archeology*. Edited by Sally R. Binford and Lewis R. Binford. Chicago: Aldine, 1968.

—"General Introduction." Pages 1–10 in *For Theory Building in Archaeology: Essays on Faunal Remains, Aquatic Resources, Spatial Analysis, and Systemic Modeling*. Edited by Lewis R. Binford. New York: Academic Press, 1977.

Biran, Avraham, and Joseph Naveh. "An Aramaic Stele Fragment from Tel Dan." *IEJ* 43 (1993): 81–98.

—"The Tel Dan Inscription: A New Fragment." *IEJ* 45 (1995): 17–18.

Bird, Phyllis A. *Missing Persons and Mistaken Identities: Women and Gender in Ancient Israel*. OBT. Minneapolis: Fortress, 1997.

Blakely, Jeffrey A. "Reconciling Two Maps: Archaeological Evidence for the Kingdoms of David and Solomon." *BASOR* 327 (2002): 49–54.

Bloch, Marc. *The Historian's Craft*. New York: Vintage, 1953.

Bloch-Smith, Elizabeth. "Israelite Ethnicity in Iron I: Archaeology Preserves What is Remembered and What is Forgotten in Israel's History." *JBL* 122 (2003): 401–25.

—*Judahite Burial Practices and Beliefs About the Dead*. JSOTSup 123. Sheffield: JSOT Press, 1992.

Booth, Wayne, Gregory G. Colomb, and Joseph M. Williams. *The Craft of Research*. 2d ed. Chicago: University of Chicago Press, 2003.

Bordreuil, Pierre, and Françoise Briquel-chatonnet. *Le temps de la Bible*. Folio histoire 122. Gallimard: Fayard, 2003.

Braudel, Fernand. *La Méditerranée et le Monde méditerranéen à l'époque de Philippe II*. 2d ed. Paris: Armand Colin, 1966. Published in English as *The Mediterranean and the Mediterranean World in the Age of Philip II*. New York: Harper & Row, 1972.

Breisach, Ernst. *Historiography: Ancient, Medieval, and Modern*. 2d ed. Chicago: University of Chicago Press, 1994.

—*On the Future of History: The Postmodernist Challenge and Its Aftermath*. Chicago: University of Chicago Press, 2003.

Brettler, Marc Zvi. "The Copenhagen School: The Historiographical Issues." *AJSR* 27 (2003): 1–22.

—*The Creation of History in Ancient Israel*. New York: Routledge, 1995.

Bright, John. *Early Israel in Recent History Writing: A Study in Method*. SBT 19. London: SCM Press, 1956.

—*A History of Israel*. 4th ed. Louisville, Ky.: Westminster John Knox, 2000; 1st ed. Philadelphia: Westminster, 1959.

Brown, William P. Introduction to John Bright, *A History of Israel* (4th ed.).

Bunimovitz, Shlomo, and Avraham Faust. "Chronological Separation, Geographical Segregation, or Ethnic Demarcation? Ethnography and the Iron Age Low Chronology." *BASOR* 322 (2001): 1–10.

—"Ideology in Stone: Understanding the Four-Room House." *BAR* 28, no. 4 (2002): 33–41, 59–60.

Burke, Peter. "History of Events and the Revival of Narrative." Pages 233–48 in Burke, ed., *New Perspectives on Historical Writing*.

—ed. *New Perspectives on Historical Writing*. University Park, Pa.: Penn State University Press, 1992.

—"Overture: The New History, Its Past and Its Future." Pages 1–23 in Burke, ed., *New Perspectives on Historical Writing*.

Burnett, Fred W. "Historiography." Pages 106–12 in *Handbook of Postmodern Biblical Interpretation*. Edited by A. K. M. Adam. St. Louis, Miss.: Chalice, 2000.

Bury, J. B. "The Science of History." Pages 3–22 in *Selected Essays of J. B. Bury*. Edited by Harold Temperley. Cambridge: Cambridge University Press, 1930.

Buss, Martin J. *Biblical Form Criticism in its Context*. JSOTSup 274. Sheffield: Sheffield Academic Press, 1999.

Carr, David. "Getting the Story Straight: Narrative and Historical Knowledge." Pages 119–33 in *Historiography between Modernism and Postmodernism: Contributions to the Methodology of Historical Research*. Edited by Jerzy Topolski. Amsterdam: Rodopi, 1994.

—"Philosophy of History." Pages 671–73 in Audi, ed., *The Cambridge Dictionary of Philosophy*.

Carroll, Robert P. "Madonna of Silences: Clio and the Bible." Pages 84–103 in Grabbe, ed., *Can a "History of Israel" Be Written?*

Carter, Charles E. "A Discipline in Transition: The Contributions of the Social Sciences to the Study of the Hebrew Bible." Pages 3–36 in *Community, Identity, and Ideology: Social Science Approaches to the Hebrew Bible*. Edited by Charles E. Carter and Carol Meyers. Sources for Biblical and Theological Study 6. Winona Lake, Ind.: Eisenbrauns, 1996.

Carter, Jonathan A. "Telling Times: History, Emplotment, and Truth." *History and Theory* 42 (2003): 1–27.

Chapman, Mark D. *Ernst Troeltsch and Liberal Theology: Religion and Cultural Synthesis in Wilhelmine Germany*. Christian Theology in Context. Oxford: Oxford University Press, 2001.

Chartier, Robert. *On the Edge of the Cliff: History, Language, and Practices*. Parallax Re-Visions of Culture and Society. Baltimore: The Johns Hopkins University Press, 1997.

Christian, David. *Maps of Time: An Introduction to Big History*. Berkeley: University of California Press, 2004.

Cohen, Rudolph. "Survey of Israel." *OEANE* 5:104–6.

Cohn, Bernard S. "Toward a Rapprochement." *Journal of Interdisciplinary History* 12 (1981): 227–52.

Cohn, Dorrit. *The Distinction of Fiction*. Baltimore: The Johns Hopkins University Press, 1999.

Collingwood, R. G. *The Idea of History*. Oxford: Clarendon, 1946.

—*The Principles of History and Other Writings in the Philosophy of History*. Edited by William Dray and W. J. van der Dussen. Oxford: Oxford University Press, 1999.

Comaroff, John, and Jean Comaroff. *Ethnography and the Historical Imagination*. Boulder, Colo.: Westview, 1992.

Cook, Albert. *History/Writing*. Cambridge: Cambridge University Press, 1988.

Cook, Deborah. *The Subject Finds a Voice: Foucault's Turn toward Subjectivity*. Revisioning Philosophy 11. New York: Peter Lang, 1993.

Coote, Robert B., and Keith W. Whitelam. *The Emergence of Early Israel in Historical Perspective*. Sheffield: Almond Press, 1987.

Craig, Edward, ed. *The Routledge Encyclopedia of Philosophy*. 10 vols. London: Routledge, 1998.

Cross, Frank Moore. *Canaanite Myth and Hebrew Epic*. Cambridge, Mass.: Harvard University Press, 1973.

Davies, Philip R. "'Ancient Israel' and History: A Response to Norman Whybray." *ExpTim* 108 (1996): 211–12.

—"Biblical Studies in a Postmodern Age." *Jian Dao* 7 (1997): 37–55.

—"The Future of 'Biblical History.'" Pages 126–41 in *Auguries: The Jubilee Volume of the Sheffield Department of Biblical Studies*. Edited by David J. A. Clines and Stephen D. Moore. JSOTSup 269. Sheffield: Sheffield Academic Press, 1998.

—"'House of David' Built on Sand: The Sins of the Biblical Maximizers." *BAR* 20 (1994): 54–55.

—*In Search of "Ancient Israel"*. JSOTSup 148. Sheffield: Sheffield Academic Press, 1992.

—"Introduction." Pages 11–21 in Fritz and Davies, eds., *The Origins of the Ancient Israelite States*.

—"Method and Madness: Some Remarks on Doing History with the Bible." *JBL* 115 (1995): 699–705.

—*Scribes and Schools: The Canonization of Hebrew Scripture*. Library of Ancient Israel. Louisville, Ky.: Westminster John Knox, 1998.

—"The Society of Biblical Israel." Pages 22–33 in *Second Temple Studies*. Vol. 2, *Temple and Community in the Persian Period*. Edited by Tamara C. Eskenazi and Kent Harold Richards. JSOTSup 175. Sheffield: JSOT Press, 1992.

—"Sociology and the Second Temple." Pages 11–19 in *Second Temple Studies*. Vol. 1, *Persian Period*. Edited by Philip R. Davies. JSOTSup 117. Sheffield: JSOT Press, 1991.

—"This Is What Happens…" Pages 106–18 in *"Like a Bird in a Cage": The Invasion of Sennacherib in 701 BCE*. Edited by Lester L. Grabbe. JSOTSup 363. Sheffield: Sheffield Academic Press, 2003.

—"What Separates a Minimalist from a Maximalist? Not Much." *BAR* 26, no. 2 (2000): 24–27, 72–73.

—"Whose History? Whose Israel? Whose Bible? Biblical Histories, Ancient and Modern." Pages 104–22 in Grabbe, ed., *Can a "History of Israel" Be Written?*

Davis, Natalie Zemon. "The Possibilities of the Past." *Journal of Interdisciplinary History* 12 (1981): 267–75.

Day, John, ed. *In Search of Pre-Exilic Israel: Proceedings of the Oxford Old Testament Seminar*. JSOTSup 406. London: T. & T. Clark, 2004.

Deist, Ferdinand E. "Contingency, Continuity and Integrity in Historical Understanding: An Old Testament Perspective." *Scriptura* Special Issue 11 (1993): 99–115.

—*The Material Culture of the Bible: An Introduction*. The Biblical Seminar 70. Sheffield: Sheffield Academic Press, 2000.

Dever, William G. "Biblical Archaeology: Death and Rebirth." Pages 706–22 in *Biblical Archaeology Today: Proceedings of the Second International Congress on Biblical Archaeology Jerusalem June–July 1990*. Edited by Avraham Biran and Joseph Aviram. Jerusalem: Israel Exploration Society, 1993.

—"Excavating the Hebrew Bible, or Burying It Again?" (review of Israel Finkelstein and Neil Asher Silberman, *The Bible Unearthed: Archaeology's New Vision of Ancient Israel and the Origin of Its Sacred Texts*). *BASOR* 322 (2001): 67–77.

—"Histories and Non-Histories of Ancient Israel: The Question of the United Monarchy." Pages 65–94 in Day, ed., *In Search of Pre-Exilic Israel*.

—"Impact of the 'New Archaeology.'" Pages 337–52 in Drinkard, Mattingly, and Miller, eds., *Benchmarks in Time and Culture*.

—"The Impact of the 'New Archaeology' on Syro-Palestinian Archaeology." *BASOR* 242 (1981): 15–29.

—"On Listening to the Text—and the Artifacts." Pages 1–23 in *The Echoes of Many Texts: Reflections on Jewish and Christian Traditions Essays in Honor of Lou H. Silberman*. Edited by William G. Dever and J. Edward Wright. Atlanta: Scholars Press, 1997.

—"Revisionist Israel Revisited: A Rejoinder to Niels Peter Lemche." *CurBS* 4 (1996): 35–50.

—"Save Us From Postmodern Malarkey." *BAR* 26, no. 2 (2000): 28–35, 68–69.

—*What Did the Biblical Writers Know and When Did They Know It? What Archaeology Can Tell Us About the Reality of Ancient Israel.* Grand Rapids: Eerdmans, 2001.

—"What Remains of the House That Albright Built?" *BA* 56 (1993): 25–35.

—*Who Were the Early Israelites and Where Did They Come From?* Grand Rapids: Eerdmans, 2003.

Dietrich, Walter. *Die frühe Königszeit in Israel: 10. Jahrhundert v. Chr.* BE 3. Stuttgart: Kohlhammer, 1997.

Donner, Herbert. *Geschichte des Volkes Israel und seiner Nachbarn in Grundzügen.* 2 vols. ATD 4. Göttingen: Vandenhoeck & Ruprecht, 1984.

Dothan, Trude. "Early Philistines." *OEANE* 4:310–11.

Dray, William. *On History and Philosophers of History.* Philosophy of History and Culture 2. Leiden: Brill, 1989.

—"Philosophy and Historiography." Pages 763–82 in Bentley, ed., *Companion to Historiography.*

Drinkard, Joel F., Gerald L. Mattingly, and J. Maxwell Miller, eds. *Benchmarks in Time and Culture: An Introduction to Palestinian Archaeology.* Archaeology and Biblical Studies. Atlanta: Scholars Press, 1988.

Edelman, Diana Vikander. "Clio's Dilemma: The Changing Face of History-Writing." Pages 247–55 in Lemaire and M. Sæbø, eds., *Congress Volume: Oslo, 1988.*

—"Doing History in Biblical Studies." Pages 13–25 in Edelman, ed., *The Fabric of History.*

—ed. *The Fabric of History: Text, Artifact and Israel's Past.* JSOTSup 127. Sheffield: JSOT Press, 1991.

Emerton, J. A. "The Value of the Moabite Stone as an Historical Source." *VT* 41 (2002): 483–92.

Evans, Richard J. *In Defense of History.* New York: Norton, 1999.

Ewald, Heinrich Georg August. *The History of Israel.* 2 vols. 2d ed. London: Longmans, Green & Co., 1869.

Faust, Avraham. "Abandonment, Urbanization, Resettlement and the Formation of the Israelite State." *NEA* 66 (2003): 147–61.

Fehling, Detlev. *Herodotus and His "Sources": Citation, Invention and Narrative Art.* ARCA Classical and Medieval Texts, Papers, and Monographs 21. Leeds: Francis Cairns, 1989. Translation of *Die Quellenangaben bei Herodot.* Berlin: de Gruyter, 1971.

Feldman, Richard. "Evidence." Pages 293–94 in Audi, ed., *The Cambridge Dictionary of Philosophy.*

Finkelstein, Israel. *The Archaeology of the Israelite Settlement.* Jerusalem: Israel Exploration Society, 1988.

Finkelstein, Israel, and Neil Asher Silberman. *The Bible Unearthed: Archaeology's New Vision of Ancient Israel and the Origin of Its Sacred Texts.* New York: Free Press, 2001.

Finley, M. I. *Ancient History: Evidence and Models.* London: Chatto & Windus, 1985.

—*Early Greece: The Bronze and Archaic Ages.* London: Chatto & Windus, 1981.

—*The Use and Abuse of History.* New York: Viking, 1975.

Førland, Tor Egil. "The Ideal Explanatory Text in History: A Plea for Ecumenism." *History and Theory* 43 (2004): 321–40.

Foucault, Michel. *The Archaeology of Knowledge.* New York: Pantheon Books, 1972. Translation of *L'archéologie du savoir.* Paris: Gallimard, 1969.

—*The History of Sexuality.* 3 vols. New York: Vintage, 1980. Translation of *Histoire de la Sexualité,* 3 vols. Paris: Gallimard, 1976.

—*Madness and Civilization: A History of Insanity in the Age of Reason.* New York: Vintage, 1973. Translation of *Folie et déraison: Histoire de la folie à l'âge classique.* Paris: Plon, 1961; 2d ed. Paris: Gallimard, 1972.

Freedman, David Noel. "W. F. Albright as an Historian." Pages 33–43 in Van Beek, ed., *The Scholarship of William Foxwell Albright.*

Frendo, Anthony J. "Back to Basics: A Holistic Approach to the Problem of the Emergence of Ancient Israel." Pages 41–64 in Day, ed., *In Search of Pre-Exilic Israel.*

Fritz, Volkmar. *Die Entstehung Israels im 12. und 11. Jahrhundert v. Chr.* BE 2. Stuttgart: Kohlhammer, 1996.

—"Israelites and Canaanites: You Can Tell Them Apart." *BAR* 28, no. 4 (2002): 28–31, 63.

Fritz, Volkmar, and Philip R. Davies, eds. *The Origins of the Ancient Israelite States.* JSOTSup 228. Sheffield: Sheffield Academic Press, 1996.

Gal, Zvi. *Lower Galilee During the Iron Age.* Winona Lake, Ind.: Eisenbrauns, 1992.

Garbini, Giovanni. *History and Ideology in Ancient Israel.* New York: Crossroad, 1988. Translation of *Storia e Ideologia nell'Israele Antico.* Brescia: Paideia, 1986.

—*Myth and History in the Bible.* JSOTSup 362. Sheffield: Sheffield Academic Press, 2003.

Gardiner, Patrick. "History, History of the Philosophy of." Pages 360–64 in Honderich, ed., *The Oxford Companion to Philosophy.*

—"History, Problems of the Philosophy of." Pages 364–67 in Honderich, ed., *The Oxford Companion to Philosophy.*

—*The Nature of Historical Explanation.* Oxford: Oxford University Press, 1952.

Geertz, Clifford. *The Interpretation of Cultures.* New York: Basic Books, 1973.

Geus, C. H. J. de. *The Tribes of Israel: An Investigation into Some of the Presuppositions of Martin Noth's Amphictyony Hypothesis.* SSN. Assen: Van Gorcum, 1976.

Ginzburg, Carlo. *Il formaggio e i vermi: Il cosmos di un mugnaio del '500.* Turin: Giulio Einaudi Editore, 1976. Published in English as *The Cheese and the Worms: The Cosmos of a Sixteenth-Century Miller.* New York: Penguin, 1982.

Gitin, Seymour. "Late Philistines." *OEANE* 4:311–13.

Glueck, Nelson. *The Other Side of the Jordan.* New Haven: American Schools of Oriental Research, 1940.

Gnuse, Robert Karl. *No Other Gods: Emergent Monotheism in Israel.* JSOTSup 241. Sheffield: Sheffield Academic Press, 1997.

Goodman, Jordan. "History and Anthropology." Pages 783–804 in Bentley, ed., *Companion to Historiography.*

Gorman, Jonathan. "Freedom and History" (review of *The Truth of History*, by C. Behan McCullagh). *History and Theory* 39 (2000): 251–62.

—*Understanding History: An Introduction to Analytical Philosophy of History.* Philosophica 42. Ottawa: University of Ottawa Press, 1992.

Gottwald, Norman K. *The Hebrew Bible in its Social World and in Ours.* Atlanta: Scholars Press, 1993.

—*The Politics of Ancient Israel.* Library of Ancient Israel. Louisville, Ky.: Westminster John Knox, 2001.

—*The Tribes of Yahweh: A Sociology of the Religion of Liberated Israel, 1250–1050 B.C.E.* The Biblical Seminar 66. Sheffield: Sheffield Academic Press, 1999. Reprinted with expanded introductory material from *The Tribes of Yahweh: A Sociology of the Religion of Liberated Israel, 1250–1050 B.C.E.* Maryknoll, N.Y.: Orbis, 1979.

—"Triumphalist Versus Anti-Triumphalist Versions of Early Israel: A Response to Articles by Lemche and Dever in Volume 4 (1996)." *CurBS* 5 (1997): 15–42.

Grabbe, Lester L. "Are Historians of Ancient Palestine Fellow Creatures—or Different Animals?" Pages 19–36 in Grabbe, ed., *Can a "History of Israel" Be Written?*

—ed. *Can a "History of Israel" Be Written?* JSOTSup, 245. Sheffield: Sheffield Academic Press, 1997.

—"Hat Die Bibel Doch Recht? A Review of T. L. *Thompson's The Bible in History.*" *SJOT* 14 (2000): 117–39.

—"Introduction." Pages 11–18 in Grabbe, ed., *Can a "History of Israel" Be Written?*

—"Reflections on the Discussion." Pages 188–96 in Grabbe, ed., *Can a "History of Israel" Be Written?*

Graham, Gordon. "History, Philosophy of." Pages 453–59 in vol. 4 of Craig, ed., *The Routledge Encyclopedia of Philosophy.*

Green, Anna, and Kathleen Troup, eds. *The Houses of History: A Critical Reader in Twentieth-Century History and Theory, Selected and Introduced by Anna Green & Kathleen Troup.* New York: New York University Press, 1999.

Grosby, Steven. *Biblical Ideas of Nationality: Ancient and Modern.* Winona Lake, Ind.: Eisenbrauns, 2002.

Gruber, Mayer I. "The Ancient Israel Debate: A Jewish Postcolonial Perspective." *ANES* 38 (2001): 3–27.

Halpern, Baruch. *David's Secret Demons: Messiah, Murderer, Traitor, King.* Grand Rapids: Eerdmans, 2001.

—"Erasing History: The Minimalist Assault on Ancient Israel." *BAR* 11, no. 6 (1995): 26–35, 47.

—"Eyewitness Testimony: Parts of Exodus Written Within Living Memory of the Event." *BAR* 29, no. 5 (2003): 50–57.

—*The First Historians: The Hebrew Bible and History.* San Francisco: Harper & Row, 1988.

Halpern, Baruch, and Deborah W. Hobson, eds. *Law and Ideology in Monarchic Israel.* JSOTSup 124. Sheffield: JSOT Press, 1991.

Halsall, Guy. "Archaeology and Historiography." Pages 805–27 in Bentley, ed., *Companion to Historiography.*

Harvey, Van A. *The Historian and the Believer: The Morality of Historical Knowledge and Christian Belief.* Toronto: MacMillan, 1969.

Hayes, John H. "The History of the Study of Israelite and Judaean History." Pages 1–69 in Hayes and Miller, eds., *Israelite and Judaean History.*

—"The Twelve-Tribe Israelite Amphictyony: An Appraisal." *Trinity University Studies in Religion* 10 (1975): 22–36.

Hayes, John H., and Sara R. Mandell. *The Jewish People in Classical Antiquity: From Alexander to Bar Kochba.* Louisville, Ky.: Westminster John Knox, 1998.

Hayes, John H., and J. Maxwell Miller, eds. *Israelite and Judaean History.* Philadelphia: Westminster, 1977.

Hengehold, Laura. "Subject, Postmodern Critique of the." Pages 196–201 in vol. 9 of Craig, ed., *The Routledge Encyclopedia of Philosophy.*

Henige, David P. "Deciduous, Perennial or Evergreen? The Choices in the Debate in 'Early Israel.'" *JSOT* 27 (2003): 387–412.

Herion, Gary A. "The Impact of Modern and Social Science Assumptions on the Reconstruction of Israelite History." *JSOT* 34 (1986): 3–33.

Herrmann, Siegfried. *A History of Israel in Old Testament Times.* 2d ed. Philadelphia: Fortress, 1981. Translation of *Geschichte Israels in alttestamentlicher Zeit.* 2d. ed. Munich: Kaiser, 1980. 1st. ed. 1973.

Hess, Richard S. "Literacy in Iron Age Israel." Pages 82–102 in Long, Baker, and Wenham, eds., *Windows into Old Testament History.*

Hjelm, Ingrid. "Whose Bible is it Anyway? Ancient Authors, Medieval Manuscripts, and Modern Perceptions." *SJOT* 18 (2004): 108–34.

Hodder, Ian, ed. *On the Surface: Çatalhöyük 1993–95.* BIAA 22. London: British Institute of Archaeology at Ankara, 1996.

—*Reading the Past: Current Approaches to Interpretation in Archaeology.* Cambridge: Cambridge University Press, 1986.

—*Symbols in Action: Ethnoarchaeological Studies of Material Culture.* New Studies in Archaeology. Cambridge: Cambridge University Press, 1982.

—"Theoretical Archaeology: A Reactionary View." Pages 1–16 in *Symbolic and Structural Archaeology.* Edited by Ian Hodder. Cambridge: Cambridge University Press, 1982.

—*Theory and Practice in Archaeology.* Material Cultures: Interdisciplinary Studies in the Material Construction of Social Worlds. London: Routledge, 1992.

Hoffmeier, James K. *Israel in Egypt: The Evidence for the Authenticity of the Exodus Tradition.* New York: Oxford University Press, 1997.

Hoffmeier, James K., and Allan Millard, eds. *The Future of Biblical Archaeology: Reassessing Methodologies and Assumptions.* Grand Rapids: Eerdmans, 2003.

Honderich, Ted, ed. *The Oxford Companion to Philosophy.* Oxford: Oxford University Press, 1995.

Howatson, M. C., ed. *The Oxford Companion to Classical Literature.* Oxford: Oxford University Press, 1989.

Huizinga, Johan. "A Definition of the Concept of History." Pages 1–10 in *Philosophy and History: Essays Presented to Ernst Cassirer.* Edited by Raymond Klibansky and H. J. Paton. Oxford: Clarendon, 1936.

Huppert, George. "The *Annales* Experiment." Pages 873–88 in Bentley, ed., *Companion to Historiography.*

Hurvitz, Avi. "The Historical Quest for 'Ancient Israel' and the Linguistic Evidence of the Hebrew Bible: Some Methodological Observations." *VT* 47 (1997): 301–15.

Iggers, Georg G. *Historiography in the Twentieth Century: From Scientific Objectivity to the Postmodern Challenge.* Hanover, N.H.: Wesleyan University Press, 1997.

Isserlin, B. S. J. *The Israelites.* London: Thames & Hudson, 1998.

Jamieson-Drake, David W. *Scribes and Schools in Monarchic Judah: A Socio-Archeological Approach.* JSOTSup109. Sheffield: Almond Press, 1991.

Jenkins, Keith. "A Postmodern Reply to Perez Zagorin." *History and Theory* 39 (2000): 181–200.

Kaiser, Walter C. *The Old Testament Documents: Are They Reliable and Relevant?* Downers Grove, Ill.: InterVarsity, 2001.

Kallai, Zecharia. "Biblical Historiography and Literary History: A Programmatic Survey." *VT* 49 (1999): 338–50.

Keel, Othmar, and Christoph Uehlinger. *Gods, Goddesses and Images of God in Ancient Israel.* Minneapolis: Fortress, 1998. Translation of *Göttinnen, Götter und Gottessymbole.* QD 134. Fribourg: Herder Verlag, 1992.

Kelle, Brad. *Hosea 2: Metaphor and Rhetoric in Historical Perspective.* Academia Biblical 20. Atlanta: Society of Biblical Literature, 2005.

Kellner, Hans. "Introduction: Describing Redescriptions." Pages 1–18 in Ankersmit and Kellner, eds., *A New Philosophy of History.*

King, Philip J., and Lawrence E. Stager. *Life in Biblical Israel.* Library of Ancient Israel. Louisville, Ky.: Westminster John Knox, 2001.

Kirkham, Richard L. "Truth, Coherence Theory of." Pages 470–72 in vol. 9 of Craig, ed., *The Routledge Encyclopedia of Philosophy.*

—"Truth, Correspondence Theory of." Pages 472–75 in vol. 9 of Craig, ed., *The Routledge Encyclopedia of Philosophy.*

—"Truth, Pragmatic Theory of." Pages 478–80 in vol. 9 of Craig, ed., *The Routledge Encyclopedia of Philosophy.*

Kitchen, Kenneth A. "The Controlling Role of External Evidence in Assessing the Historical Status of the Israelite United Monarchy." Pages 111–30 in Long, Baker, and Wenham, eds., *Windows into Old Testament History*.

—*On the Reliability of the Old Testament*. Grand Rapids: Eerdmans, 2003.

Kliever, Lonnie D., and John H. Hayes. *Radical Christianity: The New Theologies in Perspective with Readings from the Radicals*. Anderson, S.C.: Droke House, 1968.

Kloppenberg, James T. "Objectivity and Historicism: A Century of American Historical Writing" (review of Peter Novick, *That Noble Dream: The "Objectivity Question" and the American Historical Profession*). *AHR* 94 (1989): 1011–30.

Knauf, Ernst Axel. "From History to Interpretation." Pages 26–64 in Edelman, ed., *The Fabric of History*.

—"War 'Biblisch-Hebräisch' eine Sprache?" *ZAH* 3 (1990): 11–23.

Kocka, Jurgen. "Comparison and Beyond." *History and Theory* 42 (2003): 39–44.

Kofoed, Jens Bruun. "Epistemology, Historiographical Method, and the 'Copenhagen School.'" Pages 23–43 in Long, Baker, and Wenham, eds., *Windows into Old Testament History*.

Kosso, Peter. "Historical Evidence and Epistemic Justification: Thucydides as a Case Study." *History and Theory* 32 (1993): 1–13.

Krawitz, Lilian. "Separating Mythos from Logos in Biblical Archaeology." *OTE* 16 (2003): 34–46.

Krishnaswamy, Revathi. "History in Language, Language in History." *Clio* 34 (2004): 1–18.

LaBianca, Øystein S. "Sociocultural Anthropology and Syro-Palestinian Archaeology." Pages 369–87 in Drinkard, Mattingly, and Miller, eds., *Benchmarks in Time and Culture*.

Larsson, Gerhard. "Possible Hellenistic Influences in the Historical Parts of the Old Testament." *SJOT* 18 (2004): 296–311.

Leerssen, Joep, and Ann Rigney, eds. *Historians and Social Values*. Amsterdam: Amsterdam University Press, 2000.

Lemaire, André. "Hebrew and West Semitic Inscriptions and Pre-exilic Israel." Pages 366–85 in Day, ed., *In Search of Pre-Exilic Israel*.

Lemaire, André, and M. Sæbø, eds. *Congress Volume: Oslo, 1998*. VTSup. 80. Leiden: Brill, 2000.

Lemche, Niels Peter. *Ancient Israel: A New History of Israelite Society*. The Biblical Seminar 5. Sheffield: Sheffield Academic Press, 1988. Translation of *Det Gamle Israel: Det israelitiske samfund fra sammenbruddet af bronzealderkulturen til hellnistisk tid*. Aarhus: ANIS, 1984.

—"'Because They Have Cast Away The Law of the Lord of Hosts'—or: 'We and the Rest of the World': The Authors Who 'Wrote' The Old Testament," *SJOT* 17 (2003): 268–90.

—*The Canaanites in Their Land: The Tradition of the Canaanites*. JSOTSup 110. Sheffield: Sheffield Academic Press, 1991.

—*Early Israel: Anthropological and Historical Studies on the Israelite Society Before the Monarchy*. VTSup 37. Leiden: Brill, 1985.

—"Good and Bad in History: The Greek Connection." Pages 127–40 in *Rethinking the Foundations: Historiography in the Ancient World and in the Bible*. Edited by Steven L. McKenzie and Thomas Romer. BZAW 294. Berlin: de Gruyter, 2000.

—"Ideology and the History of Ancient Israel." *SJOT* 14 (2000): 165–93.

—*The Israelites in History and Tradition*. Library of Ancient Israel. Louisville, Ky.: Westminster John Knox, 1998.

—"New Perspectives on the History of Israel." Pages 42–60 in *Perspectives in the Study of the Old Testament and Early Judaism: A Symposium in Honor of Adam S. van der Woude on the Occasion of His 70th Birthday*. Edited by Florentiono García Martínez and Ed Noort. Leiden: Brill, 1998.

194   *Philosophy and Practice in Writing a History of Ancient Israel*

—"The Old Testament—a Hellenistic Book?" *SJOT* 7 (1993): 163–93.
—"On the Use of 'System Theory,' 'Macro Theories,' and 'Evolutionistic Thinking' in Modern Old Testament Research and Biblical Archaeology." *SJOT* 4 (1990): 73–88.
—"The Origin of the Israelite State: A Copenhagen Perspective on the Emergence of Critical Historical Studies of Ancient Israel in Recent Times." *SJOT* 12 (1998): 44–63.
—*Prelude to Israel's Past: Background and Beginnings of Israelite History and Identity*. Peabody, Mass.: Hendrickson, 1998.
—"Rachel and Lea, or, on the Survival of Outdated Paradigms in the Study of the Origin of Israel." *SJOT* 2 (1987): 127–53 and *SJOT* 1 (1988): 39–65.
Lemche, Niels Peter, and Thomas L. Thompson. "Did Biran Kill David? The Bible in the Light of Archaeology." *JSOT* 64 (1994): 3–22.
Le Roy Ladurie, Emmanuel. *Montaillou, village occitan de 1294 à 1324*. Paris: Gallimard, 1975. Published in English as *Montaillou: The Promised Land of Error*. Abridged and translated by Barbara Bray. New York: Vintage, 1979.
Leyden, Wolfgang von. "Categories of Historical Understanding." *History and Theory* 32 (1984): 53–77.
Lipschits, Oded. "The Rural Settlement in Judah in the Sixth Century B.C.E.: A Rejoinder." *PEQ* 136 (2004): 99–107.
Lipschits, Oded, and Joseph Blenkinsopp, eds. *Judah and the Judeans in the Neo-Babylonian Period*. Winona Lake, Ind.: Eisenbrauns, 2003.
London, Gloria. "Ethnoarchaeology and Interpretations of the Past." *NEA* 31 (2000): 2–8.
Long, Burke O. "Mythic Trope in the Autobiography of William Foxwell Albright." *BA* 56 (1993): 36–45.
—*Planting and Reaping Albright: Politics, Ideology, and Interpreting the Bible*. University Park, Pa.: The Pennsylvania State University Press, 1997.
Long, V. Philips. *The Art of Biblical History*. Foundations of Contemporary Interpretation 5. Grand Rapids: Zondervan, 1994.
—"How Reliable Are Biblical Reports? Repeating Lester Grabbe's Comparative Experiment." *VT* 41 (2002): 367–84.
Long, V. Philips, David W. Baker, and Gordon J. Wenham, eds. *Windows into Old Testament History: Evidence, Argument, and the Crisis of "Biblical Israel"*. Grand Rapids: Eerdmans, 2002.
Lyotard, Jean-François. *The Lyotard Reader*. Edited by Andrew Benjamin. Oxford: Blackwell, 1989.
MacAlister, R. A. S. *A Century of Excavation in Palestine*. London: Religious Tract Society, 1925.
Machinist, Peter. "William Foxwell Albright: The Man and His Work." Pages 385–403 in *The Study of the Ancient Near East in the Twenty-First Century: The William Foxwell Albright Centennial Conference*. Edited by Jerrold S. Cooper and Glenn M. Schwartz. Winona Lake, Ind.: Eisenbrauns, 1996.
Malamat, Abraham. "The Proto-History of Israel: A Study in Method." Pages 303–13 in *The Word of the Lord Shall Go Forth: Essays in Honor of David Noel Freedman in Celebration of His Sixtieth Birthday*. Edited by Carol Meyers and M. O'Connor. Winona Lake, Ind.: Eisenbrauns, 1983. Reprinted in Abraham Malamat, *History of Biblical Israel: Major Problems and Minor Issues*. Culture and History of the Ancient Near East 7. Leiden: Brill, 2001.
Mandelbaum, Maurice. *The Problem of Historical Knowledge: An Answer to Relativism*. 1st ed. New York: Harper & Row, 1938.
Mandell, Sara R., and David Noel Freedman. *The Relationship Between Herodotus' History and Primary History*. South Florida Studies in the History of Judaism 60. Atlanta: Scholars Press, 1993.

Martens, Elmer A. "The Oscillating Fortunes of 'History' within Old Testament Theology." Pages 312–40 in Millard, Hoffmeier, and Baker, eds., *Faith, Tradition, and History.*

Master, Daniel M. "State Formation Theory and the Kingdom of Ancient Israel." *JNES* 60 (2001): 117–31.

Matthews, Victor H. *A Brief History of Ancient Israel.* Louisville, Ky.: Westminster John Knox, 2002.

Mattingly, Gerald L. "The Exodus-Conquest and the Archaeology of Transjordan: New Light on an Old Problem." *Grace Theological Journal* 4 (1983): 245–62.

Mayes, A. D. H. "The Covenant People: Max Weber and the Historical Understanding of Ancient Israel." Pages 285–310 in *Covenant as Context: Essays in Honour of E. W. Nicholson.* Edited by A. D. H. Mayes and R. B. Salters. Oxford: Oxford University Press, 2003.

—*Israel in the Period of the Judges.* SBT 29. London: SCM Press, 1974.

—*The Old Testament in Sociological Perspective* (London: Marshall Pickering, 1989).

Mazar, Amihai. *Archaeology of the Land of the Bible 10,000–586 B.C.E.* ABRL. New York: Doubleday, 1990.

McCullagh, C. Behan. "Bias in Historical Description, Interpretation, and Explanation." *History and Theory* 39 (2000): 39–66.

—*Justifying Historical Descriptions.* Cambridge: Cambridge University Press, 1984.

—"Metaphor and Truth in History." *Clio* 23 (1993): 24–49.

—*The Truth of History.* London: Routledge, 1998.

—"What Do Historians Argue About?" *History and Theory* 43 (2004): 18–38.

McKenzie, Steven L., and M. Patrick Graham, eds. *The History of Israel's Traditions: The Heritage of Martin Noth.* JSOTSup 182. Sheffield: Sheffield Academic Press, 1994.

McNutt, Paula M. *Reconstructing the Society of Ancient Israel.* Library of Ancient Israel. Louisville, Ky.: Westminster John Knox, 1999.

Meier, John P. *A Marginal Jew: Rethinking the Historical Jesus.* 2 vols. New York: Doubleday, 1991.

Mendenhall, George E. "The Hebrew Conquest of Palestine." *BA* 25 (1962): 66–87.

Meyer, Eduard. *Geschichte Des Alterthums.* 5 vols. Stuttgart: Cotta, 1884–1902.

Meyers, Carol. *Discovering Eve: Ancient Israelite Women in Context.* New York: Oxford University Press, 1988.

—"Engendering Syro-Palestinian Archaeology: Reasons and Resources." *NEA* 66 (2003): 185–97.

Millard, Alan. "History and Legend in Early Babylonia." Pages 103–10 in Long, Baker, and Wenham, eds., *Windows into Old Testament History.*

—"Story, History, and Theology." Pages 37–64 in Millard, Hoffmeier, and Baker, eds., *Faith, Tradition, and History.*

Millard, Alan, James K. Hoffmeier, and David W. Baker, eds. *Faith, Tradition, and History: Old Testament Historiography in Its Near Eastern Context.* Winona Lake, Ind.: Eisenbrauns, 1994.

Miller, J. Maxwell. "History or Legend? Digging into Israel's Origins." *ChrCent* 121, no. 4 (2004): 42–47.

—"Is It Possible to Write a History of Israel Without Relying on the Hebrew Bible?" Pages 93–102 in Edelman, ed., *The Fabric of History.*

—"The Israelite Occupation of Canaan." Pages 213–84 in Hayes and Miller, eds., *Israelite and Judaean History.*

—"Old Testament History and Archaeology." *BA* 50 (1987): 55–63.

—"Reading the Bible Historically: The Historian's Approach." Pages 11–28 in *To Each Its Own Meaning: An Introduction to Biblical Criticism and Their Application.* Edited by Stephen R. Haynes and Steven L. McKenzie. Louisville, Ky.: Westminster John Knox, 1993.

Miller, J. Maxwell, and John H. Hayes. *A History of Ancient Israel and Judah*. Philadelphia: Westminster, 1986. Revised edition forthcoming.

Miller, Robert D. II, "Identifying Earliest Israel." *BASOR* 333 (2004): 55–68.

Mink, Louis. "The Autonomy of Historical Understanding." Pages 160–92 in *Philosophical Analysis and History*. Edited by William Dray. New York: Harper & Row, 1966.

Mitchell, W. J. T. "Representation," Pages 11–22 in *Critical Terms for Literary Study*. Edited by Frank Lentricchia and Thomas McLaughlin. Chicago: University of Chicago Press, 1995.

Momigliano, Arnaldo. "Ancient History and the Antiquarian." *Journal of the Warburg and Courtauld Institutes* 13 (1950): 285–315.

Morgan, David. "The Evolution of Two Asian Historiographical Traditions." Pages 11–22 in Bentley, ed., *Companion to Historiography*.

Mykytiuk, Lawrence J. *Identifying Biblical Persons in Northwest Semitic Inscriptions of 1200–539 B.C.E.* Society of Biblical Literature Academia Biblica 12. Atlanta: Society of Biblical Literature; Leiden: Brill, 2004.

Na'aman, Nadav. "In Search of Reality Behind the Account of David's Wars with Israel's Neighbors." *IEJ* 52 (2002): 200–24.

NEA 65, no. 1 (2002).

Nicholson, Ernest W. "Current 'Revisionism' and the Literature of the Old Testament." Pages 1–22 in Day, ed., *In Search of Pre-Exilic Israel*.

—*God and His People: Covenant and Theology in the Old Testament*. Oxford: Clarendon, 1986.

Noll, K. L. *Canaan and Israel in Antiquity: An Introduction*. The Biblical Seminar 83. New York: Continuum/Sheffield, 2001.

Noth, Martin. "As One Historian to Another" (review of John Bright, *A History of Israel*). *Int* 15 (1961): 61–66.

—*Aufsätze zur biblischen Landes- und Altertumskunde*. 2 vols. Edited by Hans Walter Wolff. Neukirchen–Vluyn: Neukirchener Verlag, 1971.

—"Der Beitrag der Archäologie zur Geschichte Israels." Pages 34–51 in vol. 1 of his *Aufsätze zur biblischen Landes- und Altertumskunde*. Reprint of pages 262–82 in *Congress Volume: Oxford, 1959*. VTSup 7. Leiden: Brill, 1960.

—*The Chronicler's History*. JSOTSup 50. Sheffield: JSOT Press, 1987. Translation of his the second part of *Überlieferungsgeschichtliche Studien I*.

—*The Deuteronomistic History*. JSOTSup 15. Sheffield: JSOT Press, 1981. Translation of his the first part of *Überlieferungsgeschichtliche Studien I*.

—*Developing Lines of Theological Thought in Germany*. Fourth Annual Bibliographical Lecture, Union Theological Seminary in Virginia. Richmond: Union Theological Seminary, 1963.

—*Gesammelte Studien zum Alten Testament II*. Edited by Hans Walter Wolff. Munich: Kaiser, 1969.

—*Geschichte Israels*. Göttingen: Vandenhoeck & Ruprecht, 1950.

—"God, King, and Nation in the Old Testament." Pages 145–78 in his *The Laws in the Pentateuch and Other Studies*. Translation of "Gott, König, Volk im Alten Testament: Eine methodologische Auseinandersetzung mit einer gegenwärtigen Forschungsrichtung." *ZTK* 47 (1950): 157–91.

—"Grundsätzliches zur geschichtlichen Deutung archäologischer Befunde auf dem Boden Palästinas." Pages 3–16 in vol. 1 of his *Aufsätze*. Reprint of *PJ* 34 (1938): 7–22.

—"Hat Die Bibel Doch Recht?" Pages 17–33 in vol. 1 of his *Aufsätze*. Reprint of pages 7–22 in *Festschrift für Günther Dehn, zum 75 Geburtstag am 18 April 1957*. Edited by Wilhelm Schneemelcher. Neukirchen: Verlag der Buchhandlung des Erziehungsvereins, 1957.

—"Die Historisierung des Mythus im Alten Testament." Pages 29–61 in his *Gesammelte Studien zum Alten Testament II*. Reprint of *Christentum und Wissenschaft* 4 (1928): 265–72, 301–9.

—*The History of Israel*. 2d ed. New York: Harper & Row, 1960. Translation of his *Geschichte Israels*.

—*A History of Pentateuchal Traditions*. Englewood Cliffs, N.J.: Prentice–Hall, 1972. Reprinted, Chico, Calif.: Scholars Press, 1981. Translation of *Überlieferungsgeschichte des Pentateuch*. Stuttgart: Kohlhammer, 1948.

—*The Laws in the Pentateuch and Other Studies*. Philadelphia: Fortress, 1966. Translation of *Gesammelte Studien zum Alten Testament*. 2d ed. Munich: Kaiser, 1960.

—*The Old Testament World*. Philadelphia: Fortress, 1966. Translation of *Die Welt des Alten Testaments: Einführung in die Grenzgebiete der alttestamentlichen Wissenschaft*. Berlin: Töpelmann, 1964.

—*Das System der Zwölf Stämme Israels*. Darmstadt: Wissenschaftliche Buchgesellschaft, 1966. Reprint of BWANT 4, no. 1. Stuttgart: Kohlhammer, 1930.

—*Überlieferungsgeschichtliche Studien I*. Tübingen: Niemeyer Verlag, 1948.

—"The Understanding of History in Old Testament Apocalyptic." Pages 194–214 in his *The Laws in the Pentateuch and Other Studies*. Translation of *Das Geschichtsverständnis der alttestamentlichen Apokalyptik*. Arbeitsgemeinschaft für Forschung des Landes Nordrhein–Westfalen: Geisteswissenschaften 21. Cologne: Westdeutscher Verlag, 1954.

Novick, Peter. *That Noble Dream: The "Objectivity Question" and the American Historical Profession*. Ideas in Context. Cambridge: Cambridge University Press, 1988.

Organ, Barbara E. *Is the Bible Fact or Fiction? An Introduction to Biblical Historiography*. New York: Paulist, 2004.

Ortner, Sherry B. "Theory in Anthropology since the Sixties." *Comparative Studies in Society and History* 26 (1984): 126–66.

Palti, Elías. "The 'Return of the Subject' as a Historico-Intellectual Problem." *History and Theory* 43 (2004): 57–82.

Parker, Simon. *Stories in Scripture and Inscriptions: Comparative Studies on Narratives in Northwest Semitic Inscriptions and the Hebrew Bible*. New York: Oxford University Press, 1997.

Pike, Dana Marston. "Israelite Theophoric Personal Names in the Bible and Their Implications for Religious History." Ph.D. diss., University of Pennsylvania, 1990.

Prins, Gwyn. "Oral History." Pages 114–39 in Burke, ed., *New Perspectives on Historical Writing*.

Pritchett, W. Kendrick. *The Liar School of Herodotos*. Amsterdam: Gieben, 1993.

Provan, Iain W. "The Historical Books of the Old Testament." Pages 198–211 in Barton, ed., *The Cambridge Companion to Biblical Interpretation*.

—"Ideologies, Literary and Critical: Reflections on Recent Writing on the History of Israel." *JBL* 114 (1995): 585–606.

—"In the Stable with the Dwarves: Testimony, Interpretation, Faith and the History of Israel." Pages 281–319 in Lemaire and M. Sæbø, eds., *Congress Volume: Oslo, 1988*.

Provan, Iain W., V. Philips Long, and Tremper Longman III. *A Biblical History of Israel*. Louisville, Ky.: Westminster John Knox, 2003.

Rainey, Anson F. "Stones for Bread: Archaeology Versus History." *NEA* 64, no. 3 (2001): 140–49.

Ramsey, George W. *The Quest for the Historical Israel*. Louisville, Ky.: Westminster John Knox, 1981.

Ranke, Leopold von. "Vorrede der ersten Ausgabe—Oktober 1824." Pages 3–5 in *Fürsten und Völker: Geschichten der romanischen und germanischen Völker von 1494–1514. Die Osmanen und die spanische Monarchie im 16. und 17. Jahrhundert*. Edited by Willy Andreas. Wiesbaden: Emil Vollmer, 1957.

Richard, Suzanne, ed. *Near Eastern Archaeology: A Reader*. Winona Lake, Ind.: Eisenbrauns, 2003.

Ricoeur, Paul. *Time and Narrative*. 3 vols. Chicago: University of Chicago Press, 1984. Translation of *Temps et récit*. 3 vols. Paris: Éditions du Seuil, 1984.

Rigney, Ann. "Narrativity and Historical Representation." *Poetics Today* 12 (1991): 591–601.

Ringer, Fritz. "Max Weber on Causal Analysis, Interpretation, and Comparison." *History and Theory* 41 (2002): 163–78.

Rogerson, John W., and Philip R. Davies. *The Old Testament World*. Englewood Cliffs, N.J.: Prentice–Hall, 1989. Rev. ed. printed as Philip R. Davies and John W. Rogerson, *The Old Testament World*. London: T&T Clark International; Louisville, Ky.: Westminster John Knox, 2005.

Rorty, Richard. *Objectivity, Relativism, and Truth*. 2 vols. Cambridge: Cambridge University Press, 1991.

Rosaldo, Renato. "From the Door of His Tent: The Fieldworker and the Inquisitor." Pages 77–97 in *Writing Culture: The Poetics and Politics of Ethnography*. Edited by James Clifford and George E. Marcus. Berkeley: University of California Press, 1986.

Roth, Guenther. Introduction to *Economy and Society: An Outline of Interpretive Sociology*, by Max Weber. 2 vols. Edited by Guenther Roth and Claus Wittich. Berkeley: University of California, 1978.

Roth, Paul A. "Narrative Explanations: The Case of History." *History and Theory* 27 (1988): 1–13.

Ruben, David-Hillel. "Explanation in History and Social Science." Pages 525–31 in vol. 3 of Craig, ed., *The Routledge Encyclopedia of Philosophy*.

Running, Leona Glidden, and David Noel Freedman. *William Foxwell Albright: A Twentieth-Century Genius*. New York: Morgan, 1975.

Sauer, James A., and Larry G. Herr. "Transjordan in the Bronze and Iron Ages." *OEANE* 5:231–35.

Saussure, Ferdinand de. *Cours de linguistique générale*. Lusanne: Payot, 1916. Published in English as *Course in General Linguistics*. Glasgow: Fontana/Collins, 1977.

Scham, Sandra. "The Days of the Judges: When Men and Women Were Animals and Trees Were Kings." *JSOT* 97 (2002): 37–64.

Scheffler, Eben. "Beyond the Judges and the Amphictyony: The Politics of Tribal Israel (1200–1020 BCE)." *OTE* 14 (2001): 494–509.

Schloen, J. David. *The House of the Father as Fact and Symbol: Patrimonialism in Ugarit and the Ancient Near East*. Studies in the Archaeology of the Levant 2. Winona Lake, Ind.: Eisenbrauns; Boston: Harvard Semitic Museum, 2001.

—"W. F. Albright and the Origins of Israel." *NEA* 65, no. 1(2002): 57–68.

Schniedewind, William M. Review of George Athas, *The Tel Dan Inscription: A Reappraisal and a New Interpretation*. No pages. Published 5 October 2003. Online: http://www. bookreviews.org/pdf/3275_3685.pdf.

Schoors, Antoon. *Die Königreiche Israel und Juda im 8. und 7. Jahrhundert v. Chr.: Die assyrische Krise*. BE 5. Stuttgart: Kohlhammer, 1998.

Shanks, Hershel. "Face to Face: Biblical Minimalists Meet Their Challengers." *BAR* 23, no. 4 (1997): 26–42, 66.

Shanks, Michael, and Christopher Tilley. *Social Theory and Archaeology*. Albuquerque: University of New Mexico Press, 1988.

Sharpe, Jim. "History from Below." Pages 24–41 in Burke, ed., *New Perspectives on Historical Writing*.

Silberman, Neil Asher. "Visions of the Future: Albright in Jerusalem, 1919–1929." *BA* 56 (1993): 8–16.

Smend, Rudolf. *Deutsche Alttestamentler in drei Jahrhunderten: mit 18 Abbildungen.* Göttingen: Vandenhoeck & Ruprecht, 1989.

—"Nachruf auf Martin Noth." Pages 137–65 in Noth, *Gesammelte Studien Zum Alten Testament II.*

Smith, D. Neel. "Herodotus and the Archaeology of Asia Minor: A Historiographic Study." Ph.D. diss., University of California, Berkeley, 1987.

Smith, Mark S. "W. F. Albright and His 'Household': The Cases of C. H. Gordon, M. H. Pope, and F. M. Cross." Pages 221–44 in *"A Wise and Discerning Mind": Essays in Honor of Burke O. Long.* Edited by Saul M. Olyan and Robert C. Culley. BJS 325. Providence: Brown University, 2000.

Soggin, J. Alberto. *A History of Israel: From the Beginnings to the Bar Kochba Revolt, AD 135.* London: SCM Press, 1984. Translation of *Storia d'Israele, dalle origini alla rivolta di Bar-Kochba, 135 d.C.* Brescia: Paideia, 1984. Now in its third edition and retitled, *An Introduction to the History of Israel and Judah.* 3d ed. London: SCM Press, 1998. Translation of *Introduzione alla Storia d'Israele e di Giuda.* Brescia: Paideia, 1998.

—*An Introduction to the History of Israel and Judah.* 3d ed. London: SCM Press, 1998. Translation of *Introduzione alla Storia d'Israele e di Giuda.* Brescia: Paideia, 1998.

Stager, Lawrence E. "The Archaeology of the Family in Ancient Israel." *BASOR* 260 (1985): 1–35.

Stanford, Michael. *An Introduction to the Philosophy of History.* Oxford: Blackwell, 1998.

Stern, Ephraim. *Archaeology of the Land of the Bible.* Vol. 2, *The Assyrian, Babylonian, and Persian Periods, 732–332 BCE.* ABRL. New York: Doubleday, 2001.

—"The Babylonian Gap: The Archaeological Reality." *JSOT* 28 (2004): 273–77.

Stoianovich, Traian. *French Historical Method: The* Annales *Paradigm.* Ithaca, N.Y.: Cornell University Press, 1976.

Stone, Lawrence. "The Revival of Narrative: Reflections on a New Old History." *Past and Present* 85 (1979): 3–24.

Talshir, Zipora. "Textual and Literary Criticism of the Bible in Post-Modern Times: The Untimely Demise of Classical Biblical Philology." *Hen* 21 (1999): 235–52.

Thompson, Thomas L. "Defining History and Ethnicity in the South Levant." Pages 166–87 in Grabbe, ed., *Can a "History of Israel" Be Written?*

—*Early History of the Israelite People from the Written and Archaeological Sources.* SHANE 4. Leiden: Brill, 1992.

—"From the Stone Age to Israel." Pages 9–32 in *Proceedings: Eastern Great Lakes and Midwest Biblical Societies.* Edited by Terrance Callan. Grand Rapids: Eastern Great Lakes Biblical Society, 1991.

—"Hidden Histories and the Problem of Ethnicity in Palestine." Pages 23–39 in *Western Scholarship and the History of Palestine.* Edited by Michael Prior. London: Melisinde, 1998.

—*The Historicity of the Patriarchal Narratives: The Quest for the Historical Abraham.* BZAW 133. Berlin: de Gruyter, 1974.

—"Historiography of Ancient Palestine and Early Jewish Historiography: W. G. Dever and the Not So New Biblical Archaeology." Pages 26–43 in Fritz and Davies, eds., *The Origins of the Ancient Israelite States.*

—"The Intellectual Matrix of Early Biblical Narrative: Inclusive Monotheism in Persian Period Palestine." Pages 107–24 in *The Triumph of Elohim: From Yahwisms to Judaisms.* Edited by Diana Vikander Edelman. Grand Rapids: Eerdmans, 1996.

—"Lester Grabbe and Historiography: An Apologia." *SJOT* 14 (2000): 140–61.

—"Martin Noth and the History of Israel." Pages 81–90 in McKenzie and Graham, eds., *The History of Israel's Traditions.*

—"Methods and Results: A Review of Two Recent Publications." *SJOT* 15 (2001): 306–25.
—*The Mythic Past: Biblical Archaeology and the Myth of Israel*. New York: Basic Books, 1999.
—"A Neo-Albrightean School in History and Biblical Scholarship?" *JBL* 114 (1995): 683–98.
—"Problems of Genre and Historicity with Palestine's Inscriptions." Pages 321–26 in Lemaire and M. Sæbø, eds., *Congress Volume: Oslo, 1988*.
—"Text, Content and Referent in Israelite Historiography." Pages 65–92 in Edelman, ed., *The Fabric of History*.
Tigay, Jeffrey H. *You Shall Have No Other Gods: Israelite Religion in the Light of Hebrew Inscriptions*. HSS 31. Atlanta: Scholars Press, 1986.
Troeltsch, Ernst. "Historiography." Pages 716–23 in vol. 6 of *Encyclopaedia of Religion and Ethics*. Edited by James Hastings. New York: Scribner's, 1908–26.
Ussishkin, David. *The Conquest of Lachish by Sennacherib*. Tel Aviv: Tel Aviv University Institute of Archaeology, 1982.
Van Beek, Gus W., ed. *The Scholarship of William Foxwell Albright: An Appraisal*. HSS 33. Atlanta: Scholars Press, 1989.
Van Seters, John. *Abraham in History and Tradition*. New York: Yale University Press, 1975.
—*In Search of History: Historiography in the Ancient World and the Origins of Biblical History*. New Haven: Yale University Press, 1983.
—*The Pentateuch: A Social-Science Commentary*. Trajectories. Sheffield: Sheffield Academic Press, 1999.
Veijola, Timo. "Martin Noth's *Überlieferungsgeschichtliche Studien* and Old Testament Theology." Pages 101–27 in McKenzie and Graham, eds., *The History of Israel's Traditions*.
Watts, James W., ed. *Persia and Torah: The Theory of Imperial Authorization of the Pentateuch*. Atlanta: Scholars Press, 2001.
Weber, Max. *Ancient Judaism*. New York: Free Press, 1952. Translation of *Gessamelte Aufsätze zur Religionssoziologie*. Vol. 3, *Das antike Judentum*. Tübingen: Mohr, 1922–23. This work originally appeared as a series of articles in the *Archiv für Sozialwissenschaft und Sozialforschung*, 1917–19.
Wesselius, Jan-Wim. *The Origin of the History of Israel: Herodotus's Histories as Blueprint for the First Books of the Bible*. JSOTSup 345. Sheffield: Sheffield Academic Press, 2002.
White, Hayden. *Metahistory: The Historical Imagination in Nineteenth-Century Europe*. Baltimore: The Johns Hopkins University Press, 1973.
—*Tropics of Discourse*. Baltimore: The Johns Hopkins University Press, 1978.
Whitelam, Keith W. "Between History and Literature: The Social Production of Israel's Traditions of Origin." *SJOT* 2 (1991): 60–74.
—"The Identity of Early Israel: The Realignment and Transformation of Late Bronze–Iron Age Palestine." *JSOT* 63 (1994): 57–87.
—*The Invention of Ancient Israel: The Silencing of Palestinian History*. London: Routledge, 1996.
—*The Just King: Monarchical Judicial Authority in Ancient Israel*. JSOTSup 12. Sheffield: Department of Biblical Studies, 1979.
—"Recreating the History of Israel." *JSOT* 35 (1986): 45–70.
—"The Search for Early Israel: Historical Perspective." Pages 41–64 in *The Origin of Early Israel—Current Debate*. Edited by Shmuel Ahituv and Eliezer D. Oren. Beer-Sheva: Ben-Gurion University of the Negev, 1998.
—"The Social World of the Bible." Pages in 35–49 in Barton, ed., *The Cambridge Companion to Biblical Interpretation*.

—"Sociology or History: Towards a (Human) History of Ancient Palestine?" Pages 149–66 in *Words Remembered, Texts Renewed: Essays in Honour of John F. A. Sawyer*. Edited by Jon Davies, Graham Harvey, and Wilfred G. E. Watson. JSOTSup 195. Sheffield: Sheffield Academic Press, 1995.

Wilcoxen, Jay A. "Narrative." Pages 57–98 in *Old Testament Form Criticism*. Edited by John H. Hayes. TUMSR 2. San Antonio: Trinity University Press, 1974.

Winther-Nielsen, Nicolai. "Fact, Fiction, and Language Use: Can Modern Pragmatics Improve on Halpern's Case for History in Judges?" Pages 44–81 in Long, Baker, and Wenham, eds., *Windows into Old Testament History*.

Wright, George Ernest. *Biblical Archaeology*. Philadelphia: Westminster, 1957.

Yamada, Shigeo. "Aram–Israel Relations as Reflected in the Aramaic Inscription from Tel Dan." *UF* 27 (1995): 611–25.

Yamauchi, Edwin. "The Current State of Old Testament Historiography." Pages 1–36 in Millard, Hoffmeier, and Baker, eds., *Faith, Tradition, and History*.

Younger, K. Lawson, *Ancient Conquest Accounts: A Study in Ancient near Eastern and Biblical History Writing*. JSOTSup 98. Sheffield: Sheffield Academic Press, 1990.

Younger, K. Lawson, and Mark W. Chavalas, eds. *Mesopotamia and the Bible: Comparative Explorations*. Grand Rapids: Baker, 2002.

Zagorin, Perez. "History and Postmodernism: Reconsiderations." *History and Theory* 29 (1990): 263–74.

—"History, the Referent, and Narrative: Reflections on Postmodernism Now." *History and Theory* 38 (1999): 1–24.

Zevit, Ziony. *The Religions of Ancient Israel: A Synthesis of Parallactic Approaches*. London: Continuum, 2000.

—"Three Debates About Bible and Archaeology." *Bib* 83 (2002): 1–27.

Zwelling, Jeremy. "The Fictions of Biblical History" (review of Thomas L. Thompson, *The Mythic Past*). *History and Theory* 39 (2000): 117–41.